Frozen Delights

FROZEN DELIGHTS

DELIGHTS

Linda Burum

CHARLES SCRIBNER'S SONS

New York

Charles Scribner's Sons
Macmillan Publishing Company
866 Third Avenue, New York, NY 10022
Collier Macmillan Canada, Inc.

Library of Congress Cataloging-in-Publication Data

Burum, Linda.
Frozen Delights.
1. Ice cream, ices, etc.   2. Desserts, Frozen.
I. Title.
TX795.B97   1986   641.8'6   86-13736
ISBN 0-684-18584-9

Macmillan books are available at special discounts for bulk purchases
for sales promotions, premiums, fund-raising, or educational use.
For details, contact:

Special Sales Director
Macmillan Publishing Company
866 Third Avenue
New York, NY 10022

10   9   8   7   6   5   4   3   2   1

Printed in the United States of America

Contents

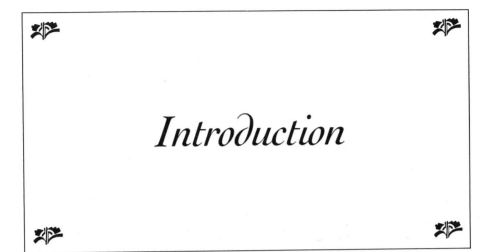

Introduction

The unrivaled sensation of something icy and flavorful melting on the tongue is not new to the world's food lovers. Though we take for granted today's cornucopia of delightful frozen sweets, such things were once reserved for nobility. History's raconteurs describe King Charles I of England's first bite of ice cream, prepared for him by his French chef. It delighted him so, he paid the fellow handsomely not to divulge the recipe. The Romans made flavored ices by pouring juice, honey, or wines over compacted snow. Slave runneres were sent to the mountains to gather the snow for these ancient refreshments. Such gastronomic frivolities vanished during the Dark Ages until Marco Polo returned from China to Venice with tales of frozen desserts made with milk. During the same period of history, other travelers back from India and the Middle East described the icy drinks served in pearwood bowls and sipped with spoons—the word for sherbet being derived from the Arabic *sharbah*, meaning a drink. Even today, serving sherbet is a sign of Middle Eastern hospitality. The sophisticated Italians were quick to adapt these first forms of *gelati* and *sorbetti*. During the Renaissance almost every banquet table held some sort of elaborate frozen refreshment molded into icy towers.

Even without mechanical refrigeration or churns, frozen desserts became a favorite of the masses soon after an enterprising Sicilian, Francesco Procopio dei Coltelli, opened the first Paris café to serve *gelato* in 1660. *Gelati* and *sorbetti* become so popular that, just sixteen years later, Paris had 260 establishments making and selling iced desserts.

In America, the first homemade ice creams were fashioned in a pot freezer requiring hand-shaking and packing of hand-chopped ice with salt—a laborious but worthwhile task. In 1846, though, preparing this fast-growing favorite became easier with the invention of the hand-cranked ice cream machine by Nancy Johnson. The rest is modern ice cream history.

It's not difficult to understand the world's passion for frozen desserts. In addition to their obvious sensual pleasures, almost everyone has a cherished ice cream memory—from a romance at the soda fountain to the taste of smooth Italian *gelato* bought from a vendor at the Trevi Fountain. Ice cream parlors with their cool marble-topped tables and swirled wrought-iron chairs lured us in for after-movie treats or Saturday afternoon outings. And ice cream was served at every birthday. Over the years, Americans became ice cream connoisseurs. Farm families inevitably owned a wooden churn to crank up batches of ice cream with fresh dairy cream and the season's harvest of fruit. Even during the heyday of "processed" ice creams with their supply of artificial fillers, flavorings, and colorings, true ice cream lovers always knew where to get "real" ice cream. In many towns someone owned an ice cream store where ice creams were made in small batches and hand-packed.

No small part of our recent good-food movement has been an emphasis on fine-quality iced desserts. In addition to the veritable explosion of quality ice cream shops, one can find a respectable selection of "upscale" products in supermarket freezers. Ice cream makers are outdoing themselves to create ever more fantastic flavors. Still, nothing compares with turning a favorite food into your own specialty.

Capture the special quality of just-churned ice creams or sorbets, or spruce up ready-made products by stirring in the likes of Truffle Chips, Cassis Ripple sauce, or crushed pralines, or combine ice cream and cake, for deliciously fanciful party desserts. Create a shaped cake such as the Spring Butterfly by layering sorbet and ice cream on a liqueur-drenched sponge cake. Chocolate lovers will always remember you if you serve them Frozen Quadruple Chocolate Suicide Cake, with its brownie foundation and chocolate meringue layers wedged between chocolate ice cream, smothered with chocolate whipped cream.

The recipes cover almost every facet of frozen desserts. Included are still-frozen dishes needing no churning, such as frozen mousses or soufflés. Elegant sorbets capture the fruit's very essence; they're made primarily of pure fruit puree or juice and judiciously sweetened. And the soft frozen yogurts can be churned in a food processor or frozen in an ice cream machine. Some frozen delights, such as the creamy dairy-free tofulatos, are prudent, and some voluptuous and wicked, such as the Amaretto–Chocolate Swirl Frozen Cheesecake and its Kahlúa-flavored cousin, or the satiny-textured Frozen Chocolate Pâté. I discovered that ice cream pies were the perfect vehicle for layering textures and flavors that meld together deliciously. Crunchy cookie or meringue crusts topped with a sorbet and then ice cream or frozen mousse have infinite possibilities, only a sampling of which are featured in the chapter on frozen pies. Others can be invented by creative cooks combining the basic recipes with a little imagination. In fact, a number of recipes serve as starting points for cooks who want to exercise their own creativity. The Coffee-Chocolate Multilayered Ice Cream Cake, for example, calls for vanilla and coffee ice cream, chocolate sorbet, and fudge sauce. The same cake could be constructed with orange and raspberry sorbet or sherbet, vanilla ice cream, and raspberry jam. Whether or not you have an ice cream machine, you can put together your own very self-indulgent creations from this range of possibilities. Some are even healthy to eat!

A Few Definitions

Churned desserts are stirred during the freezing process, which helps create their smooth texture.

CHURNED DESSERTS

Ice cream is a mixture of ice cream, flavorings, sweeteners, and sometimes stabilizers, agitated during freezing. In French-style or custard ice creams, the milk or cream is cooked with egg or egg yolk to form a custard base to which flavorings are added. This results in a rich, smooth texture.

Sorbets (*sorbetti*) are usually made from fruit puree, water, sugar, and sometimes a small amount of stabilizer such as gelatin or egg white to smooth out the texture. Some sorbets are made from fruit juice or wine.

Granitas are Italian-style flavored ices, sometimes containing fruit. They are quickly frozen to obtain a rough crystalline texture that the Italians find refreshing.

Sherbets blend milk, water, sweeteners, flavorings, and/or fruit juices to create an ice cream–like dessert. Sherbets are, however, much less rich than sorbets and not so full of fruit.

Bombes are molded frozen desserts usually composed of layerings of ice creams or sorbets and ice cream which, when cut open, result in a decorative pattern. Some bombes have still-frozen centers.

Still-frozen desserts are not stirred while they are freezing.

Frozen mousses are rich, velvety-textured desserts obtained by combining beaten eggs or egg yolks and cream, flavored with sweeteners, liqueurs, or fruit juice or puree. Nowadays there is no clear division between the composition of parfaits, soufflés, and mousses.

Parfaits are often based on beaten egg yolks that have been cooked and then have beaten cream, beaten egg white, flavorings, and sweeteners added.

Frozen soufflés are either a parfait or a mousse mixture frozen in and served from a soufflé dish.

Frappés were originally frozen ices that had been scraped or crushed and served slushy. Cream and even eggs have worked their way into some frappé mixtures.

What Makes a Great Frozen Dessert?

Of course you'll say the best chocolate, fresh ripe fruit, pure cream, and the proper balancing of ingredients. This is true, but as with many prepared foods, ingredients are only the foundation. How the elements are assembled will equally affect the final result.

Frozen mixtures, whether churned or still-frozen, have many forces working on them as they sit in a 32° F. or cooler atmosphere being transformed from a liquid mixture to a smooth solid. Understanding how these forces work can make the cook's handling of each ingredient more effective.

Large icy crystals are the enemy of smooth and creamy frozen desserts. Whether freezing low-fat yogurt, fresh fruit puree, or a mixture of whipped cream and egg yolks, you will want to do everything possible to promote the formation of only the tiniest ice crystals as the dessert freezes. Large chunky ice crystals formed by the linking up of water molecules are responsible for an unpleasant grainy feeling on the palate.

A close-up view of the microscopic arrangement of a frozen dessert's structure gives an understanding of how this crystal formation can be avoided. Though ice creams, sorbets, and still-frozen desserts are considered "frozen," they are not completely frozen. Instead, multitudes of tiny ice crystals are suspended in a binding syrup consisting of sugars, minerals, and other components such as fat or protein. While much of the water part of a dessert mixture (from milk or fruit juice) freezes, the concentration of sugar and other substances in the unfrozen part is so great it lowers the water's freezing temperature to the extent that the dessert will not solidify. Thus desserts with high percentages of these substances have a soft or slushy texture.

Emulsified fat globules; milk, egg, and gelatin proteins; cooked starches; stabilizers (usually vegetable gums); and air bubbles all work as buffers to separate tiny crystals from one another, keeping them from growing into larger ones. With this in mind, it's easy to see how various ingredients and techniques alter the texture of the dessert. A high fat content, for example, means there are many natural buffers preventing the linking up of large crystals. Beating in air can make the dessert seem smooth because many of the crystals are kept apart. But beating in too much air can make ice cream seem foamy and will make still-frozen desserts icy. (The chapter on still-frozen desserts explains this seemingly contradictory statement.) Since alcohol and certain invert sugars,★ such as the ones in honey, corn syrup, fruit preserves, and sweetened condensed milk, lower the freezing point of the mixture, desserts made with them will usually be softer; a lower percentage of the mixture will actually freeze solidly. I have used this phenomenon to advantage in a number of still-frozen desserts and pie and cake fillings where a higher alcohol or invert sugar content prevents large crystal formation and results in a velvety texture without churning.

The method of freezing also influences the dessert's texture. If a still-frozen dessert is slowly frozen—for instance, in a freezer that is frequently opened and shut—it has time to develop long links of ice molecules and larger crystals. Faster freezing usually results in a smoother texture. However, too fast freezing of ice cream—by adding too much salt to the ice used for freezing (see page 15)—allows large ice crystals to form faster

★ The term "invert sugars" refers to the chemical structure of certain sugars.

than churning can keep them apart and results in a coarse, grainy ice cream or sorbet. Agitation during freezing keeps the crystals apart and usually results in a smoother mixture than one that is still-frozen, all the other factors being equal. But perfectly grand still-frozen desserts can be made with the right ingredients and techniques. Most, however, such as parfaits and mousses, are not designed to have the same texture as ice cream.

The way frozen desserts are stored will also affect their texture. The longer they are frozen, the more time they have to develop large crystals, and raising and lowering the freezing temperature also gives water molecules the opportunity to link up.

For the most success with these recipes, take time to read the special techniques in each chapter introduction for the dessert you will be making. Wherever possible, I have also included with the recipe the best method for freezing that dessert.

Frozen Delights

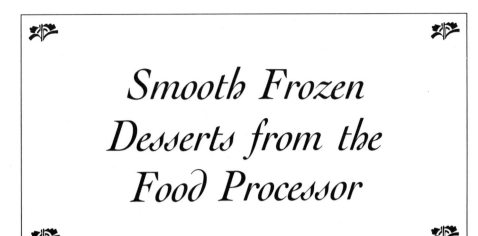

Smooth Frozen Desserts from the Food Processor

Long before I ever owned an ice cream churn, I owned a food processor. I soon learned from the recipes in the machine's accompanying booklet that one could make fine ice creams and sorbets from frozen chopped fruits, cream, and sugar. I like to think I've improved on these already good recipes. Another inspiration came from Anne Greer, a cookbook author and Cuisinart spokesperson. In her book *Cuisine of the American Southwest* she offers several processor-churned ice creams that gave me further inspiration for this chapter.

The basic method for most of these desserts is to prepare your mixture for ice creams or sorbets, freeze them in divided ice cube trays, and when you are ready to serve them, process the cubes into a fine snow and then into a finer frozen mixture. A little unflavored gelatin incorporated into many of the mixtures helps keep large crystals from forming in the churned dessert. Some desserts stay supple without gelatin if they are particularly rich or have a liqueur mixed into them.

Even now, though I have invested in a fancy ice cream machine, I like to prepare cubes of frozen yogurt and process them to a soft yogurt consistency just before serving them. My recipes are designed so that the finished products can also be held in the freezer for at least a few days. The yogurt recipes may be found in the chapter "Lighter, Healthier Delights" and may also be churned in an ice cream maker.

The "Ultra Sorbets" are among my favorite processor recipes: fruit, with a complementary liqueur and a little sugar to intensify the fruit flavor that freezing diminishes. I don't sweeten the sorbets much before freezing the mixture because the amount of sweetening needed depends on the ripeness of the fruit. The final sorbet may be sweetened to taste by sprinkling in a little sifted powdered sugar at the end of processing. These and the processor fruit sorbets may be found at the beginning of the chapter "Delectable Sorbets."

After you make the basic processor ice creams you can embellish them with any of the suggestions in this chapter or with the swirls, ripples, or stir-ins suggested in the "Basic Vanilla Ice Creams with Add-ons" section in the chapter "Ice Creams: Traditional and New."

The "Instant Fruit Ice Creams" capture summer's flavor any time of year. By simply processing together cream, frozen fruit (your own or commercially frozen), and a little sugar, fruit ice creams can be whipped up in seconds. These are very fruity, with a special character all their own. Even if you own an ice cream maker, you may want to try them.

And finally, try two of the simplest and best desserts to emerge from processor or churn—Quick Crème de Menthe–Chocolate Chip Freeze, with its Kahlúa variation, and Frozen Banana Pudding.

INSTANT FRUIT ICE CREAMS

I have seen a variety of recipes using this concept of beaten cream, sugar, and frozen fruit whirled into an instant ice cream. The desserts use a higher proportion of fruit to cream than standard ice creams would, and the result is so refreshing you may never go back to eating commercially frozen fruit ice creams again. Eat these just after you have processed them, or place them in the freezer for a few minutes. They are not as creamy once they have been stored longer than an hour. But you need not store them, since they take only minutes to make.

Instant Peach Ice Cream

1 cup heavy cream, well chilled
6 tablespoons sugar
14 ounces frozen unsweetened peach slices
1 tablespoon lemon juice

Place the cream and sugar in the food processor work bowl fitted with a steel knife. Process until the cream is very thick and slightly whipped. Watch carefully as the cream thickens so that you do not allow it to turn to butter.

Add one third of the fruit and process until it is chopped coarsely. Repeat with the remaining fruit. Then pulse the machine on and off until the mixture is the texture of coarse snow. Sprinkle the mixture evenly with the lemon juice and process continuously until the mixture attains the texture of ice cream. Freeze the ice cream about 20 minutes if you find it is too soft.

MAKES 6 SERVINGS.

Instant Strawberry Ice Cream

1 cup heavy cream, well chilled
6 tablespoons sugar
16 ounces frozen unsweetened strawberries
2 teaspoons fresh lemon juice

Place the cream and sugar in the food processor work bowl fitted with a steel knife. Process until the cream is very thick and slightly whipped. Watch carefully as the cream thickens so that you do not allow it to turn to butter.

Add one third of the fruit and process until it is chopped coarsely. Repeat with the remaining fruit. Then pulse the machine on and off until the mixture is the texture of coarse snow. Sprinkle the mixture evenly with the lemon juice and process continuously until the mixture attains the texture of ice cream. Freeze the ice cream about 20 minutes if you find it is too soft.

MAKES 6 SERVINGS.

Flavor Variations

INSTANT RASPBERRY ICE CREAM

Follow the directions for Instant Strawberry Ice Cream, substituting slightly sweetened frozen raspberries (not berries in syrup) for the strawberries. Reduce sugar to 5 tablespoons.

INSTANT BOYSENBERRY ICE CREAM

Follow the directions for Instant Strawberry Ice Cream, substituting unsweetened frozen boysenberries for the strawberries. Increase the sugar to 7 tablespoons.

INSTANT BLUEBERRY ICE CREAM

Follow the directions for Instant Strawberry Ice Cream, substituting unsweetened frozen blueberries (not berries in syrup) for the strawberries. Reduce sugar to 4½ tablespoons.

QUICK AND FANCY ICED DESSERTS

These are not quite traditional ice creams or ices, nor are they parfaits, mousses, or creams like those in the chapter "Still-Frozen Desserts." But they are so delicious you'll wonder why these remarkably simple mixtures haven't been in every cook's quick recipe file for years.

Quick Crème de Menthe–Chocolate Chip Freeze

1½ cups whole milk
½ cup sugar
2¼ cups heavy cream
½ teaspoon vanilla extract
5 tablespoons green crème de menthe

⅔ cup semisweet mini chocolate morsels or 2½ ounces finely chopped semisweet chocolate

Bring 1¼ cups of the milk to the simmering point; remove from the heat and stir in the sugar until it is completely dissolved. Cool to room temperature and add the remaining ¼ cup milk, the cream, vanilla, and crème de menthe. Pour the mixture into divided ice cube trays and freeze solid.

Just before serving or up to 3 hours ahead, place half of the frozen ice cream cubes in the food processor work bowl and pulse the machine on and off until the cubes are evenly chopped to the texture of coarse snow. Then run the machine continuously until the ice cream swirls around the blades and is creamy-looking. If the mixture is too hard to move freely around the bowl, allow it to thaw slightly or add a few drops of milk.

Stir in half the chocolate morsels by hand. Process the remaining cubes and add the remaining chocolate morsels, or save both for another time. Serve immediately or pile into 1- or 2-pint containers. Cover and freeze.

MAKES ABOUT 2½ PINTS.

Variation

COFFEE KAHLÚA CHIP FREEZE

Follow the recipe for Quick Crème de Menthe–Chocolate Chip Freeze (above). Sprinkle 1 teaspoon instant coffee granules over the hot milk before adding the sugar. Substitute ½ cup coffee liqueur for the crème de menthe.

MAKES ABOUT 2½ PINTS.

Frozen Banana Pudding

4 large very ripe bananas, peeled
2 teaspoons fresh lemon juice
⅓ cup light cream or half-and-half

Slice the bananas into 1-inch-thick slices. In a bowl, sprinkle the banana slices with lemon juice and toss to coat evenly. Arrange them on a plate and freeze solid, preferably overnight. If you wish, after they are frozen, store them in a freezer bag until ready for use.

When ready to serve, place the frozen banana slices in the food processor work bowl with 2 tablespoons of the cream. Pulse the machine on and off until the mixture is the texture of coarse snow. With the machine running, drizzle in the remaining cream until the mixture is creamy but still frozen.

Serve immediately or store in the freezer up to 1 hour.

MAKES 6 SERVINGS.

PROCESSOR VANILLA WITH ADD-ONS

The basic recipe for Processor Vanilla Ice Cream was inspired by Anne Greer's recipes in *The Cuisine of the American Southwest*. The add-ons only begin to suggest what you can do with the basic recipe. Look at the "Basic Vanilla Ice Creams with Add-ons" in the chapter "Ice Creams: Traditional and New."

Basic Processor Vanilla Ice Cream

2 cups whole milk
⅔ cup sugar
2½ teaspoons unflavored gelatin
1¾ cups heavy cream
1½ teaspoons vanilla extract

Bring 1¼ cups of the milk to the simmering point; remove from the heat. In a medium bowl, combine the sugar and gelatin thoroughly. Add the heated milk all at once and whisk until the sugar and gelatin dissolve completely. Stir in the remaining milk, cream and vanilla. Pour the mixture into divided ice cube trays and freeze solid.

Just before serving or up to 3 hours ahead, place half of the frozen ice cream cubes in the food processor work bowl and pulse the machine on and off until the cubes are evenly chopped to the texture of coarse snow. Then run the machine continuously until the ice cream swirls around the blades and is creamy-looking. If the mixture is too hard to move freely around the bowl, allow it to thaw slightly or add a few drops of milk.

Process the remaining cubes or save them for another time. Serve immediately or pile ice cream into 1- or 2-pint containers. Cover and freeze.
MAKES ABOUT 2 PINTS.

Flavor Variations

ORANGE ICE CREAM

Follow the recipe for Basic Processor Vanilla Ice Cream. Reduce the sugar to ½ cup; reduce the vanilla to ½ teaspoon; stir in ½ cup frozen orange juice concentrate, thawed, and 3 tablespoons fresh lemon juice.

ALMOND ICE CREAM

Follow the recipe for Basic Processor Vanilla Ice Cream. Reduce the vanilla to 1 teaspoon. Add ¼ teaspoon almond extract. When the ice cream cubes have been processed to the creamy stage, stir in ⅔ cup chopped unsalted roasted or unroasted almonds (or ⅓ cup into half a recipe).

MAPLE-WALNUT ICE CREAM

Follow the recipe for Basic Processor Vanilla Ice Cream, using 1½ cups milk and 2¼ cups heavy cream. Substitute ¾ cup maple syrup for the sugar, and reduce the vanilla to 1 teaspoon. When the ice cream cubes have been processed to the creamy stage, stir in ⅔ cup chopped walnuts (or ⅓ cup into half a recipe).

COFFEE ICE CREAM

Follow the recipe for Basic Processor Vanilla Ice Cream. Increase the sugar to ¾ cup, and stir in 2½ tablespoons instant coffee granules dissolved in 1 tablespoon water.

MOCHA ICE CREAM

Follow the recipe for Basic Processor Vanilla Ice Cream. Increase the sugar to ¾ cup. Blend ⅓ cup unsweetened cocoa into the sugar and gelatin mixture. Stir 2½ tablespoons instant coffee granules dissolved in 3 tablespoons water into the final mixture.

Add-ons

Add-ons come in a variety of styles. There are the sauces that are actually swirl-ins, the chunky bits ranging from truffle chips to chopped toffee, nuts, or praline or even crumbled cookies that may be stirred in, and the liqueurs that may be mixed in to give added flavor and may be used on their own or along with add-ons or stir-ins.

See "Basic Vanilla Ice Creams with Add-ons" (page 16) for suggestions.

Extra-Rich Processor Vanilla Ice Cream

1 cup sugar
8 large egg yolks
Pinch of salt
2⅔ cups light cream or half-and-half

1½ cups heavy cream
2½ teaspoons vanilla extract

Combine the sugar, egg yolks, and salt in a bowl and mix them together well. In a heavy medium saucepan, heat the light cream or half-and-half to the simmering point. Gradually stir about 1 cup of the hot cream or half-and-half into the egg yolks. Return the egg yolk mixture to the cream or half-and-half in the pan and cook, stirring with a wooden spoon, over medium heat until the mixture coats the back of a spoon and a clean path remains when your finger is drawn across the back of the spoon. Cool to room temperature. Stir in the heavy cream and vanilla. Pour the mixture into divided ice cube trays and freeze solid.

Just before serving or up to 3 hours ahead, place half of the frozen ice cream cubes in the food processor work bowl and pulse the machine on and off until the cubes are evenly chopped to the texture of coarse snow. Then run the machine continuously until the ice cream swirls around the blades and is creamy-looking. If the mixture is too hard to move freely around the bowl, allow it to thaw slightly or add a few drops of milk.

Process the remaining cubes or save them for another time. Serve immediately or pile ice cream into 1- or 2-pint containers. Cover and freeze.
MAKES ABOUT 2 PINTS.

Processor Chocolate Ice Cream

3 ounces semisweet chocolate
½ cup sugar
2 teaspoons unflavored gelatin

2 cups whole milk
1¾ cups heavy cream
1½ teaspoons vanilla extract

Cut the chocolate into 9 or 10 pieces. Turn the food processor on and add the chocolate until finely chopped. Add the sugar and process the mixture to a fine powder. Leave the chocolate in the bowl.

In a very small pan, sprinkle the gelatin over 3 tablespoons water and allow to stand until it softens, about 3 minutes. In another pan bring the milk to the boiling point. With the processor on, pour the milk over the chocolate and process until the mixture is completely smooth. Heat the gelatin over low heat, stirring until no granules remain; pour into the chocolate mixture and blend well. Stir in the cream and vanilla. Pour the mixture into divided ice cube trays and freeze solid.

Just before serving or up to 3 hours ahead, place half of the frozen ice cream cubes in the food processor work bowl and pulse the machine on and off until the cubes are evenly chopped to the texture of coarse snow. Then run the machine continuously until the ice cream swirls around the blades and is creamy-looking. If the mixture is too hard to move freely around the bowl, allow it to thaw slightly or add a few drops of milk.

Process the remaining cubes or save them for another time. Serve immediately or pile ice cream into 1- or 2-pint containers. Cover and freeze. MAKES ABOUT 2 PINTS.

Flavor Variations

BITTERSWEET CHOCOLATE ICE CREAM

Follow the recipe for Processor Chocolate Ice Cream. Add ½ ounce unsweetened chocolate to the chocolate.

CHOCOLATE RUM ICE CREAM

Follow the recipe for Processor Chocolate Ice Cream. Increase the sugar by 1 tablespoon. When the ice cream cubes have been processed to the coarse snow stage, sprinkle 2½ tablespoons (or 3¾ teaspoons to each half of the recipe) golden rum over the mixture, then continue to process to the creamy stage. Freeze for 1 hour before serving.

CHOCOLATE–CHOCOLATE CHIP–GRAND MARNIER ICE CREAM

Follow the recipe for Processor Chocolate Ice Cream. Add 2 teaspoons grated orange zest to the milk before bringing it to the boiling point. When the ice cream cubes have been processed to the coarse snow stage, sprinkle 2½ tablespoons (or 3¾ teaspoons to each half of the recipe) Grand Marnier liqueur over the mixture, then continue to process to the creamy stage. Fold in ⅔ cup (⅓ cup to each half of the recipe) semisweet mini chocolate morsels or 2 ounces (1 ounce to each half of the recipe) chopped semisweet chocolate.

MEXICAN CHOCOLATE ICE CREAM

Follow the recipe for Processor Chocolate Ice Cream, adding ⅛ teaspoon ground cinnamon and ⅛ teaspoon ground mace to the sugar.

Add-ons

CHOCOLATE–BURNT ALMOND ICE CREAM

Follow the recipe for Processor Chocolate Ice Cream (page 8) or Bittersweet Chocolate Ice Cream (page 9), increasing the sugar by 1 tablespoon. Preheat the oven to 350° F. and roast ⅔ cup unsalted almonds on a baking sheet until lightly browned. Place on a plate to cool at least 1 hour, then chop coarsely. When half the ice cream cubes have been processed to the creamy stage, fold in half the almonds. Repeat with remaining ingredients. The Burnt Almond recipe on page 46 may be used in place of the plain roasted almonds.

CHOCOLATE–CHOCOLATE CHIP ICE CREAM

Follow the recipe for Processor Chocolate Ice Cream (page 8). When the ice cream cubes have been processed to the creamy stage, fold in ⅔ cup (⅓ cup to each half of the mixture) semisweet mini chocolate morsels or 2 ounces chopped semisweet chocolate. Freeze up to 1 hour before serving.

CHOCOLATE–NUT PRALINE ICE CREAM

Follow the recipe for Processor Chocolate Ice Cream (page 8). When the ice cream cubes have been processed to the creamy stage, fold in ⅔ cup (⅓ cup to each half of the mixture) coarsely chopped nut praline of your choice (see page 26). Freeze up to 1 hour before serving.

CHOCOLATE–WHITE CHOCOLATE CHIP ICE CREAM

Follow the recipe for Processor Chocolate Ice Cream (page 8), adding ¼ teaspoon almond extract along with the vanilla. When the ice cream cubes have been processed to the creamy stage, fold in 2 ounces (1 ounce to each half of the mixture) chopped white chocolate. Freeze up to 1 hour before serving.

CHOCOLATE–CHOCOLATE MINT CHIP ICE CREAM

Follow the recipe for Processor Chocolate Ice Cream (page 8). When the ice cream cubes have been processed to the creamy stage, fold in ⅔ cup (⅓ cup to each half of the mixture) semisweet chocolate mint chips or 2 ounces (1 ounce to each half recipe) chopped Tobler mint chocolate bar. Freeze up to 1 hour before serving.

CHOCOLATE COOKIE SANDWICH ICE CREAM

Follow the recipe for Processor Chocolate Ice Cream (page 8). When the ice cream cubes have been processed to the creamy stage, fold in 8 (4 to each half of the mixture) crushed chocolate sandwich cookies. Freeze up to 1 hour before serving.

Note: For additional food processor desserts, see also "Food Processor Fruit Sorbets" (page 66) and "The Easiest Fruit-Flavored Frozen Yogurts" (page 177).

Ice Creams: Traditional and New

Many commercial ice creams have come a long way since supermarkets carried only aerated, artificially colored and flavored, overly sweet products. If you're content with commercially produced ice creams, no matter how high their quality, you probably haven't luxuriated in the sensual delights of homemade ice cream fresh from the churn. Like freshly baked bread or cookies, or sun-ripened fruit just off the vine, there really is no substitute. Besides the undeniable superiority of homemade ice cream, cooks can blend mixtures to their individual taste. Light or creamy, lots of fruit or not, dark or light chocolate—flavors unavailable commercially may be created at home to your personal whim.

If you envision making ice cream from scratch as a battle with tons of dripping ice and an investment of many hours, it's time for an update on this rewarding experience. Nowadays home ice cream makers are available in an abundant array of styles and prices. The traditional White Mountain hand-cranked pine bucket—the one that has been manufactured for over a century—is still readily available. This sturdy model boasts cast-iron gear frame and gears, enabling it to churn almost frozen ice cream to its creamiest state. White Mountain also makes an electric version. Many of its machines come in sizes from 2 to 20 quarts. Richmond Cedar Works also manufactures similar machines with wooden barrels. These are somewhat lighter but still make excellent ice cream. This company's plastic-barreled models (such as the half-gallon-capacity Mini Yum Yum Machine) are ideal for people who need to save space.

The Williamsburg line offers various sizes in wooden-bucket, electrically cranked machines. The machines provide automatic shut-off and texture meters so you don't have to stop the machine to test the ice cream. Both Osrow and the Waring Ice Cream Parlor machines use table salt and ice cubes or crushed ice in a handy countertop-size, electrically run machine. Though not as sturdy as some of the wooden-bucket models, these 2-quart models are convenient, easy to handle, and inexpensive. Both make good ice cream in about 45 minutes. The Osrow machine's motor at the bottom and translucent cover make testing the ice cream simple: you don't have to lift off the heavy motor to test the ice cream. Few salt-and-ice machines have the advantage of a motor at the bottom.

Though wooden bucket churns are charming, are better insulators than the plastic ones, and require less ice and salt, they are bulkier and are harder to maintain. Plastic is easy to clean and is light and easy to handle and store on the kitchen shelf, though the plastic bucket isn't quite as durable as wood and will crack more easily.

The innovative Donvier ice cream maker may well revolutionize Americans' attitude toward making ice cream. I call it the Volkswagen of ice cream makers. Its inner pot, with a specially designed coolant, must be frozen overnight before a pint or quart of ice cream may be churned. Although the churning must be done by hand, it need not be continuous. So, according to the directions, a few turns between courses of dinner yield a freshly churned dessert.

Actually, with low-fat mixtures such as sorbets, you'll get better results if you churn intermittently at least 10 or 15 minutes out of the 20 or 25 it takes to freeze ice cream, especially if you intend to store the dessert in your freezer. High-fat mixtures require less attention. You can buy additional inner pots for the machine to allow one to cool while the other is in use. One drawback is that you must make way for a pot in the freezer and freeze it for at least 7 hours before churning. If you don't make a lot of ice cream, this may be the machine for you. My acid test for a good machine is to see how smoothly it will churn a sorbet mixture of fruit, water, and sugar. The smoother the texture, the better the machine's function. Donvier-made sorbets, while not really grainy, do have a very slight crystalline texture. I don't find it at all offensive, however. The machine freezes ice creams, especially cooked custard-based ice creams, beautifully.

The Cadillacs of popular ice cream machines are the Simac and Gaggia brands. Both companies have recently come out with smaller and lighter machines than their original designs. Some consumers prefer the older

Simac Il Gelataio, though it is larger and the bowl is inconveniently unremovable. It churns fabulous *gelato* (which is somewhat denser than ice cream because it allows little air into the canister) in about 25 minutes. It is so sturdy you could probably make ice cream daily, then hand it down to your great-grandchildren for them to use daily, too. It is, however, expensive.

The newer smaller and lighter Simac machines have a removable bowl. Some consumers have complained that the bowl sticks because of the freezing around the bowl as the ice cream churns. One solution is to remove the ice cream from the bowl, freeze it, then remove the canister from the machine after it warms up in a few minutes. A more convenient solution is always to use a very well chilled ice cream mixture so there is no condensation during the ice cream churning. The machine makes excellent *gelato*-style ice cream. For a less dense ice cream, the lid can be propped open for about 10 minutes halfway through the churning process to let in a little air. The freezing time for the new Il Gelataio is a lengthy 35 to 55 minutes.

Gaggia is slowly replacing its reliable Millegelati ice cream maker with its smaller, newer Gelateria model. I miss the control one has over the final product with the Millegelati, which requires a simple mixture of water and table salt as a coolant, and in which you could vary the proportions of salt to water, thus controlling the texture of the frozen mixture. It also has a knob on the lid that allows control of air flow. For very rich mixtures, a little air yields a less rock-hard product. The newer Gelateria, though, is smaller and sleeker-looking. It freezes chilled ice cream or sorbet mixtures in less than 20 minutes. Though the machine is not designed for letting in air, one could prop up the lid for a few minutes midway in the freezing cycle. It also comes with two bowls and blades so two or more flavors can be churned consecutively. These features make it one of the most convenient machines. With both the Simac and Gaggia, you can toss in chocolate chips, cookies, or other additions without turning off the machine, simply by lifting the lid at the appropriate time.

Two other machines, the Bialetti and Minigel, are very expensive high-tech machines. Both make great ice cream quickly, but their size and price effectively place them out of the home consumer market.

What Every Maker of Ice Cream Should Know

Many connoisseurs insist that hand-cranked ice cream is best. Is it simply the anticipation? No, they claim. You must crank the ice cream until you cannot budge the dasher. It is this determined churning at the end of the freezing process that makes the smoothest, most seductive ice cream. Machine-driven machines shut off too soon and don't continue agitation until the last possible moment. This may be true of many machines, but the new Italian models do churn until the ice cream is almost rock-hard. Their only drawback is a high price tag.

The ingredients, too, have various effects on ice cream texture. Eggs help to add body, viscosity, and smoothness, expecially when cooked in a custard ice cream base. Eggs also help incorporate and hold air in the ice cream mixture, discouraging large-crystal growth.

Too much fat from egg yolks, chocolate, and high-fat cream can result in a heavy, sticky ice cream. Ten to 18 percent fat is ideal. This is why some makers of ice cream prefer cocoa to chocolate in a rich chocolate ice cream mixture. Nonfat milk powder also gives smoothness and stability, especially to low-fat mixtures, but too much will make them sticky and grainy. Gelatin, a good stabilizer, should be used judiciously. Too much produces a gummy ice cream or sorbet.

Since alcohol doesn't freeze, adding it to frozen mixtures will make them slightly soft. It should be used sparingly unless cooked and should be added to ice cream only when the mixture is about 90 percent frozen, otherwise the ice cream will remain very slushy.

Tips for the Kitchen

- For salt and ice machines, freeze water in milk cartons. Then hammer the ice in the cartons to get crushed ice. Shaved ice, if you can get it, makes the coldest brine.
- Use rock salt if possible. It remains distributed in the ice, while table salt tends to fall to the bottom of the mixture.
- Too much salt used in the brine can give a granular texture to the final frozen mixture. However, when freezing ices such as Italian granitas this graininess is desirable. For ice cream, the best proportions are 1 part ice to 12 parts salt by measure or 1 to 6 by weight.
- An egg custard base for ice cream should never be boiled and should be only lightly thickened, otherwise the ice cream will be gummy.

- If whipped cream is to be folded into the ice cream mixture, don't fold it into a warm mixture or the air bubbles will be deflated.
- Whip cream only until very soft peaks will hold up—not until it is stiff.
- Don't boil milk or cream when making ice cream. The heat will co-agulate the milk protein and cause a grainy texture.
- Nuts, candies, and other solid materials and alcohol should be added toward the end of the freezing period.
- Let freshly churned ice cream set in the freezer for an hour or more before eating it. This ripening period helps to develop the best flavors and texture.
- Don't thaw and refreeze ice cream. Large crystals will develop and the ice cream will become icy.
- Ice cream is best eaten the day it is made. Cooked custard ice creams will hold up longer—up to 10 days.

BASIC VANILLA ICE CREAMS WITH ADD-ONS

Easy Excellent Vanilla Ice Cream

2 eggs, at room temperature
⅔ cup sugar
1½ cups half-and-half
2½ teaspoons vanilla extract
1 cup heavy cream

In a large bowl, beat the eggs until thick and light in color. Gradually beat in the sugar until light and fluffy. Stir in the half-and-half, vanilla, and cream.

Freeze according to the directions given for your ice cream maker.

MAKES ABOUT 1 QUART. DOUBLE THE RECIPE FOR LARGE ICE CREAM MAKERS IF YOU WISH TO MAKE ½ GALLON.

Old-fashioned Vanilla Custard Ice Cream

2 cups heavy cream
1 cup half-and-half
⅔ cup plus 1 tablespoon sugar
3 egg yolks
2¼ teaspoons vanilla extract

Heat the cream, half-and-half, and sugar in a heavy saucepan, over medium heat, stirring occasionally until the sugar is dissolved and the mixture is hot. In a medium bowl, beat the egg yolks until they are pale and creamy. Continue beating while gradually pouring in the cream mixture. Return the mixture to the pan. Stirring constantly, and without boiling, cook about 8 minutes over medium-low heat until the mixture will lightly coat the back of a spoon and a path drawn across the custard will remain undisturbed. Strain into a cool bowl, mix in the vanilla, and chill.

Freeze according to the instructions for your ice cream maker.

MAKES ABOUT 1 QUART. DOUBLE THE RECIPE FOR LARGE ICE CREAM MAKERS IF YOU WISH TO MAKE ½ GALLON.

Gloriously Rich French Vanilla Ice Cream

So extravagantly rich you will want to savor it by itself.

1 cup half-and-half
2 cups heavy cream
1 vanilla bean★
6 large egg yolks, at room temperature

¾ cup sugar
4 tablespoons unsalted butter

In a medium saucepan, heat the half-and-half, 1 cup cream, and the vanilla bean to the simmering point. Remove from the heat, cover, and let steep 30 minutes or longer. Remove the vanilla bean and, using the point of a paring knife, scrape the vanilla grains from the hull into the cream. In the top of a double boiler, beat the egg yolks until they are light and very fluffy. Beat while gradually adding the sugar until the eggs are pale ivory.

★ 2 teaspoons vanilla extract may be substituted. Mix it into the cold cream.

Heat the half-and-half mixture to the simmering point. Gradually beat it into the yolks in a fine stream. Place over barely simmering water (do not allow water to touch the upper pan) and cook, stirring and scraping the sides and bottom of the pan, until the mixture is thick and will hold a little mound when dropped on itself. Whisk in the butter a tablespoon at a time. Pour through a strainer or chinoise into a cool bowl and stir a few minutes to cool. Pour in the remaining 1 cup cream all at once and blend well. Chill.

Freeze according to the instructions for your ice cream maker.

MAKES ABOUT 1 QUART. DOUBLE THE RECIPE FOR LARGE ICE CREAM MAKERS IF YOU WISH TO MAKE ½ GALLON.

Rainy Day Vanilla Ice Cream

The ingredients for this ice cream are pantry staples.

2 eggs
6 tablespoons sugar
⅛ teaspoon salt
1 (12-ounce) can evaporated milk
2¼ teaspoons vanilla extract

In a large bowl, beat the eggs until very light-colored and foamy. Gradually beat in the sugar until the mixture is very thick. Beat in the salt. Stir in the milk, ½ cup water, and the vanilla. Chill well.

Freeze according to the instructions for your ice cream maker.

MAKES ABOUT 1 QUART. DOUBLE THE RECIPE FOR LARGE ICE CREAM MAKERS IF YOU WISH TO MAKE ½ GALLON.

VANILLA WITH BASIC FLAVOR CHANGES

Just a few additions, subtractions, or changes in cooking allow a variety of flavors such as caramel, coffee, or brown sugar. While they are good on their own, these basics can be given even greater dimension with add-ons. Try the Fudge Ripple Sauce, Caramelized Walnuts in Ice Cream, or Truffle Chips given below.

Caramel Ice Cream

Follow the recipe for Old-fashioned Vanilla Custard Ice Cream (page 17). Increase the sugar to ¾ cup. In a heavy medium saucepan, stir the sugar over medium heat until dissolved. When the sugar is smooth and golden-brown, remove from the heat and, stirring constantly, *immediately* pour in ½ cup boiling water. Stir over medium heat until the mixture is smooth. Cook about 10 minutes, stirring, until it is the texture of corn syrup. Pour in the half-and-half and cream and cook until they reach the simmering point. Continue with the recipe from this point on.

Butterscotch Ice Cream

Using the recipe for Easy Excellent Vanilla Ice Cream (page 16), increase the sugar to ¾ cup. Cook the sugar with 3 tablespoons unsalted butter until melted and well browned. Remove from the heat and stir in the half-and-half all at once. Reduce the vanilla to 1½ teaspoons. Return to the heat and cook, stirring until all the sugar lumps dissolve. Beat the eggs as directed. Beat in the sugar mixture. Continue with the recipe from this point on.

Orange Ice Cream

Using the recipe for Easy Excellent Vanilla Ice Cream (page 16), stir 3 tablespoons and 1 teaspoon frozen orange juice concentrate and 4 teaspoons fresh lemon juice into the half-and-half, until the two are thoroughly blended. Decrease the vanilla to 1 teaspoon. Proceed with the recipe, using the half-and-half and orange juice mixture as you would the half-and-half alone.

Ginger Ice Cream

Using the recipe for Old-fashioned Vanilla Custard Ice Cream (page 17), heat the cream, half-and-half and sugar with 3 (¼-inch-thick) slices fresh ginger, slightly smashed. When the sugar is dissolved, cover the mixture and allow it to steep about 2 hours. Remove the ginger slices and proceed with the recipe. Stir in 1½ tablespoons chopped preserved ginger in syrup with the vanilla toward the end of the freezing time.

Cinnamon Ice Cream

Using the recipe for Old-fashioned Vanilla Custard Ice Cream (page 17), substitute 2 tablespoons golden or dark brown sugar mixed with ¾ teaspoon cinnamon for 2 tablespoons of the granulated sugar. Proceed with the recipe as directed, but add 2 tablespoons frozen unsweetened apple juice concentrate to the custard mixture just after it is strained into the cool bowl.

Nutmeg Custard Ice Cream

Using the recipe for Old-fashioned Vanilla Custard Ice Cream (page 17), mix 1½ teaspoons freshly ground nutmeg into the sugar and proceed with the recipe. Do not use preground nutmeg, since it will make the ice cream bitter.

Coffee Ice Cream

Using the recipe for Easy Excellent Vanilla Ice Cream (page 16), heat ¼ cup of the half-and-half in a small pan. Sprinkle in 2 tablespoons and ½ teaspoon instant coffee granules, and stir to dissolve. Blend the coffee mixture with the remaining half-and-half. Continue with the recipe as directed.

Brown Sugar Ice Cream

Using the recipe for Old-fashioned Vanilla Custard Ice Cream (page 17), substitute golden or dark brown sugar for the granulated sugar.

Honey-Vanilla Custard Ice Cream

Using the recipe for Easy Excellent Vanilla Ice Cream (page 16) or Old-fashioned Vanilla Custard Ice Cream (page 17), replace the sugar with the same amount of honey and heat with the half-and-half until completely dissolved. Remove from the heat and continue with the recipe.

Peanut Butter Ice Cream

Using the recipe for Easy Excellent Vanilla Ice Cream (page 16), heat ⅓ cup smooth peanut butter with the half-and-half, stirring constantly until the two are thoroughly blended. Increase the sugar by 4 teaspoons. Proceed with the recipe, using the half-and-half and peanut butter mixture as you would the half-and-half alone.

Cognac Ice Cream

Using the recipe for Old-fashioned Vanilla Custard Ice Cream (page 17), mix 3½ tablespoons Cognac into the cream, half-and-half, and sugar before heating. Simmer the mixture at least 2 minutes and proceed with the recipe.

Vanilla Bourbon Ice Cream

Using the recipe for Old-fashioned Vanilla Custard Ice Cream (page 17), increase sugar to ¾ cup. Mix ¼ cup good-quality bourbon whiskey into the cream and half-and-half mixture before heating it, and proceed with the recipe.

THE SWIRL-INS AND STIR-INS

Dress up your own or commercially made ice cream. Thick fudge sauce or raspberry liqueur ripple sauce swirling through a rich vanilla, coffee, or peanut butter ice cream is just for starters. The stir-ins include my favorite Truffle Chips, which can be made in a wide variety of flavors including Amaretto or mint. A versatile stir-in such as Almond Praline works well in many flavors, too—don't just limit yourself to vanilla. It's good in Smooth Chocolate Custard, Coffee, Orange, or Honey-Vanilla Custard ice creams. These suggestions will give you a wealth of resources to create your own frozen delights.

Amaretto–Truffle Chip Ice Cream

Using the recipe for Old-fashioned Vanilla Custard Ice Cream (page 17), Cognac Ice Cream (page 21), or your favorite high-quality vanilla ice cream, blend the following truffle chips into 2 quarts ice cream just as it comes from the churn or after you have softened it just slightly. Real chocoholics might like the chips in Smooth Chocolate Custard or another mild-flavored chocolate ice cream or in a mocha ice cream. *Bon appétit!*

Truffle Chips

3 tablespoons heavy cream	*1 teaspoon unsalted butter*
4 ounces semisweet chocolate,	*⅔ cup powdered sugar, sifted*
finely chopped	*3 teaspoons Amaretto liqueur*
⅓ ounce unsweetened chocolate,	*⅛ teaspoon almond extract*
finely chopped	

In a heavy medium saucepan, warm the cream. Remove from the heat and stir in the chocolates, butter, and sugar. Stir until the chocolate is melted and the mixture is smooth. Cool to room temperature. Blend in the Amaretto and almond extract. Line an 8-inch-square baking pan with plastic wrap. Pour the truffle mixture evenly into the pan and freeze 4 hours, or until firm enough to cut. Invert the mixture onto a cutting board. With a heavy long knife, cut the truffles into $\frac{1}{4} \times \frac{1}{2}$-inch rectangles. Stir into 2 quarts slightly softened ice cream. Eat at once or freeze.

Flavor Variations

GRAND MARNIER TRUFFLE CHIPS IN ORANGE ICE CREAM

Follow the recipe for Truffle Chips, substituting 2 teaspoons Grand Marnier for the Amaretto and omitting the almond extract. Stir half of the chips into 1 quart Orange Ice Cream (page 19).

KAHLÚA TRUFFLE CHIP ICE CREAM

Follow the recipe for Truffle Chips. Stir $\frac{1}{8}$ teaspoon instant espresso powder into the cream. Substitute $2\frac{1}{2}$ teaspoons Kahlúa for the Amaretto and omit the almond extract. Stir half of the chips into 1 quart slightly softened coffee, chocolate, mocha, or Old-fashioned Vanilla Custard Ice Cream (page 17).

MINT TRUFFLE CHIP ICE CREAM

Follow the recipe for Truffle Chips. Substitute white crème de menthe for the Amaretto and omit the almond extract. Stir half of the chips into 1 quart slightly softened Smooth Chocolate Custard Ice Cream (page 41) or vanilla ice cream flavored with $\frac{1}{8}$ teaspoon peppermint or spearmint oil or extract. Or simply use plain vanilla ice cream and serve each scoop with several teaspoons of green crème de menthe sprinkled over it.

RIPPLE ICE CREAMS

Swirl these supple sauces through compatible ice creams to create mocha chocolate swirl, Irish coffee ripple, chocolate raspberry swirl, pecan butterscotch ripple, or more.

First make the ripple sauce and allow it to cool completely. Spread 1 quart slightly softened ice cream in a chilled 8- or 9-inch-square cake pan. Pour the sauce in ribbons across the surface of the ice cream. Pull a broad knife or metal spatula in an even zigzag pattern through the ice cream to give a marbled effect. Cover with plastic wrap, then foil, and freeze until firm, 4 hours or longer.

Fudge Ripple Sauce

This makes enough for 2 quarts ice cream. If you wish, half may be frozen for future use. Thaw the sauce and bring it to room temperature before using it.

1 tablespoon unsalted butter
1½ ounces semisweet chocolate or
  ¼ cup semisweet chocolate
  chips
¼ cup sugar

2½ tablespoons unsweetened cocoa
3 tablespoons half-and-half
¼ cup light corn syrup
¼ teaspoon vanilla extract

In a very small heavy saucepan, melt the butter and chocolate together. In a bowl, blend the sugar and cocoa together. Blend in the half-and-half, corn syrup, and vanilla. Stir the chocolate and butter together smoothly. Blend in the cocoa mixture. Cook over low heat, stirring, for 3 minutes.

Butterscotch Ripple

⅓ cup golden or light brown sugar, packed
4 teaspoons light corn syrup
3 tablespoons half-and-half
2 teaspoons unsalted butter
¼ teaspoon vanilla extract

In a small saucepan, combine the sugar, corn syrup, and half-and-half. Cook and stir over medium heat until the sugar dissolves and the mixture thickens slightly. Stir in the butter. Remove from the heat. Transfer to a bowl and stir in the vanilla. Cool to room temperature before using.

MAKES ENOUGH FOR 1 QUART. RECIPE MAY BE DOUBLED FOR ½ GALLON.

Raspberry Ripple

Combine ½ cup seedless raspberry jam with 1 tablespoon Chambord liqueur. Other compatible liqueurs are kirsch, Cointreau, Triple Sec, or raspberry eau-de-vie.

Strawberry Ripple

Combine ½ cup good-quality strawberry preserves with 1 tablespoon kirsch, Cointreau, or Triple Sec liqueur. Blend well and push through a sieve to puree the strawberries.

Cassis Ripple

Combine ½ cup black currant preserves with 3½–4 teaspoons Cassis liqueur.

Ripple Ideas

BUTTERSCOTCH PECAN RIPPLE ICE CREAM

Use Butterscotch Ripple with pecan ice cream or Butter Pecan Ice Cream (page 29).

CHOCOLATE PEANUT BUTTER RIPPLE ICE CREAM

Use Fudge Ripple Sauce and Peanut Butter Ice Cream (page 21) together. If you really want to gild the lily, blend 4 ounces crushed peanut brittle into the ice cream before swirling in the sauce.

CHOCOLATE-RASPBERRY RIPPLE ICE CREAM

Use Easy Excellent Chocolate Ice Cream (page 42) and Raspberry Ripple.

IRISH COFFEE RIPPLE ICE CREAM

Make Vanilla Bourbon Ice Cream (page 21). Add 2 teaspoons instant coffee granules to the bourbon before proceeding with the recipe. Swirl in Fudge Ripple Sauce. Serve with whipped cream.

DOUBLE STRAWBERRY RIPPLE ICE CREAM

Use Strawberry Ripple and strawberry ice cream together.

JAMOCA ALMOND FUDGE ICE CREAM

Use coffee or mocha ice cream. Blend ⅔ cup chopped roasted unsalted almonds into the softened ice cream. Swirl in Fudge Ripple Sauce.

CHOCOLATE CHERRY SWIRL ICE CREAM

Quarter 1 cup drained canned dark sweet cherries. Swirl them into vanilla ice cream. Swirl in Fudge Ripple Sauce.

NUTS IN ICE CREAM

There are many ways to use nuts in ice cream. They can simply be roasted and stirred in, as in Chocolate–Burnt Almond or Honey-Almond Ice Cream, or they can be given another dimension by mixing them with caramelized sugar, as in Almond Praline, Butter Pecan, or Peanut Brittle Ice Cream. Almost any nut responds favorably to this treatment. Another very easy and elegant stir-in, given to me by my friend Martha Casselman, is chopped chestnuts that have been preserved in syrup. And I like chopped baklava in Old-fashioned Vanilla Custard or Cinnamon Ice Cream.

Almond Praline Ice Cream

½ cup sugar
⅔ cup blanched,★ toasted chopped almonds
5 cups ice cream

Lightly oil or butter a baking sheet. In a small very heavy pan or small cast-iron skillet, combine the sugar and 3 tablespoons water and cook over low heat, occasionally swirling the pan, until the sugar dissolves.

★ In a bowl, cover the almonds with boiling water. Cool to room temperature. Remove almonds one at a time and squeeze between thumb and forefinger. Almond will slip from skin. Dry on paper towels.

Continue cooking until the sugar caramelizes (it will first turn grainy and then melt) and turns a golden-amber color. Don't allow the caramel to get too dark. Stir in the nuts and blend in well. Pour onto the baking sheet and cool until hardened. In a food processor, chop the praline into pieces the size of rice grains. Or transfer to a plastic bag and pound with a mallet to crush.

Soften the ice cream slightly. Place in a large bowl, sprinkle on the praline, and blend it into the ice cream. Freeze at least 4 hours.

Pecan Praline Ice Cream

½ cup coarsely chopped pecans
6 tablespoons sugar
1½ tablespoons unsalted butter
1 quart ice cream

Lightly oil or butter a baking sheet. In a heavy medium saucepan or cast-iron skillet, combine the pecans, sugar, and butter. Cook, stirring constantly, over medium heat until the sugar melts and becomes a golden-amber color. The sugar mixture should be smooth. Drop by rounded tablespoonfuls onto the baking sheet. Let cool completely. Break up the clusters into tiny pieces, by hand or with a mallet.

Soften the ice cream slightly and stir in the praline.

Flavor Variations

PECAN BUTTERSCOTCH SWIRL ICE CREAM

Follow the recipe for Pecan Praline Ice Cream. Swirl Butterscotch Ripple into the praline ice cream, following the directions on page 24.

HAZELNUT PRALINE ICE CREAM

Follow the recipe for Almond Praline Ice Cream, substituting roasted skinned hazelnuts for the almonds. The technique for skinning hazelnuts may be found on page 172, in the recipe for Frozen Hazelnut Praline Soufflé.

MACADAMIA NUT PRALINE ICE CREEAM

Follow the recipe for Almond Praline Ice Cream, substituting roasted chopped unsalted macadamia nuts for the almonds. Good with pineapple or Tropical Mango Ice Cream (page 58).

Coconut Praline

½ cup sugar
1½ tablespoons unsalted butter
⅔ cup sweetened shredded coconut

Lightly oil or butter a baking sheet and have 2 forks ready. In a heavy saucepan over medium heat, heat the sugar and butter together, stirring occasionally until the sugar is melted and a pale golden color and the mixture is smooth. Sprinkle in the coconut and blend it with the caramel, using the forks to help separate and coat the coconut strands with caramel. When the coconut is evenly mixed in, turn the mixture out onto the baking sheet and separate the clumps with the forks or spread it into a thin layer. When the praline is cool, crumble it up, pounding any sturdy clumps with a mallet if necessary.

MAKES ABOUT 1¼ CUPS.

Praline Ice Cream Suggestions

CHOCOLATE-PRALINE ICE CREAM

Stir Almond Praline—see Almond Praline Ice Cream (page 26)—into Smooth Chocolate Custard Ice Cream (page 41).

PRALINE-FUDGE SWIRL ICE CREAM

Swirl half a recipe for Fudge Ripple Sauce (page 24) into Almond Praline Ice Cream (page 26).

PRALINE-COFFEE-FUDGE SWIRL ICE CREAM

Stir your favorite praline into Coffee Ice Cream (page 20). Swirl with Fudge Ripple Sauce (page 24).

PUMPKIN-PRALINE ICE CREAM

Stir your favorite praline into Pumpkin Ice Cream (page 58).

COGNAC PRALINE ICE CREAM

Stir your favorite praline into Cognac Ice Cream (page 21). And stir in half a recipe for Fudge Ripple Sauce (page 24) for Cognac Praline–Fudge Ripple Ice Cream.

Other Compatible Ice Creams for Almond Praline

MOCHA

COFFEE

CARAMEL

Butter Pecan Ice Cream

6½ tablespoons light brown sugar, packed
2 tablespoons unsalted butter, melted
6½ tablespoons heavy cream
¾ cup pecan halves or pieces, chopped the size of rice grains

1½ teaspoons vanilla extract
1 quart Old-fashioned Vanilla Custard Ice Cream (page 17)

Lightly butter a large heatproof plate or a baking pan. In a heavy medium saucepan, over medium-high heat, cook the sugar until it begins to melt. Reduce the heat to medium and cook, stirring, until all the sugar is melted, a light golden amber color, and completely smooth. Quickly stir in the butter and the cream. Stir until all the lumps disappear. Stir in the pecans and blend in well. Stir in the vanilla. Pour onto the plate and cool completely; the mixture will remain soft.

Soften the ice cream just slightly. Stir in the pecan mixture. Freeze until firm, about 4 hours or more.

MAKES ABOUT 1 QUART.

Honey-Almond Ice Cream

Make Honey–Vanilla Custard Ice Cream according to the directions on page 21. Fold in ⅔ cup chopped roasted unsalted almonds just when the ice cream has finished being churned.

Caramelized Walnuts in Ice Cream

This is similar to praline, but the nuts are not crushed fine. It is great with vanilla or the suggested Caramel Ice Cream.

1 cup walnuts, chopped the size
  of peas
1½ tablespoons unsalted butter

⅔ cup sugar
1 quart Caramel Ice Cream,
  (page 19) or other ice cream

Lightly oil or butter a baking sheet. In a heavy medium saucepan or cast-iron skillet, combine the nuts, butter, and sugar. Cook, stirring constantly, over medium heat until the sugar melts and becomes a golden-amber color. The sugar mixture should be smooth. Turn onto the baking sheet, using 2 forks to pull the nuts into a single thin layer. Cool completely, then break the nut pieces apart, using 2 forks to separate any stubborn clumps. Soften the ice cream slightly and stir in the nuts. Freeze until firm.

MAKES ABOUT 1 QUART.

Flavor Variations

DOUBLE CHOCOLATE WALNUT SWIRL ICE CREAM

Follow the recipe for Caramelized Walnuts in Ice Cream. Slightly soften 1 quart of a mild chocolate ice cream, or use Smooth Chocolate Custard Ice Cream (page 41). Mix in ⅔ cup of the cooled caramelized walnuts. Swirl in Fudge Ripple Sauce, following the directions on page 24.

COFFEE-WALNUT ICE CREAM

Follow the recipe for Caramelized Walnuts in Ice Cream. Stir the cooled nuts into 5 cups slightly softened Coffee Ice Cream (page 20). Freeze until firm.

GINGER-WALNUT ICE CREAM

This would complement an Oriental meal.

Follow the recipe for Caramelized Walnuts in Ice Cream. Stir a generous ½ cup of the cooled nuts into 1 quart Ginger Ice Cream (page 19) just as it is finished churning, or into a slightly softened commercially made ginger ice cream. Freeze until firm.

Marty's Quick Chestnut Ice Cream

This is a friend's delightful contribution.

Soften 1 quart vanilla or Old-fashioned Vanilla Custard Ice Cream (page 17). Drain 1 (10-ounce) jar whole chestnuts in syrup, reserving the syrup. Chop the chestnuts into pieces the size of large peanuts. Stir the chestnuts into the ice cream and freeze until firm. Blend the syrup with 1 tablespoon Cognac or brandy, or more to taste. Serve scoops of the ice cream with a little of the syrup poured over it.

Peanut Brittle Ice Cream

Soften 1 quart vanilla ice cream. Crush 6 ounces peanut brittle. Stir the peanut brittle into the softened ice cream. This is good plain or with chocolate sauce.

Meringue Nut Crunch in Ice Cream

The French have long recognized the blissful combination of meringue with ice cream. It turns up in vacherins, meringues glacés, and various tortes. The sweet, airy crunchiness is also perfect blended into ice cream.

A few hours before eating the ice cream, soften it slightly, then blend in the Meringue Nut Crunch (page 32), or simply sprinkle them on top. One recipe is enough to blend into 2 quarts of ice cream.

Meringue Nut Crunch

This is a wonderful garnish for ice cream or still-frozen desserts. It also makes a nice crust for an ice cream pie or torte.

2 large egg whites, at room temperature
½ cup sugar
½ teaspoon vanilla extract
½ cup very finely chopped nuts

Preheat the oven to 225° F. Cut baking parchment to fit 2 baking sheets and affix it to the pans with vegetable shortening. Using a 9-inch round or 8-inch-square cake pan, trace the pan shape on the parchment. Lightly film an area slightly larger than the drawn shape with shortening.

Beat the egg whites until soft peaks form. Very gradually add the sugar and beat until the meringue is stiff and glossy. Beat in the vanilla. Fold in the nuts.

Spread the meringue evenly on the shapes. Bake about 1½ hours, until the meringues are crisp and barely colored. Turn off the oven and allow the meringues to cool in the oven.

Peel the meringues from the parchment and crumble them. Serve on ice cream or store in an airtight container.

MAKES ENOUGH FOR 2 QUARTS ICE CREAM.

Flavor Variation

FUDGE RIPPLE MERINGUE ICE CREAM

Blend one recipe Meringue Nut Crunch (see above) into a slightly softened quart of vanilla, caramel, or coffee ice cream. Swirl in one-half recipe Fudge Ripple Sauce (page 24). Freeze until firm.

Baklava Ice Cream

Soften 1 quart vanilla or Cinnamon Ice Cream (page 20). Lay 4 diamond-shaped pieces baklava on their sides. Slice into ½-inch-thick slices. Cut each slice into quarters. Cut the ice cream into 4 and blend one quarter of the baklava pieces into each. Place all the Baklava Ice Cream in a large bowl. Cover with plastic wrap. Freeze until firm, about 4 hours.

Chocolate-Covered Nut Chips

These chocolate chips are filled with nuts.

*6 ounces (1 cup) semisweet choco-
     late chips
1 tablespoon unsalted butter*

*1½ tablespoons light corn syrup
1 cup finely chopped roasted or
     unroasted unsalted almonds*

Line a 9-inch-square cake pan with foil. Butter the foil. In the top of a double boiler, or in a medium pan within another pan of water, over low heat, melt the chocolate and butter together. Add the corn syrup and stir until smooth. Remove from the heat. Stir in the almonds. Spread the mixture in the pan and chill until completely firm. Break or chop into tiny chips.

MAKES ENOUGH FOR 2½ QUARTS ICE CREAM.

Marzipan Swirl Ice Cream

Swirl this into chocolate, vanilla, or peach ice cream.

*1 (7-ounce) package almond paste
2 tablespoons heavy cream
6 tablespoons light corn syrup*

*1 teaspoon fresh lemon juice
Few drops almond extract
5 cups ice cream*

Place a medium bowl in another bowl or pan of hot water about 2 inches deep. Break the almond paste into little pieces and crumble it into the bowl. Blend in the cream and the corn syrup, lemon juice, and almond extract until the mixture is completely smooth. Slightly soften the ice cream and spread it in a baking pan. Drizzle the swirl over the ice cream and swirl it in with a metal spatula or heavy knife.

MAKES ABOUT 3 PINTS.

Chocolate Marzipan Swirl Ice Cream

1 (7-ounce) package almond paste
¾ cup chocolate syrup
Few drops almond extract
2 quarts vanilla ice cream

Place a medium bowl in another bowl or pan of hot water about 2 inches deep. Break the almond paste into little pieces and crumble it into the bowl. Gradually blend in the chocolate syrup and then the almond extract, stirring until the mixture is completely smooth. Slightly soften the ice cream and spread it in a baking pan. Drizzle the swirl over the ice cream and swirl it in with a metal spatula or heavy knife.

MAKES ABOUT 2 QUARTS.

Chestnut Swirl Ice Cream

1 (8½-ounce) can sweetened chestnut spread (crème de marrons)

2 tablespoons light corn syrup
2 teaspoons Cognac or brandy
3 pints vanilla ice cream

Place the chestnut spread in the bowl and crumble it with a fork. Gradually blend in the corn syrup and then the Cognac until the mixture is completely smooth. Chill several hours or overnight. Slightly soften the ice cream and spread it in a baking pan. Drizzle the swirl over the ice cream and swirl it in with a metal spatula or heavy knife.

MAKES ABOUT 2 QUARTS.

MORE DELICIOUS STIR-INS

Some are traditional, such as Rum-Raisin or Oreo or Hydrox Cookie Ice Cream, and some, like the Florentine Ice Cream, are unconventional. Here are my flavor combination suggestions, but you might dream up a spectacular new one.

Rum-Raisin Ice Cream

⅓ cup dark raisins
⅓ cup golden raisins
About ¾ cup dark rum
⅓ cup walnuts, chopped the size
   of peas
1 quart vanilla ice cream, slightly

softened, or 1 recipe Old-
fashioned Vanilla Custard Ice
Cream (page 17) or Easy
Excellent Vanilla Ice Cream
(page 16)

Place the raisins in a small bowl. Pour in enough rum to cover them and
let soak overnight. Drain the raisins. Mix the raisins and walnuts together.
Spread out the ice cream in a large bowl or baking pan. Pour the raisin
mixture evenly over the surface, then stir into the ice cream. Freeze until
firm.

MAKES ABOUT 5 CUPS.

Oreo or Hydrox Cookie Ice Cream

Prepare a quart of any of the following ice cream flavors: vanilla, chocolate,
Smooth Chocolate Custard (page 41), Brown Sugar (page 20), Caramel
(page 19), or Cognac (page 21). Finely crush 8–10 Hydrox or Oreo cookies
to make 1 cup of large crumbs. Fold them into the ice cream when it is
almost completely churned. Freeze until firm.

   Or soften prepared ice cream, spread it in a baking dish, sprinkle the
crumbs over it, and fold them in. Freeze until firm.

MAKES ABOUT 5 CUPS.

Nut Cake Ice Cream

This delicious crumbly mixture turns ice cream into an old-fashioned
pandowdy dessert. I like it with bourbon, vanilla, or butterscotch ice
cream.

1 cup golden or light brown sugar,
    packed
1 large egg
⅓ cup all-purpose flour
½ teaspoon baking soda

½ teaspoon ground cinnamon
½ cup pecans or walnuts, chopped
    the size of peas
2 quarts ice cream

Preheat the oven to 350° F. Lightly grease an 8-inch-square cake pan. In a medium bowl, blend the sugar and egg together. Blend in the flour, baking soda, and cinnamon. Mix in the nuts. Spread in the prepared pan. Bake in the center of the oven 18 to 20 minutes, or until the sides are dry and shrink slightly from the pan sides. Cool on a rack at least 2 hours. Remove from the pan and break into pieces about the size of a pecan half.

Soften the ice cream and spread it in a baking pan. Sprinkle the cake over the ice cream and fold it in. Freeze about 4 hours. Serve the ice cream slightly softened.

MAKES ABOUT 2½ QUARTS.

Almond Macaroon Ice Cream

Coarsely crush enough chocolate or plain almond macaroons to make ⅔ cup. Use the recipes on page 211 or commercially made cookies. Soften 1 quart of your favorite ice cream and spread it in a baking pan. Sprinkle the crushed cookies over the surface of the ice cream and fold them in. Freeze until firm.

MAKES ABOUT 1 QUART.

Florentine Ice Cream

Crunchy, chocolate-coated Florentine cookies give a subtly flavored crunch to ice cream.

About 10 (3-inch-round) Florentine
    cookies
1 quart ice cream
Orange flower water (optional—see below)

Add the orange flower water if using vanilla ice cream. Or use Orange Ice Cream (page 19). Smooth Chocolate Custard (page 41) or Cognac (page 21) Ice Cream are delicious too.

Crush the cookies to about the size of peanut halves. Slightly soften the ice cream. Sprinkle 2 teaspoons orange flower water over the vanilla ice cream, if using. Sprinkle the broken cookies over the ice cream and fold everything together. Freeze until firm.

MAKES ABOUT 2½ PINTS.

VARIATION

Use 2 tablespoons Grand Marnier or Cointreau liqueur over vanilla ice cream in place of the orange flower water. The ice cream will remain slightly soft even after you have frozen it.

Crunchy Oats Ice Cream

Soften 1 quart ice cream. Spread it in a baking pan and sprinkle ½ cup granola cereal over it. Sprinkle caramelized walnuts (see Caramelized Walnuts in Ice Cream, page 30) or chopped roasted almonds over the cereal. Blend everything together and freeze until firm. Delicious in Cinnamon (page 20), Nutmeg Custard (page 20), Caramel (page 19), Maple-Walnut (page 7), Butterscotch (page 19), Old-fashioned Vanilla Custard (page 17), or Honey–Vanilla Custard Ice Cream (page 21).

MAKES ABOUT 2½ PINTS.

Nesselrode-Rum Ice Cream

Candied fruits and rum give this ice cream an old-world flavor.

Combine ¼ cup each diced glazed cherries, glazed pineapple, and golden raisins with ¾ cup walnuts, chopped the size of peas, and 2 tablespoons candied orange peel. Mix these together well and sprinkle with ½ cup dark rum. Blend in well and allow the mixture to marinate overnight. Stir the mixture very well, then drain off any unabsorbed rum.

Soften 3 pints vanilla ice cream and spread it in a baking pan. Spread the fruit and nut mixture over the ice cream and fold it in. Freeze about 6 hours.

MAKES ABOUT 2 QUARTS.

CANDIES IN ICE CREAM

Commercially made ice creams are often sold with some of the following additions stirred into them. If you are making your own ice cream, these are a nice way to extend your repertoire. Some of them, such as the Peppermint Stick, are delightful in pies and cakes of your own creation. See the cakes and pies chapter for basic recipes such as Sponge Sheet Cake (page 135) and the basic ice cream pie (page 138).

Peppermint Stick Ice Cream

Crush enough peppermint candy or candy canes to make ¾ cup. Soften 1 quart vanilla ice cream and spread it in a baking pan. Spread the crushed candy over the ice cream and fold it in. Freeze about 6 hours.

MAKES ABOUT 5 CUPS.

Toffee Chip Ice Cream

Use these chips to create Toffee Coffee or in chocolate, vanilla, honey, mocha, or ginger ice creams.

Crush enough hard English toffee to make ⅔ cup. (See the recipe on page 213 if you wish to make your own.) Soften 1 quart ice cream and spread it in a baking pan. Sprinkle the crushed candy over the ice cream and fold it in. Freeze about 6 hours.

MAKES ABOUT 5 CUPS.

Almond Roca Crunch

Cut up 10 pieces of Almond Roca candy with a heavy knife. Soften 1 quart ice cream and spread it in a baking pan. Strew the candy pieces over the ice cream and fold it in. Freeze about 6 hours. Great with chocolate or vanilla custard ice cream or coffee, bourbon, or Cognac ice creams. Or stir 2 tablespoons Amaretto or light crème de cacao liqueur into slightly softened vanilla ice cream. Then stir in the Almond Roca candy.

MAKES ABOUT 5 CUPS.

Chocolate-Covered Raisin–Nut Crunch Ice Cream

Combine ⅔ cup chocolate-covered raisins and ½ cup caramelized walnuts (see page 30). Soften 1 quart of your favorite ice cream and spread it in a baking pan. Sprinkle the mixture over the ice cream and fold it in. Freeze about 6 hours.

MAKES ABOUT 5 CUPS.

White Chocolate Chips in Deep Chocolate Ice Cream

In a food processor, using the pulsing action, or with a heavy knife, chop 1 (3-ounce) bar white chocolate into tiny chips. Soften 1 quart of your favorite chocolate ice cream and spread it in a baking pan. Sprinkle the candy pieces over the ice cream and fold it in. Freeze about 6 hours.

MAKES ABOUT 1 QUART.

Milk Chocolate Chips in Coffee Ice Cream

In a food processor, using the pulsing action, or with a heavy knife, chop 3 ounces milk chocolate into tiny chips. Soften 1 quart coffee ice cream and spread it in a baking pan. Sprinkle the candy pieces over the ice cream and fold it in. Freeze about 6 hours.

MAKES ABOUT 1 QUART.

Traditional Chocolate Chip Ice Cream

In a food processor, using the pulsing action, or with a heavy knife, chop 3 ounce semisweet chocolate into tiny chips. Soften 1 quart of your favorite ice cream and spread it in a baking pan. Sprinkle the candy pieces over the ice cream and fold it in. Freeze about 6 hours.

MAKES ABOUT 1 QUART.

Heath Bar or Butterfinger Crunch Ice Cream

Cut 3 (1⅛-ounce) Heath bars or 2 (2.6-ounce) Butterfinger bars into small pieces. Soften 1 quart any flavor ice cream and spread it in a baking pan. Sprinkle the candy pieces over the ice cream and fold it in. Freeze about 6 hours.

MAKES ABOUT 1 QUART.

Mincemeat Ice Cream

Soften 1 quart vanilla or Cognac Ice Cream (page 21). Spread it in a baking pan. Spoon 1 cup prepared mincemeat (without liquor) over the ice cream and blend it in. Freeze about 6 hours.

MAKES ABOUT 2½ PINTS.

THE CHOCOLATE ICE CREAM SERIES

Chocolate lovers are a finicky lot. Some love a smooth velvety chocolate ice cream—not too intense—with the delicious body of a custard base. Others seek out the deepest chocolate flavor but don't care for an overwhelmingly creamy mixture. Then there is the go-for-broke group, who relish the richest possible ice cream with the most chocolaty flavor. For all connoisseurs of plain chocolate ice cream, this section includes ice creams in ascending order of chocolatiness. They range from a silky rich chocolate custard to the deepest Blackout Chocolate Gelato.

To avoid boredom, some chocolate lovers switch around, depending on their mood, rather than insisting on a favorite they've cultivated. They are usually the first to sample new flavors such as chocolate raspberry or chocolate burnt almond, chocolate coconut, chocolate truffle chip, or chocolate marzipan swirl. More adventurous chocolate lovers concoct their own. Given a good basic chocolate ice cream, they might stir in some almond praline, peanut brittle, or chocolate mint candies. Though a whole section of chocolate variations follows, it merely samples the possibilities.

A Good Cocoa Ice Cream

4 large egg yolks
¾ cup sugar
1 cup half-and-half
⅛ teaspoon salt

6 tablespoons Dutch-process cocoa
    powder, sifted
2 cups heavy cream
2¼ teaspoons vanilla extract

In the top of a double boiler, combine the egg yolks and sugar, and beat until thick and light in color. Gradually beat in the half-and-half and salt. Gradually beat in the cocoa. Place the pan over simmering water and cook, beating until the mixture is thick and about double in volume, about 8 minutes. Remove from over the hot water and dip the pan into a bowl of cold water, stirring all the while. Add the cream all at once and blend it in thoroughly. Blend in the vanilla. Chill the ice cream mixture. Freeze according to the instructions for your ice cream maker. Transfer to freezer containers for storage.

MAKES ABOUT 1 QUART.

Smooth Chocolate Custard Ice Cream

1½ cups half-and-half
4 ounces semisweet or bittersweet
    chocolate, finely chopped
1½ cups heavy cream, chilled

⅔ cup plus 1 teaspoon sugar
4 large egg yolks, at room temper-
    ature
½ teaspoon vanilla extract

Chill a 2-quart or larger mixing bowl. Combine the half-and-half, chocolate, and ½ cup of the cream in a heavy medium saucepan over low heat and stir until the chocolate is completely melted. Beat the sugar and egg yolks together until the mixture is thick and the texture of whipped cream. Slowly pour the chocolate mixture in a fine stream over the yolks, beating constantly. Return the mixture to the saucepan and cook over very low heat, whisking constantly, until the mixture will coat a spoon and a path drawn across the custard will remain undisturbed. The custard should not boil. Pour the custard into the chilled bowl and stir 1 minute. Pour in the remaining 1 cup chilled cream and mix well. Mix in the vanilla. Chill if necessary. Freeze according to the instructions for your ice cream maker. Transfer to freezer containers for storage.

MAKES ABOUT 1 QUART.

Easy Excellent Chocolate Ice Cream

1½ cups half-and-half
4 ounces semisweet or bittersweet
  chocolate, chopped
2 eggs, at room temperature

⅔ cup sugar
1 teaspoon vanilla extract
1 cup heavy cream

In a heavy saucepan, combine the half-and-half and chocolate. Cook over medium-low heat, stirring occasionally, until the chocolate is completely melted and the mixture is smooth. Meanwhile, beat the eggs until they are thick and light in color. Gradually beat in the sugar until the mixture is light and fluffy. Gradually beat in the hot chocolate mixture. Stir in the vanilla and cream; chill. Freeze according to the instructions for your ice cream maker. Transfer to freezer containers for storage.

MAKES ABOUT 1 QUART.

Mexican Chocolate Ice Cream

Prepare Easy Excellent Chocolate Ice Cream (see above), mixing ⅜ teaspoon ground cinnamon into the half-and-half before adding the chocolate. After adding the cream, stir in ⅓ cup finely ground roasted unsalted almonds. Freeze according to the instructions for your ice cream maker. Transfer to freezer containers for storage.

MAKES ABOUT 1 QUART.

White Chocolate Ice Cream

This dense, rich ice cream is most delicious when served slightly softened.

2 cups half-and-half
2½ teaspoons grated orange zest
6 ounces white chocolate, chopped
 about the size of peas
2 large eggs

⅓ cup sugar
1 cup heavy cream
⅛ teaspoon almond extract
¼ teaspoon vanilla extract

Place the half-and-half and orange zest in a heavy saucepan. Scald the mixture, then simmer it 5 minutes. Remove from the heat and let stand 30 minutes or as long as overnight. Strain the half-and-half to remove the zest. Measure to be sure you have 2 cups, adding more half-and-half if necessary. Return it to the pan and mix in the chocolate. Cook, stirring occasionally, until the chocolate begins to melt. When the chocolate is about three-quarters melted, stir continuously until the mixture is completely smooth. Remove from the heat.

Beat the eggs until they are light in color. Gradually beat in the sugar until the eggs are very thick and pale ivory and the sugar is dissolved. Gradually beat in the chocolate mixture. Beat in the cream, almond extract, and vanilla. Chill the mixture. Freeze according to the instructions for your ice cream maker. Transfer to freezer containers for storage.

MAKES ABOUT 1 QUART; MAY BE DOUBLED FOR AN ICE CREAM MAKER WITH A ½-GALLON OR LARGER CAPACITY.

White Russian Ice Cream

Follow the directions for White Chocolate Ice Cream (see above). Substitute ¼ cup whole roasted coffee beans for the orange zest. Decrease the sugar to ¼ cup. Omit the almond extract. When the ice cream is almost completely frozen, add 2 tablespoons coffee liqueur and continue to freeeze until finished.

Serious Chocolate Lovers' Ice Cream

Extravagantly rich and quite dark, but not as dark as the Ultra-Dark Chocolate Ice Cream below.

2¾ cups heavy cream
Pinch of salt
5 ounces semisweet or bittersweet
    chocolate, chopped
½ ounce unsweetened chocolate,
    chopped

¾ cup sugar
2 large egg yolks, at room temper-
    ature
1 teaspoon vanilla extract

Combine ⅔ cup of the cream, the salt, and the chocolates in a heavy saucepan. Cook over medium heat, stirring occasionally, until the chocolate is completely melted and smooth. Remove from the heat. In a very small saucepan, combine the sugar and 3 tablespoons boiling water. Bring to a boil. Scrape down any sugar crystals clinging to the side of the pan and boil 4 minutes. Meanwhile, beat the egg yolks until they are light in color and fluffy. Gradually add the hot sugar syrup in a thin stream, beating at high speed until the mixture is ivory-colored and a ribbon of egg will remain on the surface when the beaters are lifted.

Place the chocolate mixture in the large bowl of an electric mixer. Gradually beat in the remaining cream. Beat in the vanilla. Fold in the egg mixture by thirds, blending everything together thoroughly. Freeze according to the instructions for your ice cream maker. Transfer to freezer containers for storage.

MAKES ABOUT 1½ QUARTS.

Ultra-Dark Chocolate Ice Cream

1½ cups milk
8 ounces semisweet chocolate,
    chopped
1 ounce unsweetened chocolate,
    chopped

4 egg yolks, at room temperature
1 cup sugar
1½ cups heavy cream

Chill a 2-quart or larger mixing bowl. Combine the milk and chocolates in a heavy medium saucepan over medium-low heat and stir until the chocolate is melted. Beat the egg yolks until they are light and fluffy.

Gradually beat in the sugar until the mixture is pale ivory and a ribbon of egg remains on the surface when the beaters are lifted. Gradually beat in the chocolate mixture. Return the mixture to the pan and cook, stirring, until it coats the back of a spoon and a path drawn across the custard remains undisturbed. Pour the mixture into the chilled bowl and stir in the cream. Press a film of plastic wrap over the surface of the mixture and chill. Freeze according to the instructions for your ice cream maker. Transfer to freezer containers for storage.

MAKES ABOUT 1½ QUARTS.

Blackout Chocolate Gelato

12 ounces bittersweet or semisweet chocolate, chopped
6 tablespoons sugar

6 egg yolks, at room temperature
1½ cups half-and-half
½ teaspoon vanilla extract

Chill a large bowl (in the freezer if possible). Melt the chocolate in the covered top of a double boiler over simmering water. Remove from the heat and stir the chocolate until it is smooth. Combine the sugar and ¾ cup water in a heavy saucepan. Cook over low heat, swirling the pan occasionally, until the sugar is dissolved. Turn up the heat and bring the mixture to a boil; remove from the heat. Beat the egg yolks until they are pale and fluffy. Beating on low speed, slowly pour the sugar syrup into the yolks in a fine stream. Return the mixture to the pan and cook, stirring, over low heat until the mixture coats the back of a spoon and a path drawn across the custard remains undisturbed. Remove from the heat and stir in the chocolate. Pour into the chilled bowl. Stir until the mixture cools to room temperature. Blend in the half-and-half and vanilla; chill. Freeze according to the instructions for your ice cream maker. Transfer to freezer containers for storage.

MAKES ABOUT 1 QUART.

Chocolate–Chocolate Chip Ice Cream

2 ounces semisweet chocolate
2 ounces unsweetened chocolate
⅛ teaspoon salt
¾ cup sugar

1 cup whole milk
2 eggs, well beaten
2 cups heavy cream
1½ teaspoons vanilla extract

Chill a large bowl (in the freezer if possible). In a food processor, using the pulsing action, or with a heavy knife, chop the semisweet chocolate into fine chips; set aside. Combine the unsweetened chocolate, salt, and ½ cup of the sugar in a food processor and pulse the machine on and off until the chocolate is finely chopped. Or chop the chocolate by hand and combine it with the salt and all of the sugar. In a heavy saucepan, combine the chopped unsweetened chocolate mixture, the remaining sugar, and the milk and cook, stirring, over medium heat, until the chocolate is completely melted and the mixture is smooth. Stir a little of the mixture into the eggs. Then gradually return the egg mixture to the pan and cook, stirring constantly, over very low heat until the mixture will coat a spoon and a path drawn through the custard will remain undisturbed. Strain into the chilled bowl and cool. Blend in the cream and vanilla.

Freeze according to the instructions for your ice cream maker until the ice cream is mushy. Blend in the semisweet chips and complete the freezing process. Transfer to freezer containers for storage.

MAKES ABOUT 1 QUART.

Flavor Variation

CHOCOLATE-BURNT ALMOND ICE CREAM

Follow the previous recipe for Chocolate–Chocolate Chip Ice Cream, adding the following Burnt Almonds to the ice cream instead of semisweet chocolate.

Burnt Almonds
Butter
⅓ cup wateer
⅓ cup sugar
½ cup whole blanched almonds

Butter a rimmed baking sheet. Combine water, sugar, and almonds in a small heavy skillet. Cook, stirring, over medium heat until the mixture boils. Reduce the heat and simmer without stirring until the almonds start to make a popping sound, about 15 to 20 minutes; remove from the heat. Stir with a wooden spoon until the mixture crystallizes and looks dry. Return the skillet to the heat and cook, stirring, over medium-high heat until the sugar mixture melts slightly and begins to cling to the almonds. Turn out onto the prepared pan and separate with a fork; cool completely. Chop the almonds coarsely.

MAKES ABOUT 1 QUART.

Rocky Road Ice Cream

Follow the recipe for A Good Cocoa Ice Cream (page 41) or Easy Excellent Chocolate Ice Cream. When the ice cream is about three-quarters frozen, stir in 1 ounce finely chopped semisweet chocolate, 1 cup mini marshmallows, and ½ cup chopped almonds, pecans, or caramelized walnuts (see page 30). Continue to freeze until the ice cream is frozen.

MAKES ABOUT 3 PINTS.

Chocolate-Praline Ice Cream

Follow the recipe for Smooth Chocolate Custard Ice Cream (page 41) or Easy Excellent Chocolate Ice Cream. Prepare 1 recipe almond praline (page 26) or pecan praline (see page 27) and fold it in, following the directions given for Pecan Praline Ice Cream.

Mandarin Chocolate Ice Cream

2 ounces semisweet chocolate
2 ounces unsweetened chocolate
2 cups heavy cream
⅛ teaspoon salt
1 cup sugar

Grated zest of 1 large orange
 (about 4 teaspoons)
2 eggs, well beaten
1 cup orange juice

Chill a 6-cup bowl. In a food processor, using the pulsing action, or with a heavy knife, chop the semisweet chocolate into fine chips; set aside. In a heavy saucepan, combine the unsweetened chocolate and 1½ cups of the cream. Cook, stirring, over medium heat, until the chocolate is completely melted and the mixture is smooth. Blend in the salt, sugar, and orange zest. Stir a little of the hot mixture into the eggs. Then gradually add the eggs to the pan and cook, stirring constantly, over very low heat until the mixture coats a spoon and a path drawn through the custard remains undisturbed. Pour into the chilled bowl and cool. Blend in the remaining cream and the orange juice; chill.

Freeze according to the instructions for your ice cream maker until the ice cream is mushy. Blend in the semisweet chips and complete the freezing process. Transfer to freezer containers for storage.

MAKES ABOUT 1 QUART.

Chocolate Marshmallow Ice Cream

¾ cup marshmallow cream
1 cup half-and-half
4 ounces semisweet or bittersweet
  chocolate, chopped

1 egg, at room temperature
½ cup less 1 tablespoon sugar
1 teaspoon vanilla extract
2 cups heavy cream

Warm the marshmallow cream in the top of a double boiler or in a pan within another pan of water. In a heavy saucepan, combine the half-and-half and chocolate. Cook, stirring occasionally, until the chocolate is completely melted and the mixture is smooth. Meanwhile, beat the egg until it is thick and light in color. Gradually beat in the sugar until the mixture is light and fluffy. Gradually beat in the hot chocolate mixture. Stir in the vanilla and cream. Fold in the marshmallow cream and chill. Freeze according to the instructions for your ice cream maker. Transfer to freezer containers for storage.

MAKES ABOUT 1 QUART.

Chocolate–Peanut Butter Ice Cream

4 ounces semisweet chocolate
1¾ cups whole milk
¾ cup plus 2 tablespoons sugar
2 tablespoons chunky peanut
  butter

1 teaspoon vanilla extract
1½ cups heavy cream

Combine the chocolate, milk, and sugar in a heavy saucepan. Cook over low heat, stirring, until the chocolate is melted and the mixture is completely smooth. Blend in the peanut butter. Pour into a cool bowl and stir in the vanilla and cream; chill. Freeze according to the instructions for your ice cream maker. Transfer to freezer containers for storage.

MAKES ABOUT 1 QUART.

Chocolate-Raspberry Ice Cream

1 (10-ounce) package frozen raspberries in syrup
2 cups heavy cream
5 ounces semisweet or bittersweet
  chocolate, chopped

1 egg
2 egg yolks
3 tablespoons sugar
1 teaspoon vanilla extract

With a long, heavy knife, cut the block of frozen raspberries in half. Thaw half of the berries and their syrup and save the remaining berries and syrup for another occasion.

In a heavy saucepan, combine the cream and chocolate and cook over low heat, stirring occasionally, until the chocolate is melted and the mixture is completely smooth. Meanwhile, beat the egg and egg yolks together until light and fluffy. Gradually beat in the sugar until the mixture is ivory-colored and thick. Pour in the chocolate mixture in a thin stream while continuing to beat the eggs. Beat until the mixture cools to room temperature. Beat in the vanilla. Fold in the thawed raspberries; chill the mixture. Freeze according to the instructions for your ice cream maker. Transfer to freezer containers for storage.

MAKES ABOUT 1 QUART.

TRADITIONAL FRUIT ICE CREAM FAVORITES

Lemon Custard Ice Cream

Grated zest of 1 lemon
⅔ cup sugar
2 cups heavy cream
¾ cup whole milk

4 egg yolks
⅓ cup fresh lemon juice, strained
   (measure after straining)

Chill a 6- to 8-cup bowl in the freezer. Combine the lemon zest and sugar in a food processor and process them together about 5 seconds so that the oil in the lemon skin permeates the sugar, or pound them in a mortar. In a heavy saucepan, combine the lemon sugar, 1½ cups of the cream, and the milk. Heat, stirring occasionally, until the sugar is dissolved. Beat the egg yolks until they are light in color. Gradually beat in the hot cream mixture. Return to the pan over very low heat and cook 6 to 8 minutes, stirring until the mixture lightly coats the back of a spoon and a path drawn across the custard remains undisturbed. Pour into the chilled bowl and stir until the custard reaches room temperature. Place in the refrigerator. Whip the remaining ½ cup cream. When the custard is chilled, stir in the lemon juice and fold in the whipped cream. Freeze according to the instructions for your ice cream maker. Transfer to freezer containers for storage.

MAKES ABOUT 1 QUART.

Wonderful Fresh Orange Ice Cream

Serve alone or with a scoop of dark chocolate ice cream or chocolate sorbet.

2 tablespoons grated orange zest
¾ cup sugar
⅛ teaspoon salt
1 cup half-and-half
1 cup heavy cream

¼ cup plus 2 tablespoons light
   corn syrup
4 egg yolks
2 cups fresh orange juice, strained
1½ tablespoons fresh lemon juice

Chill a 6- or 8-cup bowl in the freezer. Combine the orange zest and sugar in a food processor and process them together about 5 seconds so that the oil in the orange skin permeates the sugar, or pound them in a mortar. In a heavy saucepan, combine the orange sugar, salt, half-and-half and ½ cup of the cream. Heat, stirring occasionally, until the sugar is dissolved. Blend in the corn syrup. Whisk the egg yolks until they are light in color. Gradually whisk in the hot cream mixture. Return to the pan over very low heat and cook about 6 to 8 minutes, stirring until the mixture lightly coats the back of a spoon and a path drawn across the custard remains undisturbed. Pour into the chilled bowl and stir until the custard reaches room temperature. Place in the refrigerator. Whip the remaining ½ cup cream. When the custard is chilled, stir in the orange and lemon juices and fold in the whipped cream. Freeze according to the instructions for your ice cream maker. Transfer to freezer containers for storage.

MAKES ABOUT 2½ PINTS.

Classic Fresh Strawberry Ice Cream

3 cups fresh hulled small★ straw-
berries or individually frozen
unsweetened berries
1 tablespoon fresh lemon juice

1 large egg
¾ cup sugar
½ cup half-and-half
1¼ cups heavy cream

Puree the berries in a blender or food processor. Mix in the lemon juice. Beat the egg until it is light and fluffy. Gradually beat the sugar into the egg until the mixture is pale ivory and very thick. Blend in the half-and-half and cream. Blend in the berries. Freeze according to the instructions for your ice cream maker. Transfer to freezer containers for storage.

MAKES ABOUT 1 QUART.

Fresh Raspberry Ice Cream

2 pints fresh raspberries or 1 (12-
ounce) bag individually frozen
unsweetened raspberries
2 teaspoons fresh lemon juice

½ cup half-and-half
1 large egg
⅔ cup sugar
1¼ cups heavy cream

★ Cut up large berries before measuring.

Puree the berries in a blender or food processor. Strain to remove the seeds (reserve the seeds). Blend the lemon juice into the berry puree. Combine the raspberry seeds and half-and-half and whisk with a fork. Strain out the seeds, pressing down to release all the liquids. Blend the strained half-and-half with the berry puree. Beat the egg until it is light and fluffy. Gradually beat in the sugar until the mixture is pale ivory and very thick. Blend in the berry mixture and cream. Freeze according to the instructions for your ice cream maker. Transfer to freezer containers for storage.

MAKES ABOUT 1 QUART.

Fresh Boysenberry Ice Cream

Follow the recipe for Fresh Raspberry Ice Cream (above), substituting fresh or frozen boysenberries for the raspberries. Increase the sugar to ¾ cup and 2 tablespoons.

Fresh Blackberry Ice Cream

3 cups fresh blackberries or 1 (12-ounce) bag individually frozen unsweetened blackberries
¾ cup plus 1 tablespoon sugar

1 tablespoon fresh lemon juice
½ cup half-and-half
1 large egg
1¼ cups heavy cream

Combine the berries and ½ cup of the sugar in the top of a double boiler. Place over simmering water and cook until the berries soften slightly and release their juice, about 10 minutes. Puree the berries in a blender or food processor. Strain to remove the seeds; reserve the seeds. Blend the lemon juice into the berry puree. Combine the blackberry seeds and half-and-half and whisk with a fork. Strain out the seeds, pressing down to release all the liquids. Blend the strained half-and-half with the berry puree. Beat the egg until it is light and fluffy. Gradually beat in the remaining sugar until the mixture is pale ivory and very thick. Blend in the berry mixture and cream. Freeze according to the instructions for your ice cream maker. Transfer to freezer containers for storage.

MAKES ABOUT 1 QUART.

Blueberry Ice Cream

1 (12-ounce) package frozen un-
    sweetened blueberries, thawed,
    or 2½ cups fresh blueberries
¾ cup plus 1 tablespoon sugar

⅛ teaspoon salt
1⅔ cups heavy cream
2 tablespoons lemon juice
1 tablespoon kirsch

Place the berries in a wide heavy saucepan, sprinkle them with sugar, and mix in the remaining sugar. Cover and cook over low heat 5 minutes, until the sugar begins to melt. Uncover, turn up the heat to moderate, and boil, stirring, 5 minutes more. Transfer the berries to a food processor or blender and blend about 1 second, just until the centers of the berries are pureed but pieces of berry skin are visible. Strain through a coarse wire strainer, pressing down on the berries to release all the puree and juice. Discard the skins. Don't worry if little pieces of skin get into the puree. Mix in the salt, cream, and lemon juice. Chill the mixture. Freeze according to the instructions for your ice cream maker. When the ice cream is about 90 percent frozen, stir in the kirsch and finish freezing. Transfer to freezer containers for storage.

MAKES ABOUT 1½ QUARTS.

Dark Cherry Ice Cream

⅔ cup plus 1 tablespoon sugar
4 egg yolks
1¼ teaspoons vanilla extract
1½ cups heavy cream

1¾ cups fresh or frozen unsweet-
    ened dark pitted cherries, halved

Chill a 2-quart bowl. In a heavy medium saucepan, combine ⅔ cup water and the sugar and cook, stirring constantly, until the sugar dissolves. Swirl the pan to be sure no sugar crystals cling to the side of the pan. Continue to cook over medium heat until the mixture boils. Remove from the heat. Beat the egg yolks until they are pale and a ribbon of egg leaves a trail on the surface for 15 seconds. Continue to beat while pouring the sugar mixture over the yolks in a very thin stream. Return the mixture to the saucepan and cook over low heat, whisking constantly, until the mixture will lightly coat the back of a spoon and a path drawn across the custard will remain undisturbed. Transfer to the chilled bowl and stir until the custard is cool. Blend in the vanilla. Place in the refrigerator. Whip the cream until soft peaks will hold their shape. Fold the cream and cherries into the cooled custard. Chill thoroughly. Freeze according to the instructions for your ice cream maker. Transfer to freezer containers for storage. MAKES ABOUT 1 QUART.

Peaches-and-Cream Ice Cream

2 large eggs, at room temperature
1 cup sugar
⅔ cup half-and-half
4 large ripe peaches, peeled, pitted, and sliced, or 1 (16-ounce) bag frozen unsweetened peach slices, thawed

1½ tablespoons fresh lemon juice
¼ teaspoon vanilla extract
¼ teaspoon almond extract
1 cup heavy cream

Beat the eggs until they are thick and light in color. Gradually beat in the sugar until the eggs are ivory-colored and thick. Blend in the half-and-half. Puree the peaches with the lemon juice in a blender or food processor and stir them into the egg mixture. Blend in the vanilla and almond extract. Stir in the cream. Freeze according to the instructions for your ice cream maker. Transfer to freezer containers for storage. MAKES ABOUT 1½ QUARTS.

Peaches in Frozen Custard

2 large eggs, at room temperature
1 cup sugar
1 cup half-and-half
4 large ripe peaches, peeled, pitted, and sliced, or 1 (16-ounce)

bag frozen unsweetened peach slices, thawed
¼ teaspoon vanilla extract
2 tablespoons fresh lemon juice
1 cup heavy cream

Beat the eggs until they are thick and light in color. Gradually beat in the sugar until the eggs are ivory-colored and thick. Blend in the half-and-half. Transfer to a heavy saucepan and cook over low heat, stirring, until the mixture lightly coats the back of a spoon and a path drawn through the custard remains undisturbed. Pour into a bowl and chill. Puree the peaches and stir them into the custard. Stir in the vanilla, lemon juice, and cream. Freeze according to the instructions for your ice cream maker. Transfer to freezer containers for storage.

MAKES ABOUT 1½ QUARTS.

Peach Praline Ice Cream

Prepare 1 recipe Peaches in Frozen Custard (above) as directed. Prepare the following Praline for Peach Ice Cream. When the ice cream is about three-quarters churned, stir in the praline. Continue freezing until the ice cream is completed.

Praline for Peach Ice Cream

2 tablespoons unsalted butter
3 tablespoons light brown sugar, packed
¼ cup light corn syrup
⅓ cup pecan pieces

Generously butter a large baking pan. In a small heavy saucepan, combine the butter, sugar, corn syrup, ½ tablespoon water, and the pecans. Cook over medium heat, stirring, until the mixture reaches the hard-crack stage (285° F.) or will spin a hard but not brittle thread when dropped into a cup of cold water. The color should be a clear, dark amber. Remove from the heat and pour onto the baking pan, spreading as thin as possible. Cool completely and crush coarsely in a food processor or in a bag with a mallet.

Amaretto-Peach Ice Cream

Prepare 1 recipe Peaches in Frozen Custard (page 54). Sprinkle ⅔ cup crushed amaretti biscuits with 1½ tablespoons Amaretto liqueur. Allow to stand 5 minutes. When the ice cream is about 90 percent churned, stir in the Amaretto mixture and finish the churning.

Quick Apricot Ice Cream

2 (1-pound) cans apricots halves in heavy syrup
½ cup sugar
2 tablespoons fresh lemon juice
1 cup heavy cream

Drain the apricots, reserving ½ cup juice. Combine the ½ cup juice with the sugar and cook over medium heat, swirling the pan occasionally, until the sugar is dissolved; cool to room temperature. Puree the apricots with the lemon juice in a blender or food processor. Blend in the syrup and cream; chill. Freeze according to the instructions for your ice cream maker. Transfer to freezer containers for storage.

MAKES ABOUT 1 QUART.

Fresh Apricot Ice Cream

Fresh apricots vary in their sweetness, so you'll be adding sugar to taste. Oversweeten the mixture slightly, as freezing diminishes flavor intensity.

About 2 cups fresh apricot halves
2 teaspoons fresh lemon juice
1 large egg
About 1 cup powdered sugar
1½ cups heavy cream

Cut up the apricots and puree them coarsely with the lemon juice in a blender or food processor. You should have 1¼ cups puree. Beat the egg until it is light in color and thick. Gradually blend in ⅔ cup of the sugar and ¾ cup of the cream. Beat the remaining cream until soft peaks will hold their shape. Fold the egg mixture and whipped cream into the apricot mixture. Taste and add more sugar if needed by sifting or straining over the ice cream mixture, folding it gradually in. Freeze according to the instructions for your ice cream maker. Transfer to freezer containers for storage.

MAKES ABOUT 1 QUART.

Creamy Apricot Ice Cream Custard

About 1½ cups hot black tea
¾ cup dried apricots
2 tablespoons fresh lemon juice
2 eggs

1 egg yolk
¾ cup plus 2 tablespoons sugar
1½ cups half-and-half
1 cup heavy cream

In a saucepan, pour the boiling tea over the apricots and let simmer 2 minutes. Remove from the heat and allow the apricots to soak until soft and plump. Drain the apricots, reserving the liquid. Puree the apricots in a food processor, adding the lemon juice and a little liquid if necessary to make a smooth puree.

Beat the eggs and egg yolk together until thick and light in color. Gradually add the sugar, beating until the mixture is ivory-colored and thick. In a heavy saucepan, heat the half-and-half to the boiling point and slowly beat it into the eggs. Return the egg mixture to the pan and cook over low heat, stirring, until the mixture will coat a spoon and a path drawn through the custard remains undisturbed. Blend the custard into the apricots and blend in the cream. Freeze according to the instructions for your ice cream maker. Transfer to freezer containers for storage.

MAKES ABOUT 1 QUART.

Banana-Caramel-Nut Ice Cream

½ cup sugar
2 teaspoons cornstarch
1 cup half-and-half
⅔ cup whole milk
2 eggs, lightly beaten
⅔ cup heavy cream

¾ teaspoon vanilla extract
1 cup mashed banana
5 teaspoons fresh lemon juice
⅔ cup caramelized walnuts (see
  page 30)

Combine the sugar and cornstarch in a medium saucepan; blend well. Mix in the half-and-half and milk. Cook over low heat, stirring, until the mixture thickens slightly, about 1 minute. Stir about 1 cup of the hot mixture into the beaten eggs; blend well. Return the egg mixture to the pan and cook over low heat until smooth and thickened, about 3 minutes.

Pour into a bowl and blend in the cream, vanilla, banana, and lemon juice. Chill. Freeze according to the instructions for your ice cream maker until the ice cream is about 90 percent frozen. Stir in the nuts and finish the freezing. Transfer to freezer containers for storage.

MAKES ABOUT 1 QUART.

Pumpkin Ice Cream

4 large egg yolks
¾ cup mashed cooked pumpkin
¾ cup half-and-half
1 cup sugar
⅛ teaspoon salt
¼ teaspoon ground cinnamon

⅛ teaspoon ground nutmeg
⅜ teaspoon ground ginger
2 cups heavy cream

Beat the egg yolks until they are thick and light in color. In the top of a double boiler, combine the pumpkin, half-and-half, sugar, salt, and spices. Blend well and fold in the egg yolks. Cook, stirring, over simmering water about 8 minutes, until the mixture thickens slightly. Pour into a cool bowl and blend in ⅔ cup of the cream. Place in the refrigerator to cool to room temperature or chill. Whip the remaining cream until soft peaks will hold their shape. Fold one third of the cream into the pumpkin mixture, then fold in the remaining cream. Freeze according to the instructions for your ice cream maker. Transfer to freezer containers for storage.

MAKES ABOUT 2½ pints.

Tropical Mango Ice Cream

2 medium ripe mangoes
2 teaspoons grated orange zest
1½ tablespoons fresh lemon juice
½ cup fresh orange juice

1 large egg
¾ cup plus 1 tablespoon sugar
1 cup half-and-half
1 cup heavy cream

Peel the mangoes and cut the pulp from the seeds; mash or puree in a food processor. You should have about 1⅓ cups puree. Blend in the orange zest and juices; chill. Beat the egg until it is light in color and thick. Gradually beat in the sugar, beating until it dissolves. Beat in the half-and-half. Beat the cream until soft peaks will hold their shape. Fold the egg and mango mixture together. Fold in the whipped cream. Freeze according to the instructions for your ice cream maker. Transfer to freezer containers for storage.

MAKES ABOUT 1½ QUARTS.

Apple–Apple Brandy Ice Cream

Cognac may be used in place of the apple brandy in this delicious ice cream.

1¼ cups unsweetened applesauce	1 cup sugar
3 tablespoons Calvados or apple-jack	1½ cups heavy cream
	2 large egg yolks, lightly beaten
¼ teaspoon cinnamon	½ teaspoon vanilla extract

Chill a large bowl. Combine the applesauce, Calvados, and cinnamon in a heavy saucepan. Cook over medium heat until the mixture boils. Reduce the heat and simmer 3 minutes. Stir in the sugar until it is dissolved. Pour into the chilled bowl and refrigerate. Scald the cream in a heavy saucepan. Slowly add about half of the cream to the eggs, whisking all the while. Return the egg mixture to the pan and cook over low heat, stirring, until the mixture thickens slightly and lightly coats the back of a spoon and a path drawn through the custard remains undisturbed. Blend the custard into the apple pureé. Blend in the vanilla and chill the mixture. Freeze according to the instructions for your ice cream maker. Transfer to freezer containers for storage.

MAKES ABOUT 1 QUART.

NUT ICE CREAMS

Luxury Pistachio Ice Cream

I adapted this from a recipe created by the famous French *pâtissier* Lenôtre.

1 cup shelled raw unsalted pistachio nuts
1 cup whole milk
1¾ cups heavy cream
2½ tablespoons light corn syrup

5 large egg yolks, at room temperature
¾ cup sugar
½ teaspoon vanilla extract

Chill a 2-quart bowl. Place the nuts in boiling water and simmer about 1 minute. Drain and remove the nut skins. Coarsely chop ⅓ cup of the nuts and set aside. Combine the remaining nuts in a blender or food processor with ⅓ cup of the milk. Blend to the consistency of peanut butter. Set aside in a bowl. In a heavy medium saucepan, combine the remaining milk, ⅔ cup of the cream, and the corn syrup and simmer, stirring, for 2 minutes. Continue to cook over medium heat until the mixture boils 1½ minutes. Cover and remove from the heat. Beat the egg yolks until they are pale and thick. Gradually beat in the sugar until a ribbon of egg leaves a trail on the surface for 15 seconds. Continue to beat while pouring the hot cream mixture over the yolks in a very thin stream. Return the mixture to the saucepan and cook over low heat, whisking constantly, until the mixture lightly coats the back of a spoon and a path drawn through the custard remains undisturbed. Transfer to the chilled bowl and stir until the custard is cool. Blend the remaining cream, pistachio puree, and vanilla together, then blend in the custard. Chill thoroughly. Freeze according to the instructions for your ice cream maker until the ice cream is about 85 percent frozen. Stir in the ⅓ cup chopped nuts and finish the freezing. Transfer to freezer containers for storage.

MAKES ABOUT 1 QUART.

Pistachio-Berry Ripple

Prepare Strawberry Ripple (page 25), using kirsch. Swirl in the ripple following the instructions for making ripple ice creams on page 23.

Maple-Walnut Ice Cream

2 eggs
1 cup real maple syrup
2 cups heavy cream

½ teaspoon vanilla extract
⅔ cup lightly toasted, chopped
walnuts

In a large bowl, beat the eggs until thick and light in color. Gradually beat in the syrup, then the cream and vanilla. Stir in the nuts and freeze according to the instructions for your ice cream maker. Transfer to freezer containers for storage.

MAKES ABOUT 1 QUART.

Hazelnut-Mocha Ice Cream

1 cup strong black coffee, Euro-
*   pean roast preferred*
2½ cups heavy cream
1¼ cups sugar
3½ tablespoons unsweetened cocoa
*   powder*

4 egg yolks
1½ teaspoons vanilla extract
⅔ cup toasted, skinned★ hazel-
*   nuts, coarsely chopped*

Heat the coffee, cream, sugar, and cocoa in a heavy saucepan, stirring occasionally, until the sugar is dissolved and the mixture is hot. In a medium bowl, beat the egg yolks until they are pale and creamy. Beat the eggs while gradually pouring in the cream mixture. Return the mixture to the pan. Stirring constantly, and without boiling, cook about 6 minutes over medium heat until the mixture coats the back of a spoon and a path drawn through the custard remains undisturbed. Strain into a cool bowl.

★ See the directions for roasting and skinning hazelnuts in the Frozen Hazelnut Praline Soufflé recipe (page 172).

Blend in the vanilla and nuts and chill. Mix well, then freeze according to the instructions for your ice cream maker. Transfer to freeezer containers for storage.

MAKES ABOUT 1 QUART. DOUBLE THE RECIPE FOR LARGE ICE CREAM MAKERS IF YOU WISH TO MAKE ½ GALLON.

SPECIALTY COFFEE AND TEA ICE CREAMS

Cappuccino Ice Cream

2 tablespoons brandy
2 tablespoons dark rum
⅛ teaspoon ground cinnamon
3¼ teaspoons instant espresso
* powder*
1¼ cups half-and-half
½ medium or 1 small vanilla
* bean*

5 large egg yolks
¾ cup plus 2 teaspoons sugar
1 cup (4 ounces) ricotta cheese
¾ cup heavy cream
¾ ounce bittersweet or semisweet
* chocolate, grated*

In a small saucepan, combine the brandy, rum, and cinnamon. Simmer the mixture until a lit match will not ignite it. Remove from the heat and stir in the espresso powder. In a large heavy saucepan, combine the half-and-half and vanilla bean. Bring to a boil, then reduce the heat and simmer 3 minutes. Remove from the heat, cover, and allow to steep 30 minutes or longer.

In a large bowl, beat the egg yolks until they are thick and light in color. Very gradually add the sugar and continue to beat until the mixture is ivory-colored and ribbons of egg remain on the surface 15 seconds when the beaters are lifted. Bring the half-and-half to a boil and gradually beat half of it into the eggs in a fine stream. Return the mixture to the pan. Stirring constantly, and without boiling, cook 6 to 8 minutes over medium heat, until the mixture coats the back of a spoon and a path drawn through the custard remains undisturbed. Place in a cool bowl and stir until the mixture cools to room temperature. Remove the vanilla bean, slit it lengthwise with a knife, and scrape out the vanilla grains. Stir them into the custard. Stir in the ricotta, cream, and coffee mixture. Chill thoroughly. Freeze according to the instructions for your ice cream maker. When the ice cream is about 85 percent frozen, stir in the grated chocolate. Transfer to freezer containers for storage.

MAKES ABOUT I QUART.

Espresso Ice Cream

The flavor of espresso is infused from the crushed whole beans into a cream mixture to delicately permeate this unforgettable ice cream.

1¼ cups whole coffee beans, roasted for espresso
2½ cups half-and-half
1 cup heavy cream

6 egg yolks
1 cup sugar
¾ teaspoon vanilla extract

Put the beans in a heavy paper or plastic bag and crush them very coarsely with a mallet or rolling pin. In a heavy medium saucepan, combine the half-and-half, cream, and crushed beans. Cook over moderate heat until the mixture boils. Immediately reduce the heat and barely simmer 2 minutes. Cover and allow to steep 30 minutes to 1 hour.

In a medium bowl, beat the egg yolks until they are pale and creamy. Gradually beat the sugar into the eggs until the mixture is ivory-colored and ribbons of egg remain on the surface 15 seconds when the beaters are lifted. In a fine stream, beat in the cream mixture. Return the mixture to the pan. Stirring constantly, and without boiling, cook 6 to 8 minutes over medium heat, until the mixture coats the back of a spoon and a path drawn through the custard remains undisturbed. Place in a cool bowl and chill—overnight if you want a strong coffee flavor. Strain into the canister of an ice cream maker. Stir in the vanilla. Freeze according to the instructions for your ice cream maker. Transfer to freezer containers for storage.

MAKES ABOUT 1 QUART. DOUBLE THE RECIPE FOR LARGE ICE CREAM MAKERS IF YOU WISH TO MAKE ½ GALLON.

Russian Tea Ice Cream

1 cup whole milk
4 whole cloves
2 teaspoons grated orange zest
2 tablespoons black or orange
   Pekoe or Darjeeling tea leaves
1½ tablespoons fresh lemon juice

3 tablespoons fresh orange juice
1 teaspoon unflavored gelatin
2 cups heavy cream
½ cup sugar
⅓ cup honey
4 egg yolks, lightly beaten

In the top of a double boiler, scald the milk over direct heat. Add the cloves, orange zest, and tea leaves. Cover and place over hot water. Allow to steep 15 minutes. Meanwhile, combine the lemon and orange juices in a small heatproof cup. Sprinkle the gelatin over the juice and allow it to soften about 3 minutes. Place in a bowl of very hot water and stir until no gelatin granules remain; set aside. Strain the milk and return it to the top of the double boiler. Add ½ cup of the cream, the sugar, and the honey. Cook over direct heat, stirring occasionally, until the honey and sugar are dissolved. Pour about half of the milk mixture into the eggs while whisking them. Return the milk-egg mixture to the top of the double boiler and cook, stirring, over simmering water 8 to 10 minutes, until the mixture thickens slightly and coats the back of a spoon and a path drawn through the custard remains undisturbed. Stir in the gelatin mixture. Pour the custard into a cool bowl and chill. Whip the remaining 1½ cups cream until soft peaks hold their shape. Fold into the custard mixture. Freeze according to the instructions for your ice cream maker. Transfer to freezer containers for storage.

MAKES ABOUT 1 QUART.

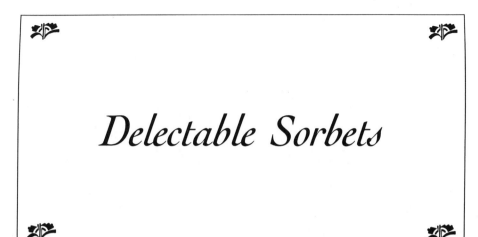

Delectable Sorbets

Nothing, not even truly ripe fruit, captures the essence of fruit flavor like a good sorbet. The sunny taste of citrus or the mellowness of pears in wine are distilled into a tiny intense scoop. Lemons taste more lemony, cherries fruitier, and cranberries more refreshing than in their natural state. Sorbets are glamorous, too. For many years they could be found only in Europe or in a handful of exclusive North American restaurants. Despite their elegant place in life, sorbets are child's play to prepare.

What makes them special is the pure fruit that goes into them. And sorbets made at home can surpass all others. Perhaps one can obtain from a nearby orchard the ripest fruit—left long enough on the tree or vine to develop the fullest fruit flavor that can't be found in supermarket produce. If necessary, fruits can be left in a warm spot to ripen fully. On the other hand, bags of individually frozen berries or peach slices are a wonderful substitute. These fruits, usually frozen shortly after picking, may have even better flavor than "fresh" supermarket fruit. More fruit and less water and sugar contribute to the really outstanding flavor and body of the best sorbets.

Because they contain no protein or butterfat, some sorbets, such as those made without the pulp of the fruit, need a little smoothing out, though Italian granitas are purposely made a bit grainy. A little gelatin, egg white, or corn syrup can give a velvety texture to the icy mixtures, especially ones that are to be churned in a food processor or stored. In addition to adding intensity, a little liqueur keeps the icy mass supple.

Remember, however, to use it moderately and add it only at the end of the freezing time.

- Recipes both for the food processor and for an ice cream maker are in this chapter, and they can be used interchangeably.
- To adapt recipes designed for the food processor for use with an ice cream maker, follow the instructions given below.
- And to adapt ice cream maker recipes for the processor, see page 80.
- The silkiest sorbet texture requires proper freezing. Begin with a well-chilled sorbet mixture and also chill the ice cream container and dasher. Sorbets need a lower ratio of salt to ice than ice creams. Use 1 cup plus 2 tablespoons salt for 6 pounds of ice cubes, or ¾ cup rock salt for 6 pounds crushed ice.
- Always heat the water and sugar together to avoid undissolved sugar granules.
- I have used a minimum of sugar in these recipes, assuming ripe fruit will be used. Taste the mixture only after it is chilled. To add sweetness, stir a little sifted powdered sugar into the mixture to taste.
- To make your own recipes, use these proportions as a guide: 2 cups chopped fruit, ⅔–1 cup liquid, plus ⅓–½ cup sugar. A teaspoon or so of fresh lemon juice often enhances the flavor. Also, ½ teaspoon unflavored gelatin or 1 tablespoon egg white helps smoothness if you are using juice or a low-pulp fruit.
- If sorbet has been stored too long and becomes icy, cut it into chunks and process in a food processor or beat it with a heavy-duty mixer only until it is barely slushy. Eat right away or refreeze 1 to 2 hours.

FOOD PROCESSOR FRUIT SORBETS

Making Processor Sorbets in an Ice Cream Machine

Follow the recipe, reducing the amount of gelatin called for by one half. Freeze according to the instructions for your ice cream maker. Transfer to containers for storage.

Very Strawberry Sorbet

3 cups fresh strawberries or berries
  frozen without sugar
½ teaspoon unflavored gelatin

3 tablespoons sugar
1½ tablespoons light corn syrup
1 tablespoon fresh lemon juice

Puree the berries and strain the puree. In a very small pan, sprinkle the gelatin over 3 tablespoons water and allow it to soak until it softens, about 3 minutes. Cook over very low heat, stirring occasionally, until the gelatin granules disappear. Remove from the heat and stir in the sugar and corn syrup until the sugar dissolves. Stir in the lemon juice and stir the mixture into the berry puree.

Pour the mixture into divided ice cube trays and freeze solid.

Several hours before serving, or up to a day ahead, place half of the frozen sorbet cubes into the food processor work bowl and pulse the machine on and off until the cubes are evenly chopped to the texture of coarse snow. Then run the machine continuously until the sorbet turns several shades paler and is creamy-looking. If the mixture is too hard to move freely around the bowl, allow it to thaw slightly or add a few drops of water.

Process the remaining sorbet cubes or save them for another time. Pile the sorbet into a 1-pint container. Cover and freeze.

MAKES ABOUT 1 PINT.

Ripe Blueberry Sorbet

4 cups fresh blueberries or berries
  frozen without sugar, thawed
1 teaspoon unflavored gelatin

⅓ cup sugar
3 tablespoons light corn syrup
1 tablespoon fresh lemon juice

Puree the blueberries. In a very small pan, sprinkle the gelatin over ⅓ cup water and allow it to soak until it softens, about 3 minutes. Cook over very low heat, stirring occasionally, until the gelatin granules disappear. Remove from the heat and stir in the sugar and corn syrup until the sugar dissolves. Stir in the lemon juice and stir the mixture into the berry puree.

Pour the mixture into divided ice cube trays and freeze solid.

Several hours before serving, or up to a day ahead, place half of the frozen sorbet cubes in the food processor work bowl and pulse the machine on and off until the cubes are evenly chopped to the texture of coarse snow. Then run the machine continuously until the sorbet turns several shades paler and is creamy-looking. If the mixture is too hard to move freely around the bowl, allow it to thaw slightly or add a few drops of water.

Process the remaining sorbet cubes or save them for another time. Pile the sorbet into 1- or 2-pint containers. Cover and freeze.

MAKES ABOUT 1½ PINTS.

Watermelon Sorbet

6 cups pitted and peeled water-
    melon, cut into 1-inch dice
    (about ¼ melon)
2 teaspoons unflavored gelatin

6–7 tablespoons sugar
¼ cup light corn syrup
3½ tablespoons fresh lemon juice

Puree the watermelon. In a very small pan, sprinkle the gelatin over ¼ cup water and allow it to soak until it softens, about 3 minutes. Cook over very low heat, stirring occasionally, until the gelatin granules disappear. Remove from the heat and stir in the sugar and corn syrup until the sugar dissolves. Stir in the lemon juice and stir the mixture into the melon puree.

Pour the mixture into divided ice cube trays and freeze solid.

Several hours before serving, or up to a day ahead, place one third of the frozen sorbet cubes in the food processor work bowl and pulse the machine on and off until the cubes are evenly chopped to the texture of coarse snow. Then run the machine continuously until the sorbet turns several shades paler and is creamy-looking. If the mixture is too hard to move freely around the bowl, allow it to thaw slightly or add a few drops of water.

Process the remaining sorbet cubes or save them for another time. Pile the sorbet into 1- to 3-pint containers. Cover and freeze.

MAKES ABOUT 2½ PINTS.

Summer Peach Sorbet

6 large ripe peaches, peeled,
   pitted, and sliced
3½ tablespoons fresh lemon juice

1¼ teaspoons unflavored gelatin
⅔ cup sugar
⅓ cup light corn syrup

Puree the peaches with the lemon juice. In a very small pan, sprinkle the gelatin over ⅓ cup water and allow it to soak until it softens, about 3 minutes. Cook over very low heat, stirring occasionally, until the gelatin granules disappear. Remove from the heat and stir in the sugar and corn syrup until the sugar dissolves. Stir the mixture into the peach puree.

Pour the mixture into divided ice cube trays and freeze solid.

Several hours before serving, or up to a day ahead, place half or one third of the frozen sorbet cubes in the food processor work bowl and pulse the machine on and off until the cubes are evenly chopped to the texture of coarse snow. Then run the machine continuously until the sorbet turns several shades paler and is creamy-looking. If the mixture is too hard to move freely around the bowl, allow it to thaw slightly or add a few drops of water.

Process the remaining sorbet cubes or save them for another time. Pile the sorbet into 1- to 3-pint containers. Cover and freeze.

MAKES ABOUT 2½ PINTS.

Santa Rosa Plum Sorbet

2 pounds ripe Santa Rosa plums
2 teaspoons fresh lemon juice
2 teaspoons unflavored gelatin
½ cup sugar
¼ cup light corn syrup

In a 4-quart pan of boiling water, blanch the plums several minutes, just until their skins split. Immediately drain the plums and rinse them in cold water. Peel and pit the plums and puree them with the lemon juice.

In a very small pan, sprinkle the gelatin over ⅓ cup water and allow it to soak until it softens, about 3 minutes. Cook over very low heat, stirring occasionally, until the gelatin granules disappear. Remove from the heat and stir in the sugar and corn syrup until the sugar dissolves. Stir the mixture into the plum puree.

Pour the mixture into divided ice cube trays and freeze solid.

Several hours before serving, or up to a day ahead, place half or one third of the frozen sorbet cubes in the food processor work bowl and pulse the machine on and off until the cubes are evenly chopped to the texture of coarse snow. Then run the machine continuously until the sorbet turns several shades paler and is creamy-looking. If the mixture is too hard to move freely around the bowl, allow it to thaw slightly or add a few drops of water.

Process the remaining sorbet cubes or save them for another time. Pile the sorbet into 1- to 3-pint containers. Cover and freeze.

MAKES ABOUT 2½ PINTS.

Lemon Sorbet

1½ teaspoons unflavored gelatin
6 tablespoons sugar
6 tablespoons light corn syrup
¾ cup fresh lemon juice

In a small pan, sprinkle the gelatin over 1½ cups water and allow it to soak until it softens, about 3 minutes. Cook over very low heat, stirring occasionally, until the gelatin granules disappear. Remove from the heat and stir in the sugar and corn syrup until the sugar dissolves. Stir the mixture into the lemon juice.

Pour the mixture into divided ice cube trays and freeze solid.

Several hours before serving, or up to a day ahead, place half of the frozen sorbet cubes in the food processor work bowl and pulse the machine on and off until the cubes are evenly chopped to the texture of coarse snow. Then run the machine continuously until the sorbet turns several shades paler and is creamy-looking. If the mixture is too hard to move freely around the bowl, allow it to thaw slightly or add a few drops of water.

Process the remaining sorbet cubes or save them for another time. Pile the sorbet into 1- to 2-pint containers. Cover and freeze.

MAKES ABOUT 1½ PINTS.

Very Mango Sorbet

2 large or 3 small very ripe
   mangoes
¾ cup fresh orange juice
¾ teaspoons unflavored gelatin

3 tablespoons sugar
2½ tablespoons light corn syrup
3 tablespoons fresh lemon juice, or
   more to taste

Peel the mangoes and puree them with the orange juice. In a very small pan, sprinkle the gelatin over ¼ cup water and allow it to soak until it softens, about 3 minutes. Cook over very low heat, stirring occasionally, until the gelatin granules disappear. Remove from the heat and stir in the sugar and corn syrup until the sugar dissolves. Stir the mixture into the mango puree. Stir in the lemon juice.

Pour the mixture into divided ice cube trays and freeze solid.

Several hours before serving, or up to a day ahead, place half or one third of the frozen sorbet cubes in the food processor work bowl and pulse the machine on and off until the cubes are evenly chopped to the texture of coarse snow. Then run the machine continuously until the sorbet turns several shades paler and is creamy-looking. If the mixture is too hard to move freely around the bowl, allow it to thaw slightly or add a few drops of water.

Process the remaining sorbet cubes or save them for another time. Pile the sorbet into 1- to 3-pint containers. Cover and freeze.

MAKES ABOUT 2½ PINTS.

Raspberry-Cantaloupe Sorbet

1 (10-ounce) package frozen raspberries in syrup, thawed
4 cups finely diced ripe cantaloupe

2 teaspoons unflavored gelatin
⅓ cup seedless raspberry jam
2 tablespoons fresh lemon juice

Pour the raspberry juice from the package into a small saucepan. Puree the raspberries and strain them. Puree the cantaloupe and mix with the raspberries; set aside.

Sprinkle the gelatin over the juice and allow it to soak until it softens, about 3 minutes. Cook over very low heat, stirring occasionally, until the gelatin granules disappear. Stir in the jam and cook, stirring, until it dissolves. Stir the mixture into the fruit puree. Stir in the lemon juice.

Pour the mixture into divided ice cube trays and freeze solid.

Several hours before serving, or up to a day ahead, place half of the frozen sorbet cubes in the food processor work bowl and pulse the machine on and off until the cubes are evenly chopped to the texture of coarse snow. Then run the machine continuously until the sorbet turns several shades paler and is creamy-looking. If the mixture is too hard to move freely around the bowl, allow it to thaw slightly or add a few drops of water.

Process the remaining sorbet cubes or save them for another time. Pile the sorbet into 2- or 3-pint containers. Cover and freeze.

MAKES ABOUT 2½ PINTS.

ULTRA SORBETS

These special sorbets are enlivened with a little liqueur or wine to deepen their fruit flavor. They are refreshing on their own and wickedly seductive with a scoop of ice cream or Velvety Vanilla Sauce (page 206). Double Kahlúa Granita partnered with rich coffee or vanilla ice cream is simple and smashing. For more ways to serve Ultra Sorbets, see the section "Making Plain Sorbets and Ice Creams Fancy."

If you have an ice cream churn and wish to use it for the Ultra Sorbets, prepare the recipe as directed, omitting the liqueur. When the sorbet is about 90 percent frozen, stir in the liqueur and finish freezing.

Ultra Raspberry Sorbet

Probably the most intense raspberry flavor you've ever tasted—and not too sweet.

2 (12-ounce) bags frozen unsweetened raspberries
¼ cup Chambord liqueur
¼ cup light corn syrup
¼ cup sugar

Thaw the berries and process to a puree. Strain to remove the seeds.

Mix the liqueur, corn syrup, sugar, and ⅓ cup hot water together. Stir until the sugar is dissolved, then mix in the puree.

Pour the mixture into divided ice cube trays and freeze solid.

Several hours before serving, or up to a day ahead, place half of the frozen sorbet cubes in the food processor work bowl and pulse the machine on and off until the cubes are evenly chopped to the texture of coarse snow. Then run the machine continuously until the sorbet turns several shades paler and is creamy-looking. If the mixture is too hard to move freely around the bowl, allow it to thaw slightly or add a few drops of water.

Process the remaining sorbet cubes or save them for another time. Pile the sorbet into 1- or 2-pint containers. Cover and freeze.

MAKES ABOUT 2 PINTS.

Ultra Orange Sorbet

Triple Sec liqueur and orange juice concentrate blended into fresh orange juice give this flavor extra impact.

2½ cups fresh orange juice
3 tablespoons frozen orange juice concentrate, thawed
3 tablespoons Triple Sec liqueur
6 tablespoons sugar

Combine the orange juice, orange juice concentrate, liqueur, and sugar and stir until the sugar dissolves. Pour the mixture into divided ice cube trays and freeze solid.

Several hours before serving, or up to a day ahead, place half of the frozen sorbet cubes in the food processor work bowl and pulse the machine on and off until the cubes are evenly chopped to the texture of coarse snow. Then run the machine continuously until the sorbet turns several shades paler and is creamy-looking. If the mixture is too hard to move freely around the bowl, allow it to thaw slightly or add a few drops of juice or water.

Process the remaining sorbet cubes or save them for another time. Pile the sorbet into 1- or 2-pint containers. Cover and freeze.

MAKES ABOUT 1¾ PINTS.

Ultra Lemon Sorbet

Icy lemon with vodka—sensational!

1½ teaspoons unflavored gelatin
6 tablespoons sugar
6 tablespoons light corn syrup
⅔ cup fresh lemon juice
¼ cup vodka

In a small pan, sprinkle the gelatin over 1⅓ cups water and allow it to soak until it softens, about 3 minutes. Cook over very low heat, stirring occasionally, until the gelatin granules disappear. Remove from the heat and stir in the sugar and corn syrup until the sugar dissolves. Stir the mixture into the lemon juice and add the vodka.

Pour the mixture into divided ice cube trays and freeze solid.

Several hours before serving, or up to a day ahead, place half of the frozen sorbet cubes in the food processor work bowl and pulse the machine on and off until the cubes are evenly chopped to the texture of coarse snow. Then run the machine continuously until the sorbet turns several shades paler and is creamy-looking. If the mixture is too hard to move freely around the bowl, allow it to thaw slightly or add a few drops of water.

Process the remaining sorbet cubes or save them for another time. Pile the sorbet into 1- or 2-pint containers. Cover and freeze.

MAKES ABOUT 2 PINTS.

Strawberries Romanoff Sorbet

The classically good combination of strawberries with orange.

1 (10-ounce) package frozen
*   strawberries in syrup*
2 tablespoons fresh lemon juice

1 cup fresh orange juice
3 tablespoons Cointreau or Triple
*   Sec*
1 tablespoon egg white

In a blender or food processor, puree the berries with the lemon juice until very smooth. Blend in the orange juice, Cointreau, and egg white.

Pour the mixture into divided ice cube trays and freeze solid.

Several hours before serving, or up to a day ahead, place one third of the frozen sorbet cubes in the food processor work bowl and pulse the machine on and off until the cubes are evenly chopped to the texture of coarse snow. Then run the machine continuously until the sorbet turns several shades paler and is creamy-looking. If the mixture is too hard to move freely around the bowl, allow it to thaw slightly or add a few drops of water or orange juice.

Process the remaining sorbet cubes or save them for another time. Pile the sorbet into 1- to 3-pint containers. Cover and freeze.

MAKES ABOUT 2½ PINTS.

Double Kahlúa Granita

A frozen slush of sweetened coffee and Kahlúa—great served with a rich vanilla or coffee ice cream.

1½ teaspoons unflavored gelatin
½ cup sugar
2¼ cups medium-strong brewed coffee

5 tablespoons Kahlúa or other coffee liqueur
¾ teaspoon vanilla extract

In a small pan, sprinkle the gelatin over ⅔ cup water and allow it to soak until it softens, about 3 minutes. Cook over very low heat, stirring occasionally, until the gelatin granules disappear. Remove from the heat and stir in the sugar until it dissolves. Combine the sugar mixture with the coffee, Kahlúa, and vanilla.

Pour the mixture into divided ice cube trays and freeze solid.

Several hours before serving, or up to a day ahead, place one third of the frozen sorbet cubes in the food processor work bowl and pulse the machine on and off until the cubes are evenly chopped to the texture of coarse snow. Then run the machine continuously until the sorbet turns several shades paler and is creamy-looking. If the mixture is too hard to move freely around the bowl, allow it to thaw slightly or add a few drops of water.

Process the remaining sorbet cubes or save them for another time. Pile the sorbet into 1- to 3-pint containers. Cover and freeze.

MAKES ABOUT 2½ PINTS.

Ultra Brandied Peach Sorbet

Peach brandy or Cognac are both good in this sorbet.

*4 large ripe peaches, peeled and
   pitted*
3 tablespoons fresh lemon juice
3 tablespoons brandy or Cognac

1 teaspoon unflavored gelatin
½ cup minus 1 tablespoon sugar
3 tablespoons light corn syrup

Process the peaches and lemon juice to a smooth puree.

Put 2 tablespoons water and 1 tablespoon brandy in a very small pan and sprinkle the gelatin over it. Allow to soak until it softens, about 3 minutes. Cook, stirring constantly, over very low heat until the gelatin granules disappear. Remove from the heat. Stir in the sugar and corn syrup until the sugar dissolves. Stir in the remaining 2 tablespoons brandy and blend the mixture into the peach puree.

Pour the mixture into divided ice cube trays and freeze solid.

Several hours before serving, or up to a day ahead, place half of the frozen sorbet cubes in the food processor work bowl and pulse the machine on and off until the cubes are evenly chopped to the texture of coarse snow. Then run the machine continuously until the sorbet turns several shades paler and is creamy-looking. If the mixture is too hard to move freely around the bowl, allow it to thaw slightly or add a few drops of water.

Process the remaining sorbet cubes or save them for another time. Pile the sorbet into 1- or 2-pint containers. Cover and freeze.

MAKES ABOUT 2 PINTS.

Ultra Melon Sorbet

Melons vary markedly in their sweetness. For a very ripe, sweet melon, start by using 3 tablespoons sugar, then taste for sweetness. Remember, you can add a little powdered sugar while processing the sorbet if you haven't sweetened it enough.

2½ cups finely diced ripe honeydew melon
3–5 tablespoons sugar
⅓ cup melon liqueur (Midori)
2 tablespoons fresh lemon juice

Process the melon together with the sugar, liqueur, and lemon juice to a smooth puree. Taste and adjust sweetness if necessary.

Pour the mixture into divided ice cube trays and freeze solid.

Several hours before serving, or up to a day ahead, place half of the frozen sorbet cubes in the food processor work bowl and pulse the machine on and off until the cubes are evenly chopped to the texture of coarse snow. Then run the machine continuously until the sorbet turns several shades paler and is creamy-looking. If the mixture is too hard to move freely around the bowl, allow it to thaw slightly or add a few drops of water.

Process the remaining sorbet cubes or save them for another time. Pile the sorbet into 1- or 2-pint containers. Cover and freeze.

MAKES ABOUT 2 PINTS.

Irish Coffee Sorbet

Great on its own or served with brandied whipped cream (page 206).

1¾ teaspoons unflavored gelatin
½ cup plus 1 tablespoon sugar
2¼ cups medium-strong brewed coffee

¼ cup Irish whiskey
¾ teaspoon vanilla extract
6 tablespoons heavy cream

In a small pan, sprinkle the gelatin over ⅔ cup water and allow it to soak until it softens, about 3 minutes. Cook over very low heat, stirring occasionally, until the gelatin granules disappear. Remove from the heat and stir in the sugar until it dissolves. Combine the sugar mixture with the coffee, whiskey, vanilla, and cream.

Pour the mixture into divided ice cube trays and freeze solid.

Several hours before serving, or up to a day ahead, place one third of the frozen sorbet cubes in the food processor work bowl and pulse the machine on and off until the cubes are evenly chopped to the texture of coarse snow. Then run the machine continuously until the sorbet turns several shades paler and is creamy-looking. If the mixture is too hard to move freely around the bowl, allow it to thaw slightly or add a few drops of water.

Process the remaining sorbet cubes or save them for another time. Pile the sorbet into 1- to 3-pint containers. Cover and freeze.

MAKES ABOUT 2½ PINTS.

Ultra Boysenberry Sorbet

2 (12-ounce) bags frozen unsweetened boysenberries
¼ cup Cassis liqueur
¼ cup light corn syrup
½ cup sugar

Thaw the berries and process to a puree. Strain to remove the seeds.

Mix the liqueur, corn syrup, sugar, and ⅓ cup hot water together. Stir until the sugar is dissolved, then mix in the puree.

Pour the mixture into divided ice cube trays and freeze solid.

Several hours before serving, or up to a day ahead, place half of the frozen sorbet cubes in the food processor work bowl and pulse the machine on and off until the cubes are evenly chopped to the texture of coarse snow. Then run the machine continuously until the sorbet turns several shades paler and is creamy-looking. If the mixture is too hard to move freely around the bowl, allow it to thaw slightly or add a few drops of water.

Process the remaining sorbet cubes or save them for another time. Pile the sorbet into 1- or 2-pint containers. Cover and freeze.

MAKES ABOUT 2 PINTS.

Nectarine and Sauternes Sorbet

5 large ripe nectarines, pitted and
*   sliced*
2 tablespoons fresh lemon juice

½ cup Sauternes wine★
1¼ teaspoons unflavored gelatin
⅔ cup sugar

Puree the nectarines with the lemon juice. Stir in the Sauternes. In a very small pan, sprinkle the gelatin over ⅓ cup water and allow it to soak until it softens, about 3 minutes. Cook over very low heat, stirring occasionally, until the gelatin granules disappear. Remove from the heat and stir in the sugar until it dissolves. Stir the mixture into the nectarine puree.

Pour the mixture into divided ice cube trays and freeze solid.

Several hours before serving, or up to a day ahead, place half or one third of the frozen sorbet cubes in the food processor work bowl and

★ Be sure to use Sauternes rather than Sauterne—a drier wine.

pulse the machine on and off until the cubes are evenly chopped to the texture of coarse snow. Then run the machine continuously until the sorbet turns several shades paler and is creamy-looking. If the mixture is too hard to move freely around the bowl, allow it to thaw slightly or add a few drops of water.

Process the remaining sorbet cubes or save them for another time. Pile the sorbet into 1- or 2-pint containers. Cover and freeze.

MAKES ABOUT 2 PINTS.

Fresh Apricot and Sauternes Sorbet

Follow the recipe for Nectarine and Sauternes Sorbet (above), increasing the water to 1 cup, the sugar to ¾ cup and decreasing the lemon juice to 1 tablespoon. Use 3 cups fresh apricot halves, pitted.

Plum Sorbet with Grenadine

2 (1-pound) cans whole purple
  plums in heavy syrup
1 tablespoon fresh lemon juice

¾ teaspoon unflavored gelatin
⅓ cup sugar
⅓ cup grenadine syrup

Drain the plums, reserving the juice, and pit them. Puree the plums with the lemon juice. In a very small pan, sprinkle the gelatin over ¼ cup water and allow it to soak until it softens, about 3 minutes. Cook over very low heat, stirring occasionally, until the gelatin granules disappear. Remove from the heat and stir in additional ¼ cup water, the sugar, syrup, and plum juice, stirring until the sugar dissolves. Stir the mixture into the plum puree.

Pour into divided ice cube trays and freeze solid.

Several hours before serving, or up to a day ahead, place half or one third of the frozen sorbet cubes in the food processor work bowl and pulse the machine on and off until the cubes are evenly chopped to the texture of coarse snow. Then run the machine continuously until the sorbet turns several shades paler and is creamy-looking. If the mixture is too hard to move freely around the bowl, allow it to thaw slightly or add a few drops of water.

Process the remaining sorbet cubes or save them for another time. Pile the sorbet into 1- to 3-pint containers. Cover and freeze.

MAKES ABOUT 3 PINTS.

FABULOUS CHURNED SORBETS

The recipes in the following section may also be used with a food processor (see instructions for freezing and storing as given in the recipe for Very Strawberry Sorbet, on page 67). As a general rule, increase any gelatin by ¼ teaspoon or use 1¼ teaspoons gelatin or 1 tablespoon egg white in recipes without either gelatin or egg white. You can omit any gelatin or egg white if you are going to eat the sorbet soon after it is churned or if the fruit you are using is pulpy, such as mango.

Poires au Vin Rouge Sorbet

The inspiration for this dish is the down-home French dessert pears braised in red wine.

3 large ripe pears, peeled, cored, and quartered	1 small vanilla bean
2½ tablespoons fresh lemon juice	The zest of ½ a large lemon
1½ cups light red wine such as Beaujolais	⅔ cup sugar
	½ teaspoon unflavored gelatin
	1 tablespoon kirsch or Cognac

Toss the pears with 2½ teaspoons of the lemon juice in a large heavy saucepan. Pour in the wine and 1½ cups water and arrange the pears so they are covered. Add the vanilla bean, lemon zest, and sugar. Cover the pan with the lid barely ajar and simmer just until the pears are tender, about 12 minutes. Let the pears cool in the liquid, to room temperature. Remove the pears from the liquid with a slotted spoon. Measure the liquid. If it measures more than 2 cups, return it to the pan and boil until it is reduced to 2 cups. If there is less than 2 cups liquid, add more water. Pour the 2 cups liquid over the pears and chill overnight.

Remove the pears to a food processor or blender with a slotted spoon. Strain and reserve the cooking liquid. In a small pan, sprinkle the gelatin over ⅓ cup of the cooking liquid. Allow it to soak until it softens, about 3 minutes. Then cook over very low heat, stirring occasionally, until the gelatin granules disappear; cool. Puree the pears. Blend in the remaining cooking liquid, remaining 5 teaspoons lemon juice, and the gelatin mixture.

Freeze according to the directions given for your ice cream maker. When the sorbet is about 90 percent frozen, stir in the kirsch and finish freezing. Transfer to freezer containers for storage.

MAKES ABOUT 1½ QUARTS.

Chocolate Sorbet

1⅓ cups sugar
⅛ teaspoon salt
5 ounces unsweetened chocolate, chopped
1 teaspoon vanilla extract

In a medium heavy saucepan, heat 4 cups water and the sugar and salt together, stirring until the sugar dissolves. Add the chocolate and simmer, stirring occasionally, until the mixture is velvety smooth, about 25 minutes. Do not allow the mixture to boil. Cool to room temperature, then stir in the vanilla. Chill, then freeze according to the instructions for your ice cream maker. Transfer to freezer containers for storage.

MAKES ABOUT 5 CUPS.

Coconut-Pineapple Sorbet

½ cup plus 2 tablespoons sugar
1 medium very ripe pineapple,
  peeled and cored
1 tablespoon fresh lemon juice

1⅓ cups frozen or canned coconut
  milk, well mixed
1 tablespoon egg white
Powdered sugar to taste

In a small pan, combine 1 cup water and the sugar and cook over medium heat, swirling the pan occasionally, until the sugar is completely dissolved. Remove from the heat and cool to room temperature. Chop the pineapple and puree it with the lemon juice in a blender or food processor until smooth. Add the coconut milk, egg white, and sugar syrup and blend thoroughly. Taste and add powdered sugar to taste if desired, mixing it in very well. Freeze according to the instructions for your ice cream maker. If your machine freezes a quart or less, divide the mixture, keeping one half chilled until you are ready to freeze it. Mix it well before freezing. Transfer to freezer containers for storage.

MAKES ABOUT 3 PINTS.

Stephen's Pear Sorbet

This is one of my husband's favorite flavor combinations: pear flavored with almond and orange and lemon zest—unexpectedly refreshing.

7 tablespoons sugar	1 tablespoon egg white
5 very ripe pears (Comice or Bosc)	1 teaspoon grated lemon zest
	1½ teaspoons grated orange zest
1 tablespoon and 2½ teaspoons fresh lemon juice	1 teaspoon almond extract

In a small pan, combine ⅔ cup water and the sugar and cook over medium heat, swirling the pan occasionally, until the sugar is completely dissolved. Remove from the heat and cool to room temperature. Peel and core the pears, dropping them into a large bowl of water with the 1 tablespoon lemon juice stirred into it.

Remove the pears from the water and puree them in a blender or food processor. Add the remaining 2½ teaspoons lemon juice, the egg white, lemon and orange zest, almond extract, and sugar syrup, blending them in thoroughly. Freeze according to the instructions for your ice cream maker.

MAKES ABOUT 1 QUART.

Quick Apricot Sorbet

½ cup sugar	3 tablespoons fresh lemon juice
2 tablespoons light corn syrup	1 teaspoon egg white
2 (1-pound) cans apricot halves in heavy syrup	

Combine ⅔ cup water and the sugar in a small pan and heat, stirring, until the sugar dissolves. Stir in the corn syrup and cool the mixture. Puree the apricots in their syrup until smooth. Add the lemon juice, egg white, and sugar syrup; chill.

Freeze according to the instructions for your ice cream maker. Transfer to freezer containers for storage.

MAKES ABOUT 1 QUART.

Fresh Lime Sorbet

1 cup sugar
¾ cup fresh lime juice
6 tablespoons fresh lemon juice
1 tablespoon egg white

Combine ¾ cup water and the sugar and cook, stirring, until the sugar dissolves; cool. Combine the remaining water, lime juice, lemon juice and egg white. Add the sugar syrup; chill.

Freeze according to the instructions for your ice cream maker. Transfer to freezer containers for storage.

MAKES ABOUT 1 QUART.

Boysenberry-Zinfandel Sorbet

4 cups Zinfandel wine
¾ cup plus 1 tablespoon sugar
1 tablespoon grated lemon zest
1½-inch cinnamon stick (optional)

1 (12-ounce) package individually frozen boysenberries
1 tablespoon lemon juice
1½ tablespoons framboise eau de vie or kirsch

In a large saucepan, combine the wine, 1⅔ cups water, the sugar, lemon zest, cinnamon stick, and boysenberries. Bring to a boil, stirring occasionally until the sugar dissolves. Reduce the heat and simmer 5 minutes. Remove the berries and cinnamon stick with a slotted spoon. Discard the cinnamon stick. Cool the liquid to room temperature. Puree the berries and strain the puree to remove the seeds. Mix the puree into the cooled wine mixture. Chill, and stir in the lemon juice. Freeze according to the instructions for your ice cream maker. When the sorbet is about three-quarters frozen, mix in the liqueur and finish freezing. Transfer to freezer containers for storage.

Soften slightly in the refrigerator, about 15 minutes, before serving.

MAKES ABOUT 1 QUART.

Tangerine Sorbet

⅔ cup sugar
3 cups freshly squeezed tangerine juice
2 teaspoons finely grated tangerine zest
5 teaspoons fresh lemon juice

In a large saucepan, combine ½ cup water and the sugar and simmer, swirling the pan occasionally, until the sugar dissolves. Cool to room temperature. Blend in the remaining ingredients and chill thoroughly.

Freeze according to the instructions for your ice cream maker. Transfer to freezer containers for storage.

MAKES ABOUT 1 QUART.

Kiwi Sorbet

⅓ cup sugar
2 tablespoons corn syrup
6 large ripe kiwi fruit, peeled
2 teaspoons fresh lime juice
1 tablespoon egg white

In a medium saucepan combine ½ cup water and the sugar and cook, swirling the pan occasionally, until the sugar dissolves. Stir in the corn syrup and cool to room temperature. Puree the kiwis with the lime juice. Strain, if desired. Stir in the egg white and cooled syrup. Chill the mixture.

Freeze according to the instructions for your ice cream maker. Transfer to freezer containers for storage.

MAKES ABOUT 1 QUART.

Blackberry Sorbet

2 pints fresh or 2 (12-ounce) bags frozen unsweetened blackberries
½ cup plus 1 tablespoon sugar
¼ cup light corn syrup
1 tablespoon egg white

Place the berries in the top of a double boiler. Sprinkle with the sugar and heat over simmering water until the sugar dissolves and juice runs from the berries. Stir well and place in a blender or food processor just long enough to puree the flesh without grinding up the seeds. Strain the puree. Place the seeds in a bowl and stir in ½ cup water. Strain the water from the seeds into the puree. Blend in the corn syrup and egg white thoroughly.

Freeze according to the instructions for your ice cream maker. Transfer to freezer containers for storage.

MAKES ABOUT 1 QUART.

Cranberry Sorbet

1½ cups plus 1 tablespoon sugar
1 quart fresh or frozen unsweetened cranberries
1 large Granny Smith apple, peeled, cored, and coarsely chopped
2 teaspoons egg white

In a large pot, combine 3½ cups water and the sugar and boil, stirring occasionally, until the sugar is dissolved. Add the berries and cook over medium heat until the berry skins begin to pop. Remove the berries to a bowl with a slotted spoon. Add the apples to the cooking liquid and simmer about 3 minutes, until they are just soft. Remove from the heat. Push the berries through a strainer or chinoise to obtain a smooth puree. Puree the apples with a little of the cooking liquid in a blender or food processor. Blend in the berry puree and remaining cooking liquid until smooth. Beat the egg white lightly with a fork and blend in. Chill the mixture. For a 1-quart capacity ice cream freezer, use half of the sorbet mixture at a time. Freeze according to the instructions for your ice cream maker. Transfer to freezer containers for storage.

MAKES ABOUT 1½ QUARTS.

Berry-Cassis Sorbet

2 (1-pound) cans blackberries in syrup
3 tablespoons fresh lemon juice
2 tablespoons sugar
1 tablespoon egg white
2½ tablespoons Cassis liqueur

Drain the berries, reserving the syrup. In a blender or food processor puree the berries just until the flesh is mushy, without grinding up the seeds. Strain the puree. Blend the seeds with the lemon juice in a small bowl. Strain the lemon juice into the puree and discard the seeds. In a saucepan, combine the sugar and ¾ cup water and cook, stirring occasionally, until the sugar dissolves. Remove from the heat and blend in the reserved syrup and berry puree. Lightly beat the egg white and blend it in. Chill the mixture.

Freeze according to the instructions for your ice cream maker. When the sorbet is about 90 percent frozen, mix in the Cassis and finish freezing. Transfer to freezer containers for storage.

MAKES ABOUT 1 QUART.

Pink Grapefruit Sorbet

2 cups strained fresh pink grapefruit juice
½ cup sugar
¼ cup light corn syrup
1 tablespoon egg white

Chill the grapefruit juice. In a small pan, combine ¼ cup water and the sugar. Cook, stirring occasionally, until the sugar dissolves. Remove from the heat and stir in the corn syrup. Blend in ¾ cup water and stir the sugar mixture into the chilled juice. Beat the egg white slightly and mix it in.

Freeze according to the instructions for your ice cream maker. Transfer to freezer containers for storage.

MAKES ABOUT 1½ PINTS.

Sweet Cherry Sorbet

1 (1-pound) bag frozen unsweet- ened, pitted Bing cherries or about 1¼ pounds fresh cherries, pitted	¾ cup sugar 2 tablespoons light corn syrup 1 tablespoon fresh lemon juice 1½ tablespoons kirsch liqueur

Thaw the cherries and puree them. Measure ¾ cup water and add a little if needed to get a smooth puree; reserve water. In a small pan, heat ½ cup additional water and the sugar until the sugar is dissolved. Stir in the corn syrup; cool. Stir the remaining ¾ cup water (or less) and the lemon juice into the cherry puree. Stir in the gelatin mixture. Chill the sorbet mixture.

Freeze according to the instructions for your ice cream maker. When the sorbet is about 90 percent frozen, stir in the kirsch and finish freezing. Transfer to freezer containers for storage.

MAKES ABOUT 1 QUART.

Fresh Apple Sorbet

A very light and refreshing sorbet.

2 pounds McIntosh, Gravenstein, or Granny Smith apples
⅓ cup sugar
1⅔ cups unsweetened apple juice
1 tablespoon fresh lemon juice

Quarter, core, and peel the apples. Slice them thickly and place them in a heavy skillet with 5 tablespoons water. Bring to a boil, reduce the heat, cover, and cook the apples over low heat just until they begin to soften, about 8 minutes. Cool to room temperature. Blend the sugar and apple juice together until the sugar is dissolved. Heat the mixture slightly if the sugar will not dissolve. Puree the apples in a blender or food processor. Blend in the apple and lemon juices; chill.

Freeze according to the instructions for your ice cream maker. Transfer to freezer containers for storage.

MAKES ABOUT 1 QUART.

Asti Spumante Sorbet

⅔ cup sugar
2 cups good-quality Asti Spumante
1 tablespoon strained fresh orange juice
1 tablespoon fresh lemon juice
1 egg white

Combine 1 cup water and the sugar in a saucepan. Boil, stirring occasionally, until the sugar is completely dissolved; cool completely. Blend in the Asti Spumante and juices; chill the mixture. Freeze according to the instructions for your ice cream maker, about 20 minutes. Beat the egg white until completely white but not stiff; fold into the sorbet and complete the freezing. Transfer to containers for storage.

MAKES ABOUT 1 QUART.

Orange-Pineapple Sorbet

⅓ cup sugar
3 tablespoons light corn syrup
⅓ fresh very ripe pineapple, peeled and cored
1 cup fresh orange juice
1½ tablespoons fresh lemon juice

Combine 1 cup water, the sugar, and the corn syrup in a heavy saucepan. Simmer, stirring occasionally, until the sugar is dissolved, then simmer 5 minutes without stirring; cool. Puree the pineapple in a blender or food processor, adding a little of the orange juice if needed. Blend in the remaining orange juice, lemon juice, and sugar syrup. Chill the sorbet mixture.

Freeze according to the instructions for your ice cream maker. Transfer to freezer containers for storage.

MAKES ABOUT 1 QUART.

Fresh Apricot Sorbet

1 cup sugar
2 tablespoons light corn syrup
4 cups pitted ripe fresh apricot halves
½ cup fresh orange juice

Combine ½ cup water, the sugar, and the corn syrup in a heavy saucepan. Simmer, stirring occasionally, until the sugar is dissolved, then simmer 2 minutes without stirring; cool. In a blender or food processor, puree the apricots, adding a little of the orange juice if needed. Blend in the juice and sugar syrup. Chill the sorbet mixture.

Freeze according to the instructions for your ice cream maker. Transfer to freezer containers for storage.

MAKES ABOUT 1 QUART.

Persimmon Sorbet

One of the most unusually textured sorbets I have ever eaten—a creamy sorbet.

7 tablespoons sugar (or more to taste)
1½ tablespoons light corn syrup
1 pound ripe persimmons (about 3 small or 2 large)
2 tablespoons fresh lemon juice
¼ teaspoon freshly grated nutmeg

In a medium saucepan, combine 1¼ cups water and the 7 tablespoons sugar and cook, swirling the pan occasionally, until the sugar dissolves completely. Stir in the corn syrup and cool the syrup to room temperature.

Peel the persimmons and puree them in a blender or food processor. Add the lemon juice, nutmeg, and syrup and blend well. Chill thoroughly. Taste and add more sugar if necessary.

Freeze according to the instructions for your ice cream maker. Transfer to containers for storage.

MAKES ABOUT 1 QUART.

Tomato and Fresh Basil Sorbet

Not a dessert but a refreshing accompaniment to meat or seafood. This sorbet may also be served as a between-courses refresher or a delightfully surprising first course.

6 large, very ripe tomatoes
1½ teaspoons unflavored gelatin
½ teaspoon sugar
⅜ teaspoon salt
3 tablespoons balsamic vinegar
⅛ teaspoon liquid red pepper
   sauce

15 turns of the pepper mill
⅔ cup fresh basil leaves, lightly
   packed
3 tablespoons vodka

Dip each tomato in a large pot of boiling water several seconds, then place in a bowl of ice water. When the tomatoes cool, cut each in half crosswise and squeeze out the seeds, using your index finger to help release them. Peel the tomatoes and puree them. Place the puree in a bowl.

In a very small pan, sprinkle the gelatin over 3 tablespoons water. Allow it to soak until it softens, about 3 minutes. Cook over low heat, swirling the pan, until the gelatin granules disappear. Stir in the sugar, salt, vinegar, pepper sauce, and ground pepper. Stir this mixture into the tomato puree. Place the basil in the food processor work bowl and pulse the machine on and off until the leaves are finely chopped; or chop the basil by hand. Stir the basil into the tomato mixture. Thoroughly chill the mixture.

Freeze according to the instructions for your ice cream maker. When the mixture is about 90 percent frozen, stir in the vodka and finish freezing. Transfer to freezer containers for storage.

MAKES ABOUT 1 QUART.

Sweet Red Pepper Sorbet with Tequila

Serve as an hors d'oeuvre, a between-courses refresher, or even as a vegetable.

2 pounds red bell peppers
   (about 6)
1¼ teaspoons unflavored gelatin
⅓ cup sugar
2 tablespoons fresh lemon juice

⅛ teaspoon salt
⅜ teaspoon liquid red pepper
   sauce, or to taste
¼ cup tequila

Cut the peppers in half lengthwise, scoop out the seeds, and remove the ribs. Place the peppers, skin side up, on a sheet of foil under a medium-high broiler flame until the skins are blistered. Wrap the peppers in foil and allow them to sit until they reach room temperature. Peel the peppers and save any juice. Process the peppers and juice together to a smooth puree.

In a small pan, sprinkle the gelatin over 6 tablespoons water and allow it to soak until it softens, about 3 minutes. Cook over very low heat, stirring occasionally, until the gelatin granules disappear. Remove from the heat and stir in the sugar, lemon juice, salt, and pepper sauce. Blend the gelatin mixture into the pepper puree.

Freeze according to the instructions for your ice cream maker. When the mixture is about 90 percent frozen, stir in the tequila and finish freezing. Transfer to freezer containers for storage.

MAKES ABOUT 1 QUART.

Cucumber-Mint Sorbet

⅓ cup fresh mint leaves, lightly
   packed
¼ cup sugar
2 pounds cucumbers, peeled,
   seeded, and cut into 1-inch
   slices

2 tablespoons fresh lemon juice
1¼ teaspoons unflavored gelatin
Pinch of salt

Combine ½ cup water, the mint, and the sugar in a small saucepan. Bring to a boil and simmer 2 minutes. Place in a blender or food processor with the cucumbers and lemon juice and puree smoothly.

In a very small pan, sprinkle the gelatin over ¼ cup water and allow it to soak until it softens, about 3 minutes. Cook over very low heat, stirring occasionally, until the gelatin granules disappear. Remove from the heat. Stir in the salt. Blend into the cucumber puree. Chill the mixture.

Freeze according to the instructions for your ice cream maker. Transfer to freezer containers for storage.

MAKES ABOUT 2½ PINTS.

MAKING PLAIN SORBETS AND
ICE CREAMS FANCY

Create your own frozen delights, starting with these suggestions, which range from simply combining a variety of ice cream and sorbet flavors

- Begin by thinking about flavor combinations that would meld into the perfect tasting experience. This, of course, is most personal, but contrast is the key. Examples: Double Kahlúa Granita (page 75) paired with Gloriously Rich French Vanilla (page 17) or Coffee Ice Cream (page 20), or Ultra Boysenberry Sorbet (page 78) and Wonderful Fresh Orange Ice Cream (page 50), or Chocolate Sorbet (page 81) served in a pool of Velvety Vanilla Sauce (page 206).
- Serving frozen mixtures in an interesting shape also adds to the glamour. Traditionally, chefs serve sorbets in the shape of an egg, which can be easily formed using two oval soup spoons. Several egg-shaped flavors arranged on a plate are quite striking. Varying the size of the scoops also makes the plainest of ice creams look professionally served. Try using a melon ball scoop to create a pile of mini balls on a pool of sauce. Or scoop up one flavor with a medium-sized scoop and top it with mini scoops of a compatible-flavor sorbet or ice cream.
- Texture contrast is another way to add excitement to a dessert: icy Ultra Orange Sorbet with a rich vanilla ice cream or a warm vanilla sauce for example. Or sprinkle Glazed Nuts (page 212) or Coconut Praline (page 28) on plain or sauced ice cream.
- Play textures against one another, crunchy against smooth or crisp with icy, by serving ice creams in edible cups. (These go beyond the cone.) Classically, the French have used Meringue Shells (page 209) to cradle ice creams or sorbets and a compatible sauce. I've also included praline and praline cookie cups, chocolate cups, and chocolate meringue shells. Hollowed citrus fruit and melons are festive containers, too.

FROZEN BOMBES

The ultimate way to combine contrasting flavors and textures is to use them in a frozen bombe. These molded, layered frozen desserts were launched in mid-nineteenth-century Paris and, true to their name, were brought aflame to the table, a brandy-soaked wick in their centers. Today bombes may be simply made by layering a variety of frozen mixtures into a fancy mold or plain bowl—it's the contrast that counts. Crushed praline, toffee, or macaroons may be wedged between a sorbet and ice cream. Or a smooth frozen mousse be complemented by a layer of refreshing sherbet. When sliced, a colorful multilayered cross section becomes the design.

Creating Bombes

- The same rules discussed in dressing up ice cream apply to bombes. Good contrast is the key.
- A real bombe mold is ideal, but gelatin molds or even a plain bowl, soufflé dish, casserole or loaf pan may be used. Before you begin, chill the mold to be used and assemble all the utensils you will need, such as a flat scoop or several large sturdy spoons.
- Measure the volume of your mold by pouring water into it from a measuring cup. This will let you know how much ice cream to use.
- Bombes must be layered and frozen in stages. It is best to layer ice cream or sorbet into the mold just as it comes from the churn or machine. If you're using commercially produced ice cream, let it soften in the refrigerator 10 to 20 minutes. Then slice the ice cream and arrange it around your mold. Smooth the slices together with the back of a spoon or flat scoop, then finish the layer, smoothing with your fingertips.

  Freeze each layer until it is rock-hard. Quality ice creams work best for bombes. Inexpensive ones never harden well enough to get a good clean slice.
- Think about contrasting both flavors and textures when you make your selection of layerings. Try filling the center of a bombe with a still-frozen mousse such as Melissa's Can't-Fail Liqueur Mousse (page 162), an easy, no-fail still-frozen dessert that is richer and creamier than ice cream and complements either ice cream or sorbet.

Combination Ideas for Creating Bombes

SORBETS, SHERBETS, AND ICE CREAMS

- Raspberry sorbet layer, vanilla layer, chocolate custard ice cream interior.
- Chocolate sorbet layer, chocolate ice cream layer, espresso or mint-chocolate chip ice cream interior.
- Lemon sorbet or sherbet layer, raspberry sorbet or sherbet layer, vanilla ice cream layer, orange sorbet or sherbet layer.

TEXTURED ICE CREAMS OR LAYERS IN BOMBES

- Coffee Ice Cream exterior (page 20), Pecan Praline Ice Cream interior (page 27).
- Vanilla ice cream exterior, Ginger-Walnut Ice Cream interior (page 31).
- Serious Chocolate Lovers' Ice Cream exterior (page 44), coarsely crushed praline layer (page 26), Gloriously Rich French Vanilla layer (page 17), Coffee Ice Cream interior.

Bombes with Still-Frozen Interiors

- Lemon Sorbet exterior (page 70), Fresh Lemon Soufflé interior (page 171).
- Ultra-Dark Chocolate Ice Cream exterior (page 44), Melissa's Can't-Fail Liqueur Mousse (Amaretto or Kahlúa variation) interior (page 162 and 163).
- Pecan Praline Ice Cream (page 27) exterior, Frozen Calvados Cream interior (page 161).
- Ultra Orange Sorbet exterior (page 73), crushed Almond Macaroon layer (page 36), Melissa's Can't-Fail Liqueur Mousse interior (Grand Marnier basic recipe) (page 162).

Ice Cream Cakes and
Other Frozen Pastries

Cakes go hand in hand with special festivities—a birthday celebration, a holiday season, or a private, small indulgence for one or two. We know, of course, that cakes are not to be gobbled down every day. When the time comes to serve them, they deserve to be gloriously rich and spectacular, filled with the finest cream and chocolate, laced with the best brandy or liqueurs, and with care lavished on them during their preparation.

Like other sinfully rich indulgences, ice cream cakes exemplify all that is splendid. They are best when showing off delicious layers of varied textures: velvety cake or crisp meringue, with the tang of sorbet and creaminess of ice cream, or a buttery nut-filled layer topped with complementary ice cream flavors stacked up into a tall icy confection.

Because almost everyone loves ice cream and cake, I've tried to include a variety for every taste. Some are light and delicate, such as the Cassis Cloud Roll (filled with frozen Cassis-flavored cream) or the layered mousse cakes, with their tang of fresh fruit or perhaps Grand Marnier. Some have airy meringue layers, and others—for example, the brownie-bottomed Frozen Quadruple Chocolate Suicide—are dense and baroque. A series of frozen, meltingly rich cheesecakes, including my favorite Amaretto–Chocolate Swirl, rounds out the collection.

Shaped cakes that can be made without fancy molds, such as the Bunny, Santa, or Sweetheart, can be created with your own choice of ice cream fillings and garnishings by following the proportions of the recipe; they will be very personal indeed.

I found the frozen cakes I liked best were based on a light sponge cake. A frozen *génoise*, though light, becomes tough because of its high butter content. Light sponge cakes, on the other hand, stay tender under layers of ice cream or frozen mousse and are great when soaked with flavorful liqueur-laced syrups.

As a matter of practicality, the more complicated cakes can be done in stages. The cakes can be baked days or even weeks ahead and frozen, and ice cream can be churned or purchased a day ahead.

- If softened ice creams are called for in the recipe, the best way to soften them is in the refrigerator. Then slice the ice cream and distribute it over the cake, spreading it with a blunt knife or spatula. Work quickly. You don't want the ice cream to melt, or the final result will be icy. Finally, smooth out each layer as evenly as possible with your fingers and freeze each layer of ice cream solid before adding another.

Amaretto–Chocolate Swirl Frozen Cheesecake

An Amaretto-laced cheesecake with an almond and amaretti crust.

crust
¾ cup plus 1 tablespoon amaretti biscuit crumbs
6 tablespoons almonds chopped almost to a powder
2½ tablespoons unsalted butter, melted

swirl mixture
4 ounces semisweet chocolate
3 tablespoons unsalted butter
2 tablespoons dark or light corn syrup
2 tablespoons Amaretto liqueur

cheesecake mixture
14 ounces cream cheese, at room
* temperature*
2 tablespoons sugar
⅔ cup sweetened condensed milk
½ cup Amaretto liqueur

1 teaspoon vanilla extract
A scant ¼ teaspoon almond
* extract*
2 cups heavy cream

Combine the crumbs and almonds and mix well. Drizzle the 2½ table-spoons butter over the mixture and mix it in thoroughly. Pat the mixture over the bottom of a 9-inch springform pan. Freeze the crust.

In a small heavy saucepan or in a double boiler, melt the chocolate and 3 tablespoons butter together over very low heat. When the chocolate is melted, stir in the corn syrup and 2 tablespoons Amaretto; mix well and remove from the heat.

Chill the beaters of an electric mixer and a bowl large enough (6-cup volume) to whip the cream. In a food processor or with an electric mixer, blend the cream cheese and sugar together until the mixture is fluffy. Add the milk, Amaretto, vanilla, and almond extract, blending them in well.

With the chilled bowl and beaters, whip the cream until curved peaks will hold their shape. Fold one fourth at a time into the cheese mixture.

If the chocolate mixture has hardened, soften it by heating it just slightly. It should be lukewarm. Pour half of the cheese mixture into the crust. Swirl half of the chocolate mixture over it and swirl it in with a knife. Repeat with the remaining cheese and chocolate. Freeze the mixture 12 hours or overnight. First cover with plastic wrap and then foil until ready to serve.

To remove the cake easily from the pan, dip a sponge in very hot water and wipe the bottom of the pan a few seconds. Repeat with the sides. Open the springform pan, remove the pan side, and smooth the sides of the cake with a small spatula.

MAKES 10 TO 12 SERVINGS.

Kahlúa Frozen Cheesecake

crust

1 cup Famous Chocolate Wafer
   crumbs
2 tablespoons unsweetened cocoa

3 tablespoons powdered sugar
3 tablespoons unsalted butter,
   melted

cheesecake mixture

14 ounces cream cheese, at room
   temperature
1½ tablespoons sugar
⅔ cup sweetened condensed milk
½ cup Kahlúa or other coffee
   liqueur

1½ teaspoons vanilla extract
2 teaspoons instant coffee granules
   mixed with 1½ teaspoons water
2 cups heavy cream

Combine the crumbs, cocoa, and powdered sugar and mix well. Drizzle the butter over the mixture and mix it in thoroughly. Pat the mixture over the bottom of a 9-inch springform pan. Freeze the crust.

Chill the beaters of an electric mixer and a bowl large enough (6-cup volume) to whip the cream. In a food processor or with an electric mixer, blend the cream cheese and sugar together until the mixture is fluffy. Add the milk, coffee liqueur, vanilla, and coffee, blending them in well.

With the chilled bowl and beaters, whip the cream until curved peaks will hold their shape. Fold one third at a time into the cheese mixture.

Pour the cheese mixture into the crust. Freeze the mixture 12 hours or overnight. Cover the cake with plastic wrap and then tightly with foil until you are ready to serve it.

To remove the cake easily from the pan, dip a sponge in very hot water and wipe the bottom of the pan a few seconds. Repeat with the sides. Open the springform pan, remove the pan side, and smooth the sides of the cake with a small spatula.

MAKES 10 TO 12 SERVINGS.

Variation

KAHLÚA FROZEN CHEESECAKE WITH CHOCOLATE GLAZE

After the cheesecake is frozen, prepare the following glaze.

Cool the glaze to a warm room temperature and drizzle it in a swirl pattern over the top of the frozen cake. Smooth the surface with a small spatula. Freeze the cake a few moments until the glaze is firm but not frozen. Score the topping into 10 equal wedges.

Freeze the cake, covered with plastic wrap and then tightly with foil, until you are ready to serve it.

Glaze

In a small heavy pan or in a double boiler, melt 2 ounces semisweet chocolate with ¼ cup unsalted butter. Mix together well and cool slightly. Stir in 2½ tablespoons heavy cream.

Daquiri Frozen Cheesecake

crust
⅔ cup butter biscuit (petit beurre) or butter cookie crumbs
6 tablespoons almonds or walnuts chopped almost to a powder
3 tablespoons unsalted butter, melted

cheesecake mixture
14 ounces cream cheese, at room temperature
½ cup sugar
2 large egg yolks
1¼ cups (1 [14-ounce] can) sweetened condensed milk

1 cup fresh lime juice
⅓ cup amber or light rum
1¼ teaspoons vanilla extract
2 cups heavy cream

Combine the crumbs and nuts and mix well. Drizzle the butter over the mixture and mix it in thoroughly. Pat the mixture over the bottom of a 9-inch springform pan. Freeze the crust.

Chill the beaters of an electric mixer and a bowl large enough (6-cup volume) to whip the cream. In a food processor or with an electric mixer, blend the cream cheese, sugar, and egg yolks together until the mixture is fluffy. Add the milk, lime juice, rum, and vanilla, blending them in well.

With the chilled bowl and beaters, whip the cream until curved peaks will hold their shape. Fold one third at a time into the cheese mixture.

Pour the cheese mixture into the crust. Freeze the mixture 12 hours or overnight. Cover the cake with plastic wrap and then tightly with foil until you are ready to serve it.

To remove the cake easily from the pan, dip a sponge in very hot water and wipe the bottom of the pan a few seconds. Repeat with the sides. Open the springform pan, remove the pan side, and smooth the sides of the cake with a small spatula.

MAKES 10 TO 12 SERVINGS.

Fruit-Topped Frozen Cheesecake

crust
¾ cup butter biscuit (petit beurre) or butter cookie crumbs
6 tablespoons almonds or walnuts chopped almost to a powder
3 tablespoons unsalted butter, melted

cheesecake mixture

12 ounces cream cheese, at room temperature

1 large egg, separated and at room temperature

2 tablespoons sugar

1¼ cups (1 [14-ounce] can) sweetened condensed milk

¼ cup fresh lemon juice

1½ teaspoons vanilla extract

2 cups heavy cream

Combine the crumbs and nuts and mix well. Drizzle the butter over the mixture and mix it in thoroughly. Pat the mixture over the bottom of a 9-inch springform pan. Freeze the crust.

Chill the beaters of an electric mixer and a bowl large enough (6-cup volume) to whip the cream. In a food processor or with an electric mixer, blend the cream cheese, egg yolk, and sugar together until the mixture is fluffy. Add the milk, lemon juice, and vanilla, blending them in well. In a clean bowl, beat the egg white just until curved peaks will hold their shape; set aside. With the chilled bowl and beaters, whip the cream until curved peaks will hold their shape. Fold in one third of the cheese mixture, then the egg white, then the remaining cheese mixture, one half at a time.

Pour the mixture into the crust and freeze 12 hours or overnight. Cover the cake with plastic wrap and then tightly with foil until you are ready to serve it.

To remove the cake easily from the pan, dip a sponge in very hot water and wipe the bottom of the pan a few seconds. Repeat with the sides. Open the springform pan, remove the pan side, and smooth the sides of the cake with a small spatula. Pour several spoonfuls of Berry Topping over the top of each cake serving. Pass the remaining topping at the table.
MAKES 10 TO 12 SERVINGS.

Berry Topping

Thaw 2 (10-ounce) packages frozen sliced strawberries or raspberries in syrup. Mix in 3 tablespoons raspberry eau de vie or kirsch and 2 tablespoons Cointreau or Triple Sec liqueur.

Frozen Chocolate Cheesecake

crust

1 cup Chocolate-Almond Macaroons or Almond Macaroons
  (page 211), crumbled, or amaretti biscuit crumbs

cheesecake mixture

8 ounces semisweet chocolate
8 ounces cream cheese, at room
  temperature
½ cup plus 2 tablespoons sugar
1 teaspoon vanilla extract
2 large egg yolks, at room temperature

6 tablespoons almonds chopped
  almost to a powder
3 tablespoons unsalted butter,
  melted

3 large egg whites, at room temperature
1 cup heavy cream
Chocolate Leaves (page 213) or
  shaved semisweet chocolate

Combine the crumbs and almonds and mix well. Drizzle the butter over the mixture and mix it in thoroughly. Pat the mixture over the bottom of a 9-inch springform pan. Freeze the crust.

Chill the beaters of an electric mixer and a bowl large enough (6-cup volume) to whip the cream. In a small pan within another pan or in a double boiler over simmering water, melt the chocolate. Cool to room temperature. In a food processor or with an electric mixer, blend the cream cheese and ⅓ cup of the sugar together until the mixture is fluffy. Add the vanilla and egg yolks, blending them in well. Mix in the melted chocolate. Beat the egg whites until very soft peaks form. Gradually add the remaining sugar, beating until the whites are glossy and stiff. Fold one third of the whites into the chocolate mixture, then fold in the remaining whites.

With the chilled bowl and beaters, whip the cream until curved peaks will hold their shape. Fold the cream into the chocolate mixture, one third at a time.

Pour mixture into the crust and freeze at least 8 hours or overnight. First cover the cake with plastic wrap and then tightly with foil until you are ready to serve it.

To remove the cake easily from the pan, dip a sponge in very hot water and wipe the bottom of the pan a few seconds. Repeat with the sides.

Open the springform pan, remove the pan side, and smooth the sides of the cake with a small spatula.

Before serving, garnish with Chocolate Leaves or shaved chocolate.

MAKES 12 SERVINGS.

Frozen Mocha Cheesecake

crust
1⅓ cups Famous Chocolate Wafer crumbs
1 teaspoon powdered instant espresso coffee
⅓ cup powdered sugar
3 tablespoons unsalted butter, melted

cheesecake mixture
2 ounces semisweet chocolate
8 ounces cream cheese, at room temperature
⅔ cup sugar
1 teaspoon vanilla extract
2 tablespoons dark rum
3 large eggs, separated and at room temperature

2½ teaspoons instant coffee powder dissolved in ½ tablespoon water
1 cup heavy cream
Chocolate Leaves (page 213) or shaved semisweet chocolate

Combine the crumbs, espresso, and powdered sugar and blend them together well. Drizzle the butter over the mixture and mix it in thoroughly. Pat the mixture over the bottom of a 9-inch springform pan. Freeze the crust.

Chill the beaters of an electric mixer and a bowl large enough (6-cup volume) to whip the cream. In a small pan within another pan or in a double boiler over simmering water, melt the chocolate. Cool to room temperature. In a food processor or with an electric mixer, blend the cream cheese and ⅓ cup sugar together until the mixture is fluffy. Add the vanilla, rum, and egg yolks, blending them in well. Mix in the dissolved coffee powder and melted chocolate. Beat the egg whites until very soft peaks form. Gradually add the remaining ⅓ cup sugar, beating until the whites are glossy and stiff. Fold in the whites, one third at a time, into the cheese mixture.

With the chilled bowl and beaters, whip the cream until curved peaks will hold their shape. Fold the cream into the cheese mixture, one third at a time.

Pour the mixture into the crust and freeze at least 8 hours or overnight. Then cover the cake with plastic wrap and then tightly with foil until you are ready to serve it.

To remove the cake easily from the pan, dip a sponge in very hot water and wipe the bottom of the pan a few seconds. Repeat with the sides. Open the springform pan, remove the pan side, and smooth the sides of the cake with a small spatula.

Before serving, garnish with Chocolate Leaves or shaved chocolate.
MAKES 12 SERVINGS.

Brownie Ice Cream Cake

The first version of this cake, using chocolate and mint chocolate chip ice creams, could be called Brownie Chocolate Mint Cake. However, it could be transformed into any number of incredible desserts simply by using different ice cream combinations. Try vanilla and black walnut together, or strawberry and vanilla. Caramel and mocha almond fudge ripple would be another marvelous alternative.

brownie layer
2 ounces semisweet chocolate
3 tablespoons unsalted butter
¼ cup all-purpose flour
2 teaspoons unsweetened cocoa
¼ teaspoon baking powder
Pinch of salt

½ cup sugar
1 large egg
½ teaspoon vanilla extract
6 tablespoons walnuts or pecans, chopped about the size of peas

filling
3 cups chocolate ice cream
1 quart Chocolate–Chocolate Mint Chip Ice Cream (page 10), or quick mint–chocolate chip dessert (page 4)

1 cup heavy cream whipped with 2 tablespoons sugar and ¾ teaspoon vanilla extract
Thin chocolate mints, broken up

Preheat the oven to 350° F. Line a 9-inch round cake pan with wax paper or parchment. Butter the paper. In a small pan within another pan or in a double boiler over simmering water, melt the chocolate and butter together. Stir until smooth and well blended. Cool slightly. Sift the flour, cocoa, baking powder, and salt together. In a medium bowl, blend the sugar, egg, and vanilla together. Blend in the chocolate. Blend in the flour mixture only until blended. Do not overmix. Blend in the nuts. Spread the batter evenly in the pan and bake in the center of the oven 15 to 18 minutes, or until a wooden pick inserted 1½ inches from the center comes out dry. Cool on a rack in the pan. Invert onto a plate and peel away the paper.

assembly

Place the brownie layer in the bottom of a 9-inch springform pan. Let the chocolate ice cream soften slightly and spread it evenly over the brownie layer, smoothing it with your fingers. Freeze until firm. Repeat with the Chocolate–Chocolate Mint Chip Ice Cream. Top with the whipped cream.

When ready to serve, remove the sides of the springform pan. Trim and smooth the sides of the cake. Decorate the top with the broken mints. Cut the cake with a long, very sharp knife dipped in hot water.

MAKES 10 SERVINGS.

Flavor Variations

BLACK WALNUT BROWNIE CAKE

Follow the recipe (above) for Brownie Ice Cream Cake, substituting 1 pint fudge ripple ice cream for the chocolate and black walnut ice cream for the Chocolate–Chocolate Mint Chip.

COFFEE AND CHOCOLATE BROWNIE ICE CREAM CAKE

Replace the Chocolate–Chocolate Mint Chip Ice Cream with coffee ice cream.

CARAMEL AND MOCHA ALMOND–FUDGE RIPPLE BROWNIE ICE CREAM CAKE

Replace the chocolate ice cream with Caramel Ice Cream (page 19) and the Chocolate–Chocolate Mint Chip Ice Cream with Jamoca Almond Fudge Ice Cream (page 26).

Cassis Cloud Roll

Frozen Cassis-flavored cream fills this delicate cake.

Roll Cake (recipe below)
2 egg yolks
⅓ cup sugar
About 7 tablespoons black currant
   preserves

About ½ cup Cassis liqueur
2 cups heavy cream
2 teaspoons light corn syrup
Sliced almonds

Prepare the cake. Chill a bowl large enough (6-cup volume) to whip the cream.

In a bowl partially submerged in very hot water, beat the egg yolks until fluffy and light in color. Gradually add the sugar and beat until the yolks are thick and ivory-colored. Remove the bowl from the water. Blend 3 tablespoons of the preserves smoothly with 5 tablespoons of the Cassis and fold into the beaten eggs. In the chilled bowl, with clean beaters, whip the cream until soft peaks will hold a shape. Fold the whipped cream into the egg yolk mixture. Freeze until the mixture is semifrozen and will hold its shape on a spoon, about 3 hours.

Blend ¼ cup water, the remaining 4 tablespoons of the Cassis, and the corn syrup together. Unroll the cake. Sprinkle the Cassis-syrup mixture evenly over the inside surface of the cake. Spread the cake with ¼ cup of the preserves to within ¼ inch of the cake edges.

Spread half of the semifrozen cream mixture over the cake, leaving a ¼-inch border. Carefully roll up the cake. Place the cake on a platter, seam side down. Frost the roll with the remaining cream mixture and freeze. Decorate the roll by making a row of 6 tiny dots of preserves in a line down the center of the cake. Make a row of flowers, using the sliced almonds as petals and the dots of preserves as the flower centers. Freeze at least 2 hours or overnight. Slice to serve.

MAKES 8 TO 10 SERVINGS.

Roll Cake

4 large egg yolks, at room temperature
⅔ cup sugar
5 large egg whites, at room temperature
½ cup sifted all-purpose flour

3 tablespoons cornstarch
½ teaspoon baking powder
⅛ teaspoon salt
1 teaspoon grated lemon zest
2 tablespoons melted butter
Powdered sugar

Preheat the oven to 350° F. Butter a 15½ × 10½-inch rimmed baking sheet and line it with wax paper or parchment. Butter the paper.

Beat the egg yolks with an electric mixer until thick and lemon-colored. Gradually add ⅓ cup of the sugar, beating until ribbons falling on the surface from the raised beaters leave a visible trail for 15 seconds. With clean beaters, beat the egg whites until they are foamy and white. Gradually beat in the remaining ⅓ cup sugar until the whites are glossy and stiff. Fold one third of the whites into the egg yolks, then fold in the flour, next the cornstarch, baking powder, salt, lemon zest, and butter. Fold in the remaining egg whites, one third at a time.

Pour the batter into the prepared pan and distribute it evenly. Bake in the center of the oven about 15 minutes, or until the cake begins to pull away from the sides and a wooden toothpick inserted into the center comes out clean. Cool in the pan 5 minutes. Run a thin spatula around the cake edge and under the bottom of the cake. Invert onto a towel lightly sprinkled with sifted powdered sugar. Immediately peel away the paper and, starting at the narrow end, roll the cake and towel together. Cool on a rack until ready to fill.

Variation

ICE CREAM CAKE ROLL

Prepare the Roll Cake (above). Spread the cake either with chocolate syrup (about ⅓ cup) or fruit preserves. Soften 1 quart ice cream and spread it to within ½ inch of the cake edges. Roll up the cake and freeze until firm, about 4 hours. Whip 1 cup heavy cream with 3 tablespoons sifted powdered sugar and ½ teaspoon vanilla extract. You can frost the cake just after it is rolled up. When the frosting is firm, about 1 hour after freezing, cover the cake with plastic wrap and then foil.

Coffee-Chocolate Multilayered Ice Cream Cake

Any number of ice cream combinations would make this a special dessert.

¾ cup butter cookie or butter biscuit (petit beurre) crumbs
2½ cups sliced almonds
¼ cup light brown sugar, packed
½ cup unsalted butter, melted
3 pints vanilla ice cream
3 tablespoons fudge sauce (page 198) mixed with 2 teaspoons coffee-flavored liqueur or

crème de cacao or Amaretto
1 pint Chocolate Sorbet (page 81) or Ultra-Dark Chocolate Ice Cream (page 44)
2 pints Coffee Ice Cream (page 20)
Chopped or slivered almonds
Mocha candy coffee beans (optional, for garnish)

Preheat the oven to 350° F. Combine the crumbs, sliced almonds, sugar, and butter and mix together thoroughly. Reserve ⅔ cup of the crumb mixture and pat the rest into the bottom of a 9-inch springform pan. Bake 12 to 15 minutes, until the nuts are lightly toasted. Chill the crust.

In the refrigerator, soften all but 1½ cups of the vanilla ice cream slightly. Spread the vanilla ice cream over the crust, smoothing the layer with your fingers; do not allow the ice cream to melt. Swirl in 2 tablespoons of the chocolate-liqueur mixture. Freeze until very firm. Soften the chocolate sorbet and spread it smoothly over the vanilla ice cream. Sprinkle with the remaining nut-crumb mixture; freeze until firm. Soften the coffee ice cream and spread over the sorbet; freeze until firm. Soften the remaining vanilla ice cream and spread it over the coffee ice cream. Swirl the remaining chocolate-liqueur sauce over the vanilla ice cream; freeze until firm.

Wipe the side of the springform pan with a warm sponge, open the pan, and remove the side. Firmly pat the nuts into the sides of the cake. Freeze until ready to serve.

MAKES 10 TO 12 SERVINGS.

Variation

RAINBOW CAKE

Follow the directions for Coffee-Chocolate Multilayered Ice Cream Cake (recipe above), substituting fruit-flavored ice creams or sherbets for the chocolate sorbet and coffee ice cream. In place of the chocolate sauce, use raspberry or strawberry sauce and a compatible liqueur or kirsch.

Berry Obsttorten

1 (12-inch) sponge cake tart shell
½ cup Chambord liqueur or
   Cassis liqueur
1 quart vanilla or compatible
   fruit-flavored ice cream

3 cups fresh berries
Meringue Nut Crunch (page 32)
   (optional)

Sprinkle the tart shell evenly with ¼ cup of the liqueur and set aside. Soften the ice cream slightly and swirl in 2 tablespoons of the liqueur. Spoon the ice cream into the tart shell and freeze. Hull the berries if necessary. Puree half the berries in a blender or food processor. If they have large seeds, such as raspberry, strain to remove the seeds. Stir the remaining liqueur into the puree. When ready to serve, mound the remaining berries in the center of the tart. Pour the puree around the berries and drizzle a little puree over the berries. Sprinkle with Meringue Nut Crunch if you like.

MAKES 10 SERVINGS.

Black Forest Ice Cream Cake

1 (16-ounce) can pitted Bing
   cherries in heavy syrup
2 tablespoons sugar
6 tablespoons and ½ teaspoon
   kirsch liqueur
Black Forest Chocolate Sponge
   Cake Layer (recipe below)
¼ cup heavy cream
3 ounces semisweet chocolate,
   chopped

2½ tablespoons light corn syrup
3 pints Old-fashioned Vanilla
   Custard Ice Cream (page 17)
   or good-quality purchased ice
   cream
12 mini Chocolate Leaves (page
   213) (optional)

Drain the cherries, reserving the juice, and place them in a glass or ceramic container. In a medium saucepan, combine the cherry juice and sugar and boil until the syrup is reduced to ½ cup. Remove from the heat and stir in 3½ tablespoons of the kirsch. Pour the syrup over the cherries and allow to stand overnight, or refrigerate as long as several weeks, until ready to assemble the cake.

Prepare the cake layer, and if you are working more than a day in advance, freeze it until ready to assemble the entire dessert.

At least 6 hours before serving, assemble the cake as follows: In a small pan, heat the cream to a simmer. Add the chocolate and cook over very low heat, stirring constantly, until the chocolate is melted. Remove from the heat and stir in the corn syrup and 2 teaspoons of the kirsch. Cool completely.

Drain the soaked cherries, reserving the syrup and 13 whole cherries. Quarter the remaining cherries. Remove the ice cream from the freezer and refrigerate it until it softens slightly.

With a thin, long serrated knife, carefully cut the cake into 2 layers. (I place a sheet of plastic wrap over the top of the cake to keep my hand from sticking to it as I cut.) Place 1 layer, cut side up, in an 8-inch springform pan, and sprinkle half of the reserved cherry syrup over it. Place the other cake layer on a plate, cut side up, and sprinkle the remaining syrup over it. Stir 2 tablespoons of the kirsch into the softened ice cream and return 1½ cups of the mixture to the freezer for the topping. Spread the remaining ice cream in a baking dish, swirl the cooled chocolate mixture over it, and with a knife swirl it throughout the ice cream. Spoon half the ice cream mixture over the cake layer in the pan and top with half of the quartered cherries, the remaining ice cream mixture, and the remaining cherries. Invert the second cake layer over the ice cream, pressing down gently. Freeze the cake until it is firm.

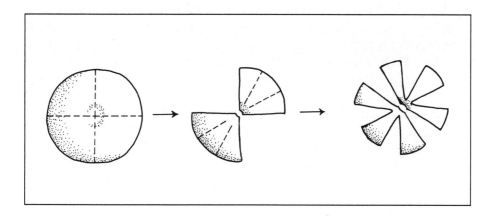

Soften the reserved 1½ cups ice cream slightly and spread it over the top of the cake. Press 12 of the reserved whole cherries at even intervals around the top edge of the cake. Place a mini chocolate leaf next to each cherry. Place the cake in the freezer. Cut the last cherry in half. Discard one half and cut remaining half into two semicircles. From the rounded edge, cut each semicircle into three equal wedges, barely reaching the center of the straight edge. Repeat with second semicircle. Fan out to form petals. Arrange the cherry flower on the center of the cake.

To serve the cake, wipe a sponge soaked with hot water over the bottom and side of the cake pan, then open the pan, remove the side, and place the cake on a plate.

MAKES 12 SERVINGS.

Black Forest Chocolate Sponge Cake Layer

3 large egg yolks, at room temperature
½ cup sugar
4 large egg whites, at room temperature
6 tablespoons sifted all-purpose flour

3 tablespoons unsweetened cocoa
½ teaspoon baking powder
⅛ teaspoon salt
1 teaspoon vanilla extract
2 tablespoons butter, melted

Preheat the oven to 350° F. Butter a 9-inch round cake pan and line it with a circle of wax paper or parchment. Butter the paper.

Beat the egg yolks with an electric mixer until thick and lemon-colored. Gradually add 5 tablespoons of the sugar, beating until ribbons falling on the surface from the raised beaters leave a visible trail for 15 seconds. With clean beaters, beat the egg whites until they are foamy and white. Gradually beat in the remaining sugar until the whites are glossy and stiff.

Combine the flour, cocoa, baking powder, and salt and sift or blend together well.

Fold one third of the egg whites into the yolks, then fold in half of the flour mixture. Fold in another third of the egg whites, then the remaining flour mixture, vanilla, butter, and remaining egg whites.

Pour the batter into the prepared pan and distribute it evenly. Bake in the center of the oven about 15 to 18 minutes, or until the cake begins to pull away from the sides and a wooden toothpick inserted into the center comes out clean. Cool in the pan 5 minutes. Run a thin spatula around the cake edge and under the bottom of the cake. Invert onto a rack to cool.

Wrap the cake in plastic wrap and refrigerate it, or wrap it in plastic wrap and foil and freeze until ready to use.

Lemon Meringue Baked Alaska

I discovered, while experimenting with meringues, that they can be successfully frozen. So, unlike standard meringue desserts, which require that the meringue be made just before serving, this cake can be taken from the freezer shortly before being served.

Lemon Sponge Cake (recipe below) or commercially baked round sponge cake layer
1 pint Lemon Sorbet (page 70) or sherbet
3 pints Lemon Custard Ice Cream (page 50) or vanilla ice cream

5 large egg whites, at room temperature
⅛ teaspoon cream of tartar
⅔ cup sugar

Remove the side of an 8-inch springform pan and line the bottom with foil; attach the pan's rim. Place the cake in the pan. Soften the sorbet just enough to spread it over the cake, evening it out with your fingertips. Freeze until firm. Repeat with the Lemon Custard Ice Cream.

Beat the egg whites and cream of tartar until soft peaks barely hold their shape. Gradually beat in the sugar until stiff glossy peaks form. Remove the cake from the freezer. Remove the side of the springform pan. Working quickly with a spatula, frost the cake with the meringue. Be sure to completely seal in the cake and ice cream with the meringue. You can bake and serve the cake right away or for best results, cover lightly with plastic wrap and place the cake in the freezer for at least 1 hour or up to 24 hours.

Heat the oven to 450° F. Cover a baking sheet with foil. Remove the cake from the freezer and bake about 1½ minutes, until meringue tips are golden brown. Serve at once or freeze at least an hour to firm the ice cream. Slice with a serrated knife dipped in hot water.

MAKES 8 SERVINGS.

Lemon Sponge Cake

3 large egg yolks, at room temper-
  ature
7 tablespoons sugar
4 large egg whites, at room tem-
  perature
⅓ cup sifted all-purpose flour

3 tablespoons cornstarch
½ teaspoon baking powder
⅛ teaspoon salt
1½ teaspoons grated lemon zest
3 teaspoons fresh lemon juice

Preheat the oven to 350° F. Butter a 9-inch round cake pan and line it with a circle of wax paper or parchment. Butter the paper.

Beat the egg yolks with an electric mixer until thick and lemon-colored. Gradually add 4 tablespoons of the sugar, beating until ribbons falling on the surface from the raised beaters leave a visible trail for 15 seconds. With clean beaters, beat the egg whites until they are foamy and white. Gradually beat in the remaining sugar until the whites are glossy and stiff.

Fold one third of the whites into the egg yolks, then fold in the flour, next the cornstarch, baking powder, salt, and lemon zest and juice. Fold in the remaining egg whites, one third at a time.

Pour the batter into the prepared pan and distribute it evenly. Bake in the center of the oven about 15 minutes, or until the cake begins to pull away from the sides and a wooden toothpick inserted into the center comes out clean. Cool in the pan 5 minutes. Run a thin spatula around the cake edge and under the bottom of the cake. Invert onto a rack to cool.

Wrap the cake in plastic wrap and refrigerate it, or wrap it in plastic wrap and foil and freeze until ready to use.

Meringue Ice Cream Towering Torte

In this most delectable torte, three delicate crunchy layers support an ice cream filling. And for chocolate addicts, a chocolate version with a brownie base follows. Try this strawberry version or your own combination of flavors.

3 cups strawberry sorbet
3 Nut-Meringue Layers
 (recipe below)
½ cup seedless strawberry
 preserves
1 quart strawberry or vanilla ice
 cream
1 cup vanilla ice cream

1 cup heavy cream
2 tablespoons Cointreau or kirsch
 liqueur
⅔ cup almond praline (page 26)
 or finely chopped almonds
Fresh fruit, chocolate-dipped
 almond slices, or candies for
 decoration

Soften the sorbet slightly. Place one of the meringue layers in a 9-inch springform pan and spread one third of the preserves to within ½ inch of the edge. Dot the sorbet over the preserves, then smooth it to an even layer with a knife or your fingertips. Place another meringue layer over the sorbet and press it down gently. Spread with one third of the preserves. Freeze until the sorbet is firm. Soften the 1 quart ice cream. Spread it over the meringue and sorbet layers. Top with the remaining preserves and the final meringue layer, pressing down gently to secure the layer. Freeze until firm, about 3 hours.

To soften the cup of vanilla ice cream. In a chilled bowl, whip the cream until firm peaks will hold their shape. Fold in the liqueur. Fold in the ice cream in thirds. Frost the cake with the cream mixture and freeze until firm.

To decorate the cake, press the praline over the sides of the torte. Decorate the top with the fresh fruit and brush it lightly with preserves.

MAKES 12 SERVINGS.

Nut-Meringue Layers

5 large egg whites, at room temperature
⅔ cup sugar
½ cup sifted powdered sugar
1 tablespoon cornstarch
½ cup very finely chopped toasted almonds (optional)

Preheat the oven to 200° F. Cut parchment paper to fit 3 cookie sheets or 2 cookie sheets and the bottom of 1 (9-inch) springform pan. Affix the paper with light dabs of vegetable shortening. Trace 3 (9-inch) round circles on the parchment.

In a large bowl, beat the egg whites until soft peaks will hold their shape. Very gradually beat in the sugar until the egg whites are very stiff and glossy. Thoroughly blend the powdered sugar and cornstarch together. Beat the mixture into the meringue, a tablespoon at a time, beating just until blended. Fold in the almonds.

Spread the meringue evenly over the circles on the baking pans. Bake about 1½ hours, until the meringues are barely golden and almost dry. Turn off the oven and allow the meringue disks to cool in the oven. Peel away the paper.

The disks may be stored in an airtight container for several days.

Variation

CHOCOLATE MERINGUES

Increase the powdered sugar to ¾ cup. Blend 5 tablespoons sifted, unsweetened cocoa into the powdered sugar mixture. The meringue may be made with or without nuts.

Frozen Quadruple Chocolate Suicide Cake

Four layers of different-textured chocolate combine in this chocoholic's dream come true: a brownie layer and two chocolate meringue layers topped with chocolate custard ice cream and frosted with chocolate whipped cream.

*1 recipe Chocolate Meringues
(recipe above)
1¼ cups heavy cream
3 ounces semisweet chocolate,
chopped up
⅓ cup powdered sugar*

*2 quarts Smooth Chocolate Custard Ice Cream (page 41) or
purchased ice cream
1 recipe brownie layer (see recipe
for Brownie Ice Cream Cake,
page 103)*

Make the meringue batter as directed. Using three quarters of the batter, make only 2 (9-inch) layers as directed. Using 2 teaspoons or a pastry bag fitted with a medium star tip, pipe or drop ½-inch meringue "kisses" on the empty portions of the parchment. Make 20 kisses. Bake the kisses 1 hour, or until crumbly and dry when broken. Remove the kisses from the oven and continue to bake the meringue layers.

In a heavy pan, combine the cream and chocolate together and cook over low heat, stirring occasionally, until the chocolate melts and the mixture is completely smooth. Stir in the powdered sugar. Cool, then float a film of plastic wrap over the surface of the cream. Chill at least 4 hours.

When the chocolate cream has chilled and the meringues are cool, slightly soften half of the ice cream. Place the brownie layer in the bottom of a 9-inch springform pan. Spread half of the ice cream over the brownie layer. Freeze until firm. Top with a meringue layer, the remaining ice cream, and the remaining meringue layer. Freeze again.

When the torte is frozen, whip the chocolate cream mixture until medium-soft peaks will hold their shape. Remove the torte from the freezer and wipe the pan with a sponge dipped in hot water. Remove the side of the pan from the torte. Frost the torte with the whipped cream mixture and decorate the top with the meringue kisses. Freeze the torte until ready to serve.

MAKES 12 TO 14 SERVINGS.

Apricot Ice Cream Cobbler

⅔ cup sugar
1¼ cups dried apricots, snipped
   into small pieces
⅛ teaspoon salt
1¼ cups all-purpose flour
1¼ cups quick-cooking oats

¾ teaspoon baking powder
⅔ cup unsalted butter
¼ cup light brown sugar, packed
3 pints vanilla or Fresh Apricot
   (page 56) or Quick Apricot Ice
   Cream (page 56)

Preheat the oven to 375° F. Butter a 9-inch-square baking pan. In a saucepan, combine ¾ cup water, the sugar, and the apricots. Simmer about 15 minutes, until thickened. Combine the salt, flour, oats, and baking powder and blend well. With an electric mixer, beat the butter until it is fluffy. Beat in the sugar until creamy. Mix in the flour mixture. Reserve 1½ cups of the mixture and pat the remaining mixture over the bottom of the buttered pan. Spread on the apricot mixture and crumble the reserved oat mixture evenly over the filling. Bake about 25 minutes, until browned lightly. Cool.

To serve, cut the cobbler into 9 pieces and top with a scoop of ice cream.

MAKES 9 SERVINGS.

Frozen Macadamia Nut Roll with Chocolate Whipped Cream Filling

filling
3 cups heavy cream
1 teaspoon instant coffee powder
4 ounces semisweet chocolate, chopped
2 tablespoons dark rum
¾ cup and 2 tablespoons powdered sugar

cake

3 large eggs, separated and at room temperature
1¼ teaspoons vanilla extract
¼ teaspoon salt
½ cup sugar

3 tablespoons all-purpose flour
6 tablespoons lightly toasted, finely chopped unsalted macadamia nuts
Sifted powdered sugar

assembly

3½ tablespoons light corn syrup
2½ tablespoons dark rum
⅓ cup chocolate syrup

About ½ cup lightly toasted, finely chopped macadamia nuts
12 macadamia nut halves for garnish

filling

In a heavy medium pan, scald the cream, sprinkle on the coffee, and mix it in. Add the chocolate and rum. Cook over low heat, stirring, until the chocolate is completely melted. Stir in the sugar until it dissolves. Press a piece of plastic wrap directly onto the surface of the cream. Chill 4 hours or longer.

cake

Preheat the oven to 375° F. Line a 15½ × 10½-inch rimmed baking sheet with wax paper or parchment. Affix the paper to the pan with vegetable shortening. Grease and lightly flour the paper.

Beat the egg yolks, vanilla, and salt together until thick and light in color. Very gradually add 2 tablespoons of the sugar and beat until the yolks have the texture of whipped cream. Clean the beaters thoroughly. Beat the whites until very soft peaks form. Gradually add the remaining sugar, beating until stiff peaks form. Fold the egg yolks into the whites. Sprinkle the flour over the eggs and fold it in. Gently fold in the 6 tablespoons nuts.

Spread the batter in the prepared pan and bake about 14 minutes, or until the cake begins to shrink away from the sides of the pan and the center springs back when lightly touched.

Immediately loosen the cake sides and turn it out onto a towel sprinkled with the sifted powdered sugar. Peel away the wax paper. Starting at the narrow end, roll up the cake and towel together; chill.

Beat the chocolate cream until soft peaks will hold their shape. Freeze until half-frozen, about 1 hour.

assembly

Combine ⅔ cup water, the corn syrup and the rum. Unroll the cake and evenly sprinkle the syrup mixture over the cake, then spread with the chocolate syrup. Spread half of the chocolate cream to within ¼ inch of the cake edges. Sprinkle on 3 tablespoons of the ½ cup chopped nuts. Roll up the cake and place it on a platter, seam side down. Frost the cake with the remaining chocolate cream and sprinkle with a spray of finely chopped nuts. Place a single row of macadamia nut halves in a row along the center of the roll. Freeze at least 6 hours.

MAKES 10 SERVINGS.

VARIATION: CHOCOLATE-ALMOND NUT ROLL

Replace the macadamia nuts with unroasted unsalted almonds. Increase the chocolate to 5 ounces.

Fabulous Strawberry Pavé

This cake can be made entirely from purchased cake and ice cream or created from scratch.

1 (10¾-ounce) loaf-shape sponge cake or angel food cake
⅓ cup kirsch or Cointreau liqueur
2 teaspoons light corn syrup
About 1 pint strawberry sorbet (page 67) slightly softened
⅓ cup strawberry preserves

About 1 quart (3⅓ cups) straw-berry ice cream (page 51)
5 tablespoons coarse almond pra-line (page 26) or chopped roasted unsalted almonds
Fresh strawberries for garnish

Slice the cake lengthwise into 6 even slices. Blend ½ cup water, the Cointreau, and the corn syrup together. Lay the cake slices out on a baking sheet and sprinkle evenly with the Cointreau mixture. Spread 4 of the slices evenly with 4 tablespoons of the preserves (1 tablespoon for each layer). Set the remaining preserves aside. Using a pancake turner to lift the cake slices, place a jam-covered cake slice on a plate; repeat with another slice. Top each slice with ¾ cup sorbet, smoothing it out with your fingertips. Top each of the sorbet-covered cake slices with another cake slice, jam side up. Freeze the 2 sorbet and cake "sandwiches."

When the sorbet has hardened (at least 3 hours later), place a 2½-foot piece of foil on a work surface. Soften 1¼ cups of the ice cream very slightly. Working very quickly, spread half the ice cream over the jam

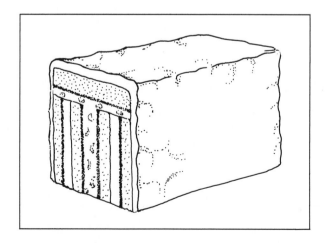

on 1 sorbet "sandwich." (I slice the ice cream, then position it on the layers and spread it with my fingertips.) Repeat with the other sandwich. Sandwich the layers together with the 2 portions of ice cream facing each other in the center of the arrangement. There will be 1 thick ribbon of ice cream in the center of the layers. Center the cake, with the layers running vertically, over the foil. Trim the final 2 cake layers to fit the top of the cake. Set aside. Bring the foil up around the cake to form a nice compact rectangle. Freeze the cake about 1 hour or more.

Top the final cake layers with the remaining preserves. Remove the cake from the freezer and spread ¾ cup ice cream smoothly over the top. Top the cake with the remaining cake layers, jam side down. Wrap the cake again and freeze until firm. When the cake is firm, place it on a platter and frost with about 1½ cups ice cream. Pat the praline onto the sides of the cake. Just before serving the cake, decorate with the fresh berries.

MAKES 12 SERVINGS.

Flavor Variations

CHOCOLATE-COFFEE PAVÉ

Follow the recipe above for Fabulous Strawberry Pavé. Try coffee ice cream in place of the sorbet, chocolate ripple ice cream in place of the strawberry ice cream, and chocolate sauce in place of the preserves. Substitute crème de cacao or coffee liqueur for the kirsch or Cointreau.

TROPICAL PAVÉ

Follow the recipe above for Fabulous Strawberry Pavé. Substitute orange sherbet or sorbet for the strawberry sorbet and pineapple or coconut ice cream for the strawberry ice cream. Use Cointreau or Triple Sec for the liqueur. Decorate the cake with fresh orange slices or pineapple wedges.

BLACK WALNUT PAVÉ

Follow the recipe above for Fabulous Strawberry Pavé. Substitute 3 tablespoons brandy or Cognac and 1 tablespoon water for the kirsch. Substitute chocolate syrup or apple butter for the preserves. Use chocolate or vanilla ice cream instead of the sorbet. Replace the strawberry ice cream with black walnut ice cream. Replace the praline or almonds with chopped black walnuts.

Easy Elegant Ice-Cream-Filled Angel Food Cake

Cut down into the center of this cake and find it filled with ice cream, sherbet, or sorbet. The cake may be frosted with whipped cream—plain or flavored with a liqueur—and decorated with toasted coconut, a spray of finely chopped nuts, or shards of chocolate (below). Create your own specialty.

1 cup flaked coconut (about 3½ ounces)
5½ tablespoons Grand Marnier or other liqueur compatible with the ice cream you have selected
1½ tablespoons light corn syrup

1 (13-ounce) prebaked tube angel food cake
2 pints orange sorbet or sherbet, slightly softened
1¼ cups heavy cream

Toast the coconut in a preheated 350° F. oven about 15 minutes, stirring occasionally, until it is pale golden. Cool on a plate. Combine 3 table-spoons water, 3 tablespoons of the liqueur, and the corn syrup; blend well. With a long serrated knife cut a 1-inch-thick layer from the top of the cake. Then remove a center ring of cake with a small sharp knife, by cutting around the inside of the cake ½ inch from the outer edge, then ½ inch from the inner edge, and hollow out the cake. It is easiest to do this by gently pulling out the inside of the cake in half circles. Leave a ½-inch-thick cake layer at the tunnel bottom. Save the cake inside for another use. Evenly sprinkle the liqueur-syrup mixture over the top and inside of the cake.

Fill the cake cavity with the sorbet and replace the top of the cake. Freeze the cake while you prepare the frosting. The cake may be frosted a day before serving if you can position it so it remains undisturbed, or it may be frosted shortly before serving.

To frost the cake, beat the cream in a chilled bowl until stiff peaks will hold their shape when the beaters are lifted. Fold in the remaining 2½ tablespoons liqueur. Remove the cake from the freezer and, with a small spatula, frost the top and sides of the cake. Gently press the toasted coconut onto the top and sides of the cake.

MAKES 10 SERVINGS.

Variations

MINT CHIP OR MOCHA ALMOND FUDGE–FILLED CAKE

Follow the recipe for Easy Elegant Ice-Cream-Filled Angel Food Cake. Replace the mixture of water, liqueur, and corn syrup with ½ cup chocolate syrup (not fudge sauce). Fill the cake cavity with mint chocolate chip or mocha almond ripple or similar ice cream. Frost the cake as directed with the 1¼ cups heavy cream, whipped with 2 tablespoons either white or green crème de menthe or crème de cacao folded into it. Decorate with grated semisweet chocolate, swirls of chocolate sauce, or the following Chocolate Shards.

Chocolate Shards

Line a 15½ × 10½-inch unrimmed baking sheet with plastic wrap. In the top of a double boiler, over barely simmering water, melt 5 ounces semisweet or bittersweet chocolate; stir until smooth. Remove the double boiler top and allow the chocolate to cool until it begins to thicken again and is cool. Quickly pour the chocolate over the plastic wrap. Cover with another layer of plastic wrap and roll out the chocolate to a 1¹⁄₁₆-inch-thick slab. Cool until hard at room temperature or in the refrigerator. Peel away the plastic wrap and break the chocolate into large pieces. Insert the pieces into the top of the cake randomly.

THE MOUSSE CAKE SERIES

Here are four elegant cakes that combine light liqueur-drenched sponge layers with a soufflé-like filling and frosting. The texture is angelically light but the cakes are devilishly rich.

The cakes may be made in stages. The layers can be baked and frozen and the mousses made and frozen ahead if you like. Be sure, if you do freeze the mousses, to soften them slightly in the refrigerator about 30 minutes before assembling the cake so they are spreadable. Do not thaw them completely. Then cut them into pieces and distribute them over the cake, working them into a smooth layer with a fork.

Since the mousses are still-frozen desserts, read the introduction to that chapter for useful tips on making these desserts a success.

Luxury Lemon Mousse Cake

cake

*3 large egg yolks, at room temper-
ature*

*4 large egg whites, at room tem-
perature*

7 tablespoons sugar

⅓ cup sifted all-purpose flour

3 tablespoons cornstarch

½ teaspoon baking powder

⅛ teaspoon salt

1 teaspoon grated lemon zest

2 teaspoons fresh lemon juice

Preheat the oven to 350° F. Butter a 9-inch round cake pan and line it with a circle of wax paper or parchment. Butter the paper.

Beat the egg yolks with an electric mixer until thick and lemon-colored. Gradually add 4 tablespoons of the sugar, beating until ribbons falling on the surface from the raised beaters leave a visible trail for 15 seconds. With clean beaters, beat the egg whites until they are foamy and white. Gradually beat in the remaining 3 tablespoons sugar until the whites are glossy and stiff.

Fold one half of the whites into the egg yolks, then fold in the flour, next the cornstarch, baking powder, salt, and lemon zest and juice. Fold in the remaining egg whites, one third at a time.

Pour the batter into the prepared pan and distribute it evenly. Bake in the center of the oven about 15 minutes, or until the cake begins to pull away from the sides and a wooden toothpick inserted into the center comes out clean. Cool in the pan 5 minutes. Run a thin spatula around the cake edge and under the bottom of the cake. Invert onto a rack to cool.

Wrap the cake in plastic wrap and refrigerate it, or wrap in plastic wrap and foil and freeze until ready to use.

mousse

5 large egg yolks, at room temperature
1¼ cups sugar
⅔ cup fresh lemon juice

2 teaspoons grated lemon zest
4 large egg whites, at room
  temperature
2 cups heavy cream

Chill beaters and a bowl large enough (6-cup volume) to whip the cream.
Beat the egg yolks until thick and light in color. Gradually add ¾ cup of
the sugar and beat until the yolks are ivory-colored and very thick. Fold
in the lemon juice and zest.

With clean beaters, beat the egg whites until they are white and foamy.
Gradually add the remaining ½ cup sugar and beat until the whites are
glossy and curved peaks will hold their shape. Be sure all the sugar has
dissolved in the egg white. Beat the cream in the chilled bowl with the
chilled beaters just until curved peaks hold their shape.

Fold half of the egg white into the lemon mixture. Fold in half of the
cream, the remaining whites and the remaining cream. Freeze the mousse
in a covered container at least 1 hour or until you are ready to assemble
the cake.

syrup

¼ teaspoon unflavored gelatin
2 tablespoons sugar
2 tablespoons light corn syrup
¼ cup fresh lemon juice
2 tablespoons whiskey

In a small saucepan, sprinkle the gelatin over 6 tablespoons water and
allow it to stand until it softens, about 3 minutes. Cook over very low
heat, stirring occasionally, until the gelatin granules disappear. Stir in the
sugar, corn syrup, lemon juice, and whiskey.

assembly

If the mousse has been frozen, remove the mousse from the freezer and
refrigerate until it is pliable but not thawed, about 20 minutes.

Cut the cake into 2 thin layers with a long, thin serrated knife. Place
1 cake layer, cut side up, in an 8-inch springform pan and sprinkle it with
half of the syrup. Place the other cake layer on a plate, cut side up, and
sprinkle with the remaining syrup.

Evenly distribute two thirds of the mousse over the cake layer in the
pan, reserving the remaining mousse for frosting the cake. Place the re-

served mousse in the freezer. Invert the second cake layer over the mousse and gently press it into the mousse. Freeze the cake until firm.

Soften the remaining mousse in the refrigerator about 20 minutes. Wipe the edges of the springform pan with a sponge dipped in hot water to loosen the side of the cake from the pan. Remove the pan's side. Frost the top and sides of the cake with the remaining mousse. Freeze the cake until the frosting is firm. Cover with plastic wrap until ready to serve.
MAKES 12 SERVINGS.

Grand Marnier Mousse Cake

I have used this combination of flavors—Grand Marnier, Cointreau, and apricot—over and over again, and it is always extraordinary.

cake
Follow the cake recipe for Luxury Lemon Mousse Cake (page 122), substituting 2 teaspoons frozen orange juice concentrate, thawed, for the lemon juice and 2 teaspoons grated orange zest for the lemon zest.

mousse

5 large eggs, separated and at room temperature	2½ tablespoons Grand Marnier
	1 tablespoon grated orange zest
¾ cup sugar	A pinch of salt
4 teaspoons frozen orange juice concentrate, thawed	2 cups heavy cream

Chill beaters and a bowl large enough (6-cup volume) to whip the cream. Beat the egg yolks until thick and light in color. Gradually add ½ cup of the sugar and beat until the yolks are very thick and ivory-colored. Fold in the orange juice, Grand Marnier, orange zest and salt.

With clean beaters, beat the egg whites until they are white and foamy. Gradually add the remaining ¼ cup sugar and beat until the whites are glossy and curved peaks will hold their shape. Beat the cream in the chilled bowl with the chilled beaters until curved peaks hold their shape.

Fold half of the egg whites into the orange mixture. Fold in half of the cream, the remaining whites, and the remaining cream. Freeze the mousse in a covered container at least 1 hour or until you are ready to assemble the cake.

syrup and glaze

4 tablespoons Cointreau liqueur

2 tablespoons light corn syrup

⅓ cup apricot jam, sieved to a
puree

4 tablespoons coarse almond praline (page 26) or almonds
chopped medium-fine

Combine ⅓ cup water, 2 tablespoons of the Cointreau, and the corn syrup and set aside. Mix the jam and the remaining 2 tablespoons Cointreau together until well blended.

assembly

If the mousse has been frozen, remove the mousse from the freezer and refrigerate until it is pliable but not thawed, about 20 minutes.

Cut the cake into 2 thin layers with a long, thin serrated knife. Place 1 cake layer in an 8-inch springform pan, cut side up, and sprinkle it with half of the syrup. Place the other cake layer on a plate, cut side up, and sprinkle with the remaining syrup. With a small spatula, spread one third of the jam–Cointreau mixture over the cut surface of each cake layer.

Evenly distribute three fourths of the mousse over the cake layer in the pan, reserving the remaining mousse for frosting the cake. Place the reserved mousse in the freezer. Invert the second cake layer over the mousse and gently press it into place. Freeze the cake until it is firm.

Soften the remaining mousse in the refrigerator about 20 minutes. Wipe the edges of the springform pan with a sponge dipped in hot water to loosen the sides of the cake from the pan. Remove the pan's side. Spread the remaining jam–Cointreau mixture over the top of the cake (I use my index finger to spread it thinly). Frost the sides of the cake with the remaining mousse. Pat the praline or almonds around the sides of the cake. Freeze the cake until the frosting is firm. Cover with plastic wrap until ready to serve.

MAKES 12 SERVINGS.

Raspberry Mousse Cake

A cloudlike mousse between raspberry-jam-and-kirsch-laced cake layers.

cake
Follow the cake recipe for Luxury Lemon Mousse Cake (page 122).

mousse
¼ cup seedless raspberry jam

1 (12-ounce) bag lightly sweetened, individually frozen raspberries, thawed, or 3 cups fresh
raspberries

8 large egg yolks, at room temperature

3 egg whites, at room temperature

¾ cup sugar★

3 tablespoons raspberry eau de vie
liqueur or kirsch

2 cups heavy cream

Chill beaters and a bowl large enough (6-cup volume) to whip the cream. In a very small pan over hot water, heat the jam, stirring occasionally, until it melts; cool slightly. Puree the berries in a blender or food processor and strain to remove the seeds.

In the top of a double boiler, beat the egg yolks until thick and light in color. Place over very hot but not quite simmering water and gradually add ½ cup of the sugar★ and beat until the yolks are very thick. Fold in the berry puree, liqueur, and cooled jam. With clean beaters beat the egg whites until they are white and foamy. Gradually add the remaining ¼ cup sugar and beat until the whites are glossy and curved peaks will hold their shape. Beat the cream in the chilled bowl with the chilled beaters until curved peaks hold their shape.

Fold half of the egg whites into the berry mixture. Fold in half of the cream, the remaining whites, and the remaining cream. Freeze the mousse in a covered container at least 1 hour or until you are ready to assemble the cake.

syrup and glaze
4 tablespoons raspberry eau de vie
or kirsch

3 tablespoons light corn syrup

7 tablespoons seedless raspberry
jam

4 tablespoons coarse almond praline (page 26) or almonds
chopped medium-fine (optional)

★Increase the sugar by 2 teaspoons if using fresh berries.

Blend 6 tablespoons water, 2 tablespoons of the liqueur, and the corn syrup and set aside. In a small saucepan over hot water or very low heat, melt the jam to a syrup, stirring occasionally. Mix the jam and the remaining 2 tablespoons liqueur together until well blended. Strain to remove any lumps.

assembly

If the mousse has been frozen, remove the mousse from the freezer and refrigerate until it is pliable but not thawed, about 20 minutes.

Cut the cake into 2 thin layers with a long, thin serrated knife. Place 1 cake layer, cut side up, in an 8-inch springform pan and sprinkle it with half of the liqueur syrup. Place the other cake layer on a plate, cut side up, and sprinkle with the remaining syrup. With a small spatula, spread one third of the jam-liqueur mixture over the cut surface of each cake layer.

Evenly distribute two thirds of the mousse over the cake layer in the pan, reserving the remaining mousse for frosting the cake. Place the reserved mousse in the freezer. Invert the second cake layer over the mousse and gently press it into place. Freeze the cake until it is firm.

Soften the remaining mousse in the refrigerator about 20 minutes. Wipe the edges of the springform pan with a sponge dipped in hot water to loosen the sides of the cake from the pan. Remove the pan's side. Frost the top and sides of the cake with the remaining mousse. Swirl the remaining jam mixture over the top of the cake. Pat the praline or almonds onto the sides of the cake. Freeze the cake until the frosting is firm. Cover with plastic wrap until ready to serve.

MAKES 12 SERVINGS.

Chocolate-Almond Mocha Mousse Cake

cake

½ cup roasted unsalted almonds
½ cup sugar
¼ cup sifted all-purpose flour
2 tablespoons unsweetened cocoa
½ teaspoon baking powder
⅛ teaspoon salt
3 large eggs, separated at room temperature
4 tablespoons unsalted butter, melted

Preheat the oven to 350° F. Butter a 9-inch round cake pan and line it with a circle of wax paper or parchment. Butter the paper.

Chop the almonds coarsely, add 2 tablespoons sugar, and chop almost to a powder. Combine the flour, cocoa, baking powder, salt, and almond mixture, blending them together well.

Beat the egg yolks with an electric mixer until thick and lemon-colored. Gradually add 4 tablespoons of the sugar, beating until ribbons falling on the surface from the raised beaters leave a visible trail for 15 seconds. With clean beaters, beat the egg whites until they are foamy and white. Gradually beat in the remaining 2 tablespoons sugar until the whites are glossy and stiff.

Fold one fourth of the whites into the egg yolks, then fold in one third of the flour-nut mixture, one fourth of the whites, one third of the nut mixture, one fourth of the whites, the remaining nut mixture, the butter, and the remaining whites.

Pour the batter into the prepared pan and distribute it evenly. Bake in the center of the oven about 20 minutes, or until the cake begins to pull away from the sides and a wooden toothpick inserted into the center comes out clean. Cool in the pan 5 minutes. Run a thin spatula around the cake edge and under the bottom of the cake. Invert onto a rack to cool.

Wrap the cake in plastic wrap and refrigerate it, or wrap in plastic wrap and foil and freeze until ready to use.

mocha mousse

4 ounces semisweet chocolate
2/3 cup milk
3/4 teaspoon instant coffee granules
5 egg yolks, at room temperature
3/4 cup sugar
1/2 cup coffee-flavored liqueur

3/4 teaspoon vanilla extract
2 egg whites, at room temperature
1 1/3 cups heavy cream
1 tablespoon light or dark corn
   syrup
15 candy coffee beans

Chill beaters and a bowl large enough to whip the cream (4-cup volume). In a double boiler or in a small pan within another pan partially filled with barely simmering water, melt the chocolate. In a heavy saucepan, heat the milk to simmering. Add the coffee and stir to dissolve. With a fork, beat the egg yolks and 1/2 cup of the sugar together until well mixed but not foamy. Add the milk, stirring all the while. Return the egg-milk mixture to the saucepan and cook over low heat, stirring, until the mixture thickens slightly and clings to the back of a spoon, about 5 minutes.

Combine the custard and the melted chocolate, blending them together smoothly. Cool completely. Stir in ¼ cup of the coffee liqueur and the vanilla.

Beat the egg whites until white and foamy. Gradually add the remaining ¼ cup sugar and beat until stiff and glossy. In the chilled bowl with chilled beaters, beat the cream only until curved peaks hold their shape. Fold half the cream into the chocolate mixture, fold in the egg whites, then the remaining cream. Chill the mousse in the freezer until it will hold its shape in a mound on a spoon, about 1½–2 hours.

assembly

Blend together the remaining ¼ cup coffee liqueur, 4 tablespoons water, and the corn syrup.

Cut the cake into 2 thin layers with a long, thin serrated knife. Place 1 cake layer, cut side up, in a 9-inch springform pan and sprinkle it with half of the liqueur mixture. Place the other cake layer on a plate, cut side up, and sprinkle with the remaining mixture.

Evenly distribute half of the mousse over the cake layer in the pan. Invert the second cake layer over the mousse. Cover with the remaining mousse, smoothing the top. Freeze until firm.

To remove the cake from the pan, wipe the bottom of the pan with a sponge dipped in hot water. Repeat with the pan's side. Remove the pan's side and smooth the cake sides with a spatula. Decorate the cake edges with 12 of the candy coffee beans and arrange the remaining 3 beans in the center of the cake. Freeze until ready to serve.

MAKES 12 SERVINGS.

FANCIFUL ICE CREAM CAKE SHAPES

Without fancy-shaped pans or other exotic equipment, festive ice cream cakes can be made for any holiday. A 9-inch round cake turns into a bunny or heart shape, and a standard 9×13 pan metamorphoses into Santa, a snowman, or a butterfly. If you simply want a large sheet ice cream cake, I've provided instructions for that, too. These are not so much recipes as suggestions to turn simple shapes into wondrous holiday creations.

Ice Cream Bunny Cake

2 (9-inch) Round Sponge Cake
  layers (page 136)
6 cups (3 pints), ice cream
  slightly softened
6 additional cups ice cream of a
  compatible flavor
1¾ cups heavy cream

1 teaspoon vanilla extract
⅓ cup sifted powdered sugar
About 1 cup flaked coconut
Red food coloring, or any berry
  juice
Multicolored gumdrops
Thin licorice strips

Bake and cool the sponge cake layers. Remove the cakes from the pans.
Clean the pans. Pack half of the first flavor of ice cream into each pan,
smoothing the layers evenly with your fingertips; freeze until firm. Soften
the second ice cream flavor slightly and layer it evenly over the first.
Freeze until firm.

Remove the cake pans from the freezer. Wipe each pan a few seconds
with a sponge dipped in hot water. Center cake over the ice cream and
press layers onto the ice cream in the pan. Invert the ice cream and cake
onto a plate. Trim ice cream layer to fit the cake evenly. Freeze at least
½ hour to firm up ice cream.

Cut the ears and bow tie from 1 layer, as illustrated. Assemble the
bunny. Whip the cream with the vanilla until curved peaks will hold their
shape, beating in the powdered sugar toward the end of the beating time.
Frost the cake with the whipped cream and freeze it while you prepare
the decoration.

Tint ¼ cup of the coconut pink with red coloring or juice. Remove the
cake from the freezer. Arrange on the ears as illustrated. Create the eyes,

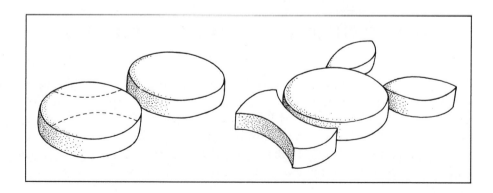

nose, and polka dots on the tie with the gum drops. Create the whiskers and mouth with the licorice. Freeze until ready to serve.

MAKES 16 SERVINGS.

Brownie Ice Cream Sweetheart Cake

2 recipes of the brownie layer (page 103), one baked in a 9-inch round pan, the other in an 8-inch-square pan
2 pints raspberry sorbet
About ½ cup chocolate syrup
3½ pints chocolate or vanilla ice cream

1½ cups flaked coconut (optional)
Red food coloring or berry juice (optional)
1½ cups heavy cream
4 tablespoons Chambord or Cassis liqueur
Tiny candy hearts or dots or chocolate hearts

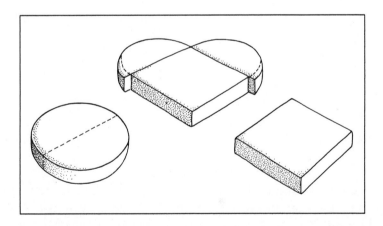

Bake and cool the brownie layers and remove them from the pans. Peel away the paper. Clean the pans. Spread the sorbet in the pans and top evenly with the chocolate syrup. Freeze until firm. Top the sorbet evenly with the ice cream and freeze until firm. If you are using the coconut for decoration, tint it pink with the red coloring. Whip the cream until soft peaks hold their shape. Fold in the liqueur.

Remove the cake pans from the freezer and wipe each pan a few seconds with a sponge dipped in hot water. Center the brownie layers over the ice cream and press layers onto the ice cream in the pan; invert the ice cream and cake onto a plate. Trim ice cream to fit the brownie layers evenly. Freeze at least ½ hour to firm up the ice cream. Arrange the shapes to form a heart and trim the edges to perfect the heart shape. Frost the cake with the whipped cream and decorate with the coconut and candy; freeze again.

MAKES 16 SERVINGS.

Spring Butterfly Ice Cream Cake

1 recipe Sponge Sheet Cake (page 135)
7½ tablespoons Cointreau or Triple Sec liqueur
1½ tablespoons light corn syrup
2 quarts plus 1 cup Old-fashioned Vanilla Custard Ice Cream (page 17)
½ cup apricot preserves

3 cups lemon or orange sorbet or sherbet
⅔ cup marshmallow cream
1¼ cups heavy cream
Yellow food coloring or carrot juice (optional)
Shoestring licorice, gumdrops, and slivered almonds for decoration

Bake and cool the cake. Remove it from the pan and peel away the paper. Clean the pan. Combine 3½ tablespoons of the liqueur, the corn syrup, and 3 tablespoons water. Sprinkle evenly over the cake. Soften the ice cream slightly and spread it evenly in the cake pan, smoothing it with your fingertips. Combine 1 tablespoon of the liqueur with the preserves and spread it over the ice cream. Freeze until the ice cream is firm. Soften the sorbet slightly and spread it evenly over the ice cream layer. Freeze again. Wipe the bottom of the ice cream pan with a sponge dipped in hot water. Invert the sorbet and ice cream layers onto the cake. Trim the ice cream layers to fit evenly on the cake. Freeze about ½ hour while you prepare the frosting. In a large bowl with a wire whisk, whisk the remaining 3 tablespoons liqueur and 2 tablespoons of the cream into the marshmallow cream until smooth. Whip the remaining cream until stiff peaks hold their shape. Fold the cream into the marshmallow mixture. Tint the frosting light yellow if you wish. Chill until ready to assemble cake.

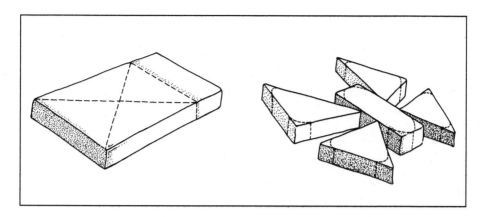

Using a long knife, cut a 3-inch wide rectangle along the width of the slightly frozen cake. Cut diagonals across the larger remaining rectangle. Assemble butterfly as shown, trimming butterfly wings to fit body.

Frost the cake and create a butterfly design using the nuts and candies. Freeze until ready to serve.

MAKES 14 TO 16 SERVINGS.

Snowman Ice Cream Cake

1 plain or chocolate Sponge Sheet
    Cake (page 135)
3 pints Pecan Praline Ice Cream
    (page 27) or another flavor of
    your choice
About 1 cup chocolate sauce
1 cup Meringue Nut Crunch
    (page 32) (optional)
3 pints dark chocolate ice cream or
    another flavor of your choice

2 cups heavy cream, well chilled
4 tablespoons light corn syrup
1¾ teaspoons vanilla extract
1 cup flaked, sweetened coconut
    (optional)
Black and red gumdrops, candy
    cane, and a toy paper hat, if
    desired

Bake and cool the cake. Remove the cake from the pan and peel away the paper. Clean the pan. Soften the praline ice cream slightly. Spread the ice cream evenly in the bottom of the cake pan. Evenly drizzle on ½ cup of the sauce. Sprinkle on the meringue nut crunch if you are using it. Freeze until the ice cream is firm. Slightly soften the chocolate ice cream.

Dot it over the praline ice cream and spread it evenly with your fingertips. Spread the remaining sauce over the cake. Freeze until firm. Wipe the ice cream pan with a wet sponge dipped in hot water. Invert the ice cream onto the cake. Trim away any excess ice cream. Freeze again. Cut the cake into the snowman shape and assemble as illustrated. Trim the arms about ¾ inch. Round off the square edges.

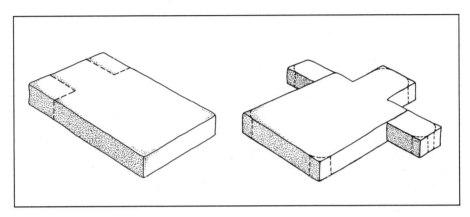

In a chilled bowl, beat the cream until soft peaks hold their shape. Beat in the corn syrup and vanilla. Frost the cake with the whipped cream, and sprinkle with the coconut if you wish. Decorate, using black gumdrops for the eyes, nose, and coat buttons and a red gumdrop for the mouth. Add the cane and hat at jaunty angles. Freeze until ready to serve. MAKES 12 TO 16 SERVINGS.

Santa Cake

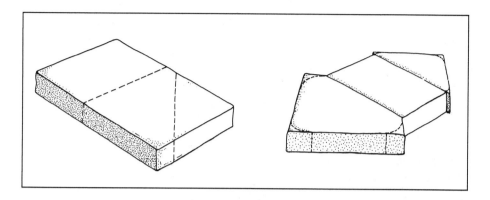

Follow the directions for the Snowman Ice Cream Cake (above), using your favorite ice cream flavor combination. Cut and assemble the Santa as illustrated. Round off the square edges. Tint one third of the whipped cream frosting with a mixture of red and yellow food coloring or berry and carrot juices. Use the colored frosting for the face. Sprinkle the beard, hat rim, and tassel with sweetened, flaked coconut. Use blue hard candy mints for the eyes and a gumdrop each for the nose and mouth. Sprinkle the hat with red cake decorating sprinkles.

Sponge Sheet Cake for Ice Cream Cakes

This thin layer cake, especially designed to accommodate an ice cream topping, tastes uncommonly good frozen.

½ cup sifted all-purpose flour
1 teaspoon baking powder
¼ teaspoon salt
3 large eggs, at room temperature

½ cup sugar
1 teaspoon vanilla extract
2½ tablespoons unsalted butter, melted

Preheat the oven to 400 ° F. Grease a 13 × 9-inch cake pan and line it with wax paper, parchment, or foil. Combine the flour, baking powder, and salt; blend well. With an electric mixer, beat the eggs until they are light and lemon-colored. Very gradually add the sugar, beating until the eggs are light and thick and a trail of egg dropped from the raised beaters leaves a ribbon for 15 seconds. Beat in the vanilla. Gently fold in the flour mixture only until combined. Fold in the butter. Spread the batter in the prepared pan and bake until the top springs back when lightly touched, about 10 minutes. Cool the pan on a rack until you are able to peel off the paper. Remove the paper and cool completely on a rack.

Variation

CHOCOLATE SPONGE SHEET CAKE

Blend 3 tablespoons cocoa into the flour mixture. Increase the sugar to ⅔ cup. Decrease the flour to ⅓ cup.

Round Sponge Cake for Ice Cream Cakes

⅓ cup sifted all-purpose flour
½ teaspoon baking powder
¼ teaspoon salt
2 large eggs, at room temperature

⅓ cup sugar
1 teaspoon vanilla extract
2 tablespoons unsalted butter, melted

Preheat the oven to 375° F. Grease a 9-inch round cake pan and line it with wax paper, parchment, or foil. Combine the flour, baking powder, and salt; blend well. With an electric mixer, beat the eggs until they are light and lemon-colored. Very gradually add the sugar, beating until the eggs are light and thick and a trail of egg dropped from raised beaters leaves a ribbon for 15 seconds. Beat in the vanilla. Gently fold in the flour mixture only until combined. Fold in the butter. Spread the batter in the prepared pan and bake until the top springs back when lightly touched, about 12 minutes. Cool the pan on a rack until you are able to peel off the paper. Remove the paper and cool completely on a rack.

Variation

CHOCOLATE ROUND SPONGE CAKE

Blend 2 tablespoons unsweetened cocoa powder into the flour mixture. Increase the sugar by 1 tablespoon. Decrease the flour to ¼ cup.

Frozen Dessert Pies

It's not likely Grandma would have a recipe for anything resembling these pies. Though inspired by the original pie shape and contrast of flaky pastry to fruit chunks or smooth custard of traditional pies, these have taken off in new directions. A fruit-studded mousse livened with a dash of liqueur, or tiers of ice cream flavors spun throughout with a satiny glaze, sit neatly in their crunchy crusts. A pie base, fashioned from a crystalline layer of bright sorbet, may hold a smooth custard ice cream or gossamer parfait filling.

Because the pie's crust is its foundation, I departed from tried-and-true graham cracker or chocolate wafer crusts in search of combinations that might add a little more sparkle to layers of ice cream or a still-frozen mousse filling. A simple mixture of sugar, egg whites, and nuts blended to form a thin meringue-like shell for the basic ice cream pie is one of my favorites. I like the way it softens just slightly under ice cream or sorbet without losing its special crunch. Pecan praline spread over a graham cracker crust adds another delicious texture to the velvety Frozen Pumpkin Pie, while macaroon crumbs or amaretti biscuits remain magically crisp under their ice cream or mousse fillings. And a mixture of butter biscuits such as petit beurre with finely chopped nuts and a little unsalted butter is a good standby crust for almost any frozen filling.

Once you have successfully made a basic pie, such as the Double Blackberry or the White Russian Ice Cream Pie with Chocolate Sorbet Crust, let your imagination take flight. Try various combinations of ice creams or sorbets and ice cream that seem appealing.

Keep these suggestions in mind to ensure success:

• Freeze unbaked crumb crusts before layering them with ice cream or sorbet. They will firm up and the crumbs will not mix with the ice cream layer.
• To spread a thin layer of ice cream over a crust, soften it in the refrigerator just slightly. Slice or cut it up and distribute it in small portions over the crust. Smooth the layer using your fingers.
• Be careful not to oversoften the ice cream, and work quickly spreading it in the crust. If the ice cream melts, the pie will be icy.
• Always freeze an ice cream or sorbet layer until it is firm before adding another one.
• Sprinkle toppings that add textural interest over one of the layers. Try praline or English toffee or crushed meringue, macaroons, or good preserves.
• If you want to drizzle a little liqueur over one layer of ice cream, remember it will not freeze. Therefore, swirl it into the ice cream layer so it will not sit in a puddle on the surface.
• When the pie is frozen solid, cover it with plastic wrap, then foil. Foil alone tends to crunch up and dig into the pie.
• You'll find the pie easier to cut and serve if you wipe the bottom of the pie pan with a sponge dipped in hot water for a few seconds.
• Ice cream pies will cut more neatly if you dip your knife in a glass of hot water, then wipe it dry before each cut.

THE BASIC ICE CREAM PIE AND VARIATIONS

An example of what you can do with a nice crunchy meringue and some sorbet and ice cream. The sauce is optional.

Raspberry Chocolate Pie with Chocolate Chambord Sauce

1 egg white
⅛ teaspoon salt
¼ cup sugar
1½ cups chopped nuts
1½ cups Ultra Raspberry Sorbet (page 72) or other raspberry sorbet

3½ cups Smooth Chocolate Custard Ice Cream (page 41)
Chocolate Chambord Sauce (recipe below)

Preheat the oven to 400° F. Thoroughly grease a 9-inch pie pan.

Beat the egg white and salt until frothy and opaque. Gradually beat in the sugar until soft peaks will hold their shape. Fold in the nuts. Spread over the bottom and sides of the prepared pan but not up onto the rim. Wipe any meringue from the rim. Prick with a fork. Bake in the center of the oven 10 to 12 minutes until firm. Cool, then chill.

Soften the sorbet slightly. Dot the sorbet evenly over the surface of the pie crust and spread it evenly over the bottom and up the sides. Freeze until firm. Soften the chocolate ice cream slightly and spread it over the sorbet. Freeze until firm.

Serve the pie with Chocolate Chambord Sauce or your favorite chocolate sauce.

MAKES 8 SERVINGS.

Chocolate Chambord Sauce

2 ounces unsweetened chocolate, chopped
⅔ cup half-and-half
⅔ cup sugar

1 tablespoon unsalted butter
1½ tablespoons light corn syrup
1½ tablespoons Chambord liqueur

In a small heavy pan over low heat, combine the chocolate and half-and-half. Cook over low heat, stirring occasionally, until the chocolate is melted and the mixture is completely smooth. Stir in the sugar and cook until it dissolves. Stir in the butter. Remove from the heat and stir in the corn syrup and liqueur.

Grand Marnier Mousse Pie in a Chocolate-Almond Shell

A special dream for lovers of chocolate-with-orange.

1 cup unsalted almonds
6 ounces (1 cup) semisweet choco-
late chips
1 tablespoon vegetable shortening
1 tablespoon light corn syrup
¼ cup plus 1 tablespoon Grand
Marnier liqueur
1 large orange
⅔ cup sugar

5 large egg yolks, at room temper-
ature
2 teaspoons frozen orange juice
concentrate, thawed
1⅔ cups heavy cream, well
chilled
Chocolate Leaves (page 213) or
grated semisweet chocolate

Line a 9-inch pie pan smoothly with aluminum foil, folding the edges over the pan rim. Chop the almonds finely to the size of large rice grains.

In the top of a double boiler or in a medium pan within another pan of simmering water, melt the chocolate chips and shortening. Remove from the heat and stir them together until smooth, then stir in the corn syrup and 1 tablespoon of the Grand Marnier. Mix the nuts in well and spread evenly over the bottom and up the sides of the foil-lined pan. Chill the shell in the refrigerator until firm, at least 1 hour. Gently loosen the foil from the pan edges and lift the shell from the pan. Peel the foil from the shell and return it to the pan.

Chill beaters and a bowl large enough (6-8-cup volume) to whip the cream. Peel only the orange part of the peel from the orange with a very sharp paring knife. Combine the peel and sugar in a deep bowl and, with a pestle or small jar, lightly pound the orange peel and sugar together to release the orange oil into the sugar. Lift the orange peel out of the sugar, shaking off any clinging sugar; discard the peel.

Beat the egg yolks until they are light in color. Gradually add the sugar and continue beating until the mixture is thick and a ribbon of egg yolk dropped from the raised beaters will remain 15 seconds. Fold in the orange juice concentrate. Beat the cream in the chilled bowl with the chilled beaters until soft peaks will hold their shape. Fold half of the cream into the egg mixture. Fold in the Grand Marnier and then the remaining cream. Pile the mousse evenly into the chocolate shell and freeze.

Serve the pie within 24 hours, garnishing it with Chocolate Leaves or grated chocolate.

MAKES 8 SERVINGS.

Variation

AMARETTO MOUSSE IN A CHOCOLATE-ALMOND SHELL

Follow the recipe for Grand Marnier Mousse Pie in a Chocolate-Almond Shell, substituting Amaretto liqueur for the Grand Marnier and omitting the orange rind. Beat ¼ teaspoon almond extract into the egg yolks.

Southern Comfort–Peach Pie

A measure of Southern hospitality. Peach ice cream lovers are wild about this pie.

½ cup graham cracker crumbs
1 cup very finely chopped pecans
3 tablespoons golden or light brown sugar, packed
¼ cup butter, melted
3 medium ripe peaches, peeled and pitted, or 12 ounces individually frozen peach slices
5 teaspoons fresh lemon juice
¼ cup plus 2 teaspoons Southern Comfort

1¾ teaspoons unflavored gelatin
2 large egg yolks, at room temperature
½ cup plus 1 tablespoon sugar
3 tablespoons light corn syrup
1 cup heavy cream
6 tablespoons peach preserves
Fresh peach slices or glazed pecans (see page 212)

Preheat the oven to 350° F. Combine the crumbs, pecans, and brown sugar in a bowl; blend thoroughly. Blend in the melted butter. Pat the mixture into a 9-inch pie plate and bake about 8 minutes, until very lightly toasted. Cool and then chill the crust.

Chill beaters and a bowl large enough (6-cup volume) to whip the cream. Chop the peaches to about the size of peas and sprinkle with the lemon juice and 1 tablespoon Southern Comfort. Chill the peaches. In a small heatproof cup, sprinkle the gelatin over 3 tablespoons of the Southern Comfort and allow to soften, about 3 minutes. Place in a pan of very hot water and stir until the gelatin granules dissolve. Beat the egg yolks until they are thick and light in color. Gradually beat in the sugar until the eggs are ivory-colored and as thick as whipped cream. Gradually beat in the corn syrup. Fold in the gelatin mixture and place in the refrigerator. In the chilled bowl with the chilled beaters, whip the cream until soft peaks will hold their shape. Fold the whipped cream and then the peaches into the egg mixture. Freeze the peach mixture at least 2 hours, stirring twice, until it holds its shape but is not yet frozen. Spoon half of the peach filling into the pie shell. Blend the preserves and the remaining 2 teaspoons Southern Comfort and spoon it over the filling in the shell. Distribute the remaining filling evenly over the preserves and smooth the top. Freeze at least 4 hours.

Garnish the pie with sliced peaches arranged like a flower on top of the pie or with a ring of glazed pecans.

MAKES 8 SERVINGS.

Fudgy Black Bottom Banana-Nut Pie

An intense fudgy baked bottom and a light but very banana-flavored filling.

2½ ounces semisweet chocolate,
*   chopped*
6 tablespoons unsalted butter, at
*   room temperature*
½ cup plus 6 tablespoons sugar
2 large eggs
1¾ teaspoons vanilla extract
2 tablespoons all-purpose flour
¼ cup semisweet mini chocolate
*   morsels*

½ cup chopped walnuts
3 medium-large bananas (about 26
*   ounces unpeeled)*
2 teaspoons fresh lemon juice
1 cup heavy cream, well chilled
¼ cup very finely chopped
*   walnuts*
Chocolate fudge sauce or shaved
*   semisweet chocolate, for garnish*

Oil a 9-inch glass pie pan. Preheat the oven to 325° F.

Melt the chocolate in 2 tablespoons water over very low heat. Remove from the heat and stir until smooth. Blend the butter and 6 tablespoons of the sugar together until they are thoroughly mixed. Beat in the eggs, one at a time, until the mixture is well blended. Beat in the melted chocolate and 1 teaspoon of the vanilla. Fold in the flour and the chocolate morsels and the ½ cup nuts. Spread the mixture evenly in the prepared pan and bake in the center of the oven about 15 minutes, until the edges are set and the center is slightly soft. Cool to room temperature, then place the pie in the freezer before continuing.

Chill beaters and a bowl large enough to whip the cream. In a blender or food processor, puree the bananas with the lemon juice and ¼ cup of the sugar until they are smooth. Place in a shallow dish in the freezer until the edges of the puree begin to freeze and the mixture is very well chilled. In the chilled bowl, beat the cream, gradually adding the remaining ¼ cup sugar until soft peaks will hold their shape. Beat the banana purée and the remaining ¾ teaspoon vanilla together until the purée is smooth. Fold in half of the whipped cream, then the remaining cream.

Pile the banana mixture over the baked fudge and sprinkle with the ¼ cup finely chopped nuts. Freeze at least 4 hours or overnight. About 20 minutes before serving, place the pie in the refrigerator. Just before serving, wipe the bottom of the pie with a sponge dipped in very hot water. Cut the pie with a knife dipped in hot water and wiped clean after each cut.

MAKES 8 TO 10 SERVINGS.

White Russian Ice Cream Pie with Chocolate Sorbet Crust

A dynamite combination of crunchy almond macaroons, lined with bittersweet chocolate sorbet and rich white-chocolate ice cream, subtly flavored with a hint of coffee. If you don't have time to make the sorbet and can't buy it, use a good bittersweet chocolate ice cream.

1⅓ cups almond macaroon crumbs (commercial or homemade, page 211)
¼ cup unsalted butter, melted
1¼ cups Chocolate Sorbet (page 81)

1 quart White Russian Ice Cream (page 43)
Chocolate Leaves (page 213)

Blend the crumbs and melted butter together and pat into a lightly buttered 9-inch pie pan; freeze until firm. Soften the sorbet slightly and dot it all over the crumb crust. Using your fingertips, smooth the sorbet evenly over the crust and around the sides. Freeze several hours, until firm.

Soften the White Russian Ice Cream and pile it into the sorbet-lined pie shell, mounding it up in the center and smoothing the top. Freeze the pie until firm. Cover with plastic wrap and then foil until you are ready to serve. Remove the pie from the freezer about 7 minutes before serving and garnish with the Chocolate Leaves.

MAKES 8 SERVINGS.

Double Blackberry Pie

1 large egg white
⅛ teaspoon salt
¼ cup sugar
1½ cups chopped almonds or
    walnuts
1½ cups Blackberry Sorbet (page
    85)

2 tablespoons Cassis liqueur
3½ cups Fresh Blackberry Ice
    Cream (page 52)
Whipped cream and fresh black-
    berries (if available) for the
    garnish

Preheat the oven to 400° F. Thoroughly grease a 9-inch pie pan.

Beat the egg white and salt until frothy and opaque. Gradually beat in the sugar until soft peaks will hold their shape. Fold in the nuts. Spread over the bottom and sides of the prepared pan but not on the rim. Prick with a fork. Bake in the center of the oven 10 to 12 minutes, until firm. Cool, then chill.

Soften the sorbet and spread it over the crust and around the sides; drizzle evenly with the Cassis, stirring the liqueur in slightly. Freeze several hours, until firm. Slightly soften the Blackberry Ice Cream and dot it over the top of the sorbet-lined crust. Smooth the ice cream and freeze until firm.

Before serving, pipe rosettes of whipped cream around the edge of the pie and in the center, using a pastry bag fitted with a star tip. Place a fresh berry in the center of each rosette.

MAKES 8 OR 9 SERVINGS.

Variation

DOUBLE BLACKBERRY PIE BAKED ALASKA

3 egg whites, at room temperature
⅛ teaspoon cream of tartar
6 tablespoons sugar
1 tablespoon Cassis liqueur
1 recipe Double Blackberry Pie (above)

Preheat the oven to 450° F.

Beat the egg whites and cream of tartar together until soft peaks hold their shape. Gradually beat in the sugar until the eggs are glossy and all the sugar is dissolved. Blend in the Cassis only until lightly blended. Spread the meringue over the pie, sealing the edges with meringue. Bake the pie 2 to 3 minutes, until the meringue starts to turn golden. Freeze immediately until the ice cream is firm, about 4 hours. If covered with plastic wrap after 4 hours in the freezer, the pie may be stored 2 days before serving.

MAKES 8 TO 9 SERVINGS.

Chocolate-Pecan Ice Cream Pie

To get the right consistency, it is essential to use a 10-inch pie plate for this crunchy pecan and chocolate-custard-bottomed pie topped with ice cream.

2 large eggs
⅔ cup light corn syrup
6 tablespoons golden or light brown sugar, packed
4 tablespoons unsalted butter, melted
¼ teaspoon salt
2 tablespoons all-purpose flour
1½ cups chopped pecans
6 ounces (1 cup) semisweet chocolate morsels
1 quart vanilla ice cream
Chocolate sauce (optional)

Preheat the oven to 325° F. Generously grease a 10-inch pie pan with vegetable shortening. Line the pan with tin foil, folding the foil over the pan edges. Grease the foil.

In a large bowl, beat the eggs and corn syrup together until smooth.

Blend in the sugar, melted butter, salt, and flour. Blend in the pecans and chocolate morsels until evenly mixed. Pour into the prepared pan. Bake in the center of the oven 35 to 40 minutes, until the edges are set. The center will be barely firm.

Cool the pie to room temperature, then chill it thoroughly. When the pie is chilled, wipe the underside of the pie pan with a sponge or cloth dipped in very hot water. Loosen the foil from the pie pan and lift the pie out of pan; clean the pan and dry it very well. Loosen the pie from the foil and return pie and foil to the pan. Trim the foil even with the pie if you wish. Keep the pie at room temperature.

About 30 minutes before serving, soften the ice cream and spread it over the pie. Return to the freezer just to allow the ice cream to firm, not longer than 45 minutes. Garnish the pie with swirled chocolate sauce if you wish.

MAKES 8 TO 10 SERVINGS.

Orange-Cranberry Mousse Pie

Delightfully refreshing, something different for the holidays.

1 large egg white	5 tablespoons Cointreau or Triple
1/8 teaspoon salt	Sec liqueur
1/4 cup sugar	1 1/2 teaspoons unflavored gelatin
1 1/2 cup chopped walnuts or	1 (16-ounce) can whole-berry
pecans	cranberry sauce
1 1/4 cups Wonderful Fresh Orange	1 cup heavy cream, chilled
Ice Cream (page 50)	1 tablespoon corn syrup

Preheat the oven to 400° F. Thoroughly grease a 9-inch pie pan.

Beat the egg white and salt until frothy and opaque. Gradually beat in the sugar only until very soft peaks will hold their shape. Fold in the nuts. Spread over the bottom and sides of the prepared pan just below the rim. Prick with a fork. Bake in the center of the oven 10 to 12 minutes, until firm. Cool, then chill.

Soften the orange ice cream slightly. Dot the ice cream evenly over the pie crust and spread it evenly with your fingertips over the bottom and up the sides. Sprinkle 1 tablespoon of the Cointreau over the ice cream and swirl it in slightly. Freeze until firm.

Place 2½ tablespoons of the Cointreau in a heatproof cup and sprinkle the gelatin over the surface. Place in a pan or bowl of very hot water and stir until no gelatin granules remain. Remove 3 cranberries from the sauce and set aside for the garnish. Blend the gelatin mixture into 1¼ cups of the cranberry sauce. In a chilled bowl, whip the cream just until soft peaks hold their shape. Fold one third of the cream into the cranberry sauce, then fold in the remaining whipped cream. Freeze the cranberry mousse until it is firm enough to mound in the pie shell but is not completely frozen. Blend the remaining cranberry sauce, the corn syrup, and remaining 1½ tablespoons Cointreau together. Pour the cranberry and corn syrup mixture over the ice cream in the pie shell. Cover with the cranberry mousse. Place the 3 whole cranberries in the center of the pie. Freeze about 4 hours, then cover with plastic wrap and foil. Let the pie sit in the refrigerator about 15 minutes before serving.

MAKES 8 TO 9 SERVINGS.

Lemon Dream Pie

1⅓ cups almond macaroon
   crumbs, commercial or homemade, or butter cookie crumbs
¼ cup unsalted butter, melted
1½ cups lemon sorbet or sherbet
2 large eggs, separated and at
   room temperature

⅔ cup sugar
⅓ cup fresh lemon juice
2 teaspoons finely grated lemon
   zest
1 cup plus 2 tablespoons heavy
   cream, well chilled
Lemon slice (for garnish)

Blend the crumbs and melted butter together and pat into a lightly buttered 9-inch pie pan; freeze until firm. Soften the sorbet slightly and dot it over the crumb crust. Smooth the sorbet over the crust and around the sides; freeze several hours, until firm.

Chill a bowl large enough (4–6-cup volume) to whip the cream. In the top of a double boiler over barely simmering water, beat the egg yolks until they are light and very fluffy. Place over hot water (not boiling) and gradually beat in 2 tablespoons of the sugar, beating until the yolks are the consistency of whipped cream. Gradually beat in the lemon juice and then the zest until the mixture thickens slightly once again. Remove from the heat. In a clean bowl with clean beaters, beat the egg whites just until very soft peaks hold their shape. Very gradually beat in the remaining sugar until the whites are glossy and curved peaks will hold their shape when the beaters are lifted.

Whip the cream in the chilled bowl until very soft peaks hold their shape. Fold the yolks into the whites, one quarter at a time. Fold in the whipped cream in thirds. Freeze until the mixture holds its shape in a spoon. Spoon into the sorbet-lined pie shell and freeze until firm. Cover with plastic wrap and then foil until ready to serve. Garnish with a very thin lemon slice.

MAKES 8 SERVINGS.

Triple-Peanut Crunch Pie

A nutty peanut crust topped with peanut brittle ice cream and a peanut-butter-laced fudgy sauce.

¾ cup graham cracker crumbs, finely crushed

2 tablespoons golden or light brown sugar, packed

⅔ cup roasted unsalted peanuts, very finely chopped

½ cup plus 3 tablespoons smooth peanut butter, at room temperature

2 tablespoons unsalted butter, melted

5 cups vanilla ice cream, slightly softened

6 ounces peanut brittle, crushed into small pieces

⅔ cup semisweet chocolate morsels

7 tablespoons heavy cream

3 tablespoons powdered sugar

Combine the crumbs, sugar, and peanuts and blend them together well. Stir in the ½ cup peanut butter and the melted butter. Pat the mixture into a greased 9-inch pie pan.

Blend the ice cream and all but 3 tablespoons of the crushed peanut brittle together. Spread the ice cream into the pie shell and freeze.

Combine the chocolate morsels and cream in a small saucepan. Cook over very low heat, stirring occasionally, until the morsels melt; stir until very smooth. Blend in the 3 tablespoons peanut butter and powdered sugar. Cool the mixture almost to room temperature. Spread the chocolate mixture over the frozen pie and sprinkle with the remaining peanut brittle. Freeze until firm. Cover with plastic wrap, then foil.

MAKES 8 SERVINGS.

Frozen Pumpkin Pie with a Pecan Praline Crust

A crunchy, buttery, nutty crust with velvety pumpkin filling, garnished with glazed pecans.

1⅓ cups butter biscuit crumbs (petit beurrre)
⅔ cup unsalted butter, melted
¾ cup chopped pecans
½ cup plus ⅓ cup golden or light brown sugar, packed
¼ cup Frangelico or other nut liqueur
¾ teaspoon ground cinnamon
¼ teaspoon ground ginger
¼ teaspoon freshly grated nutmeg
⅛ teaspoon ground cloves
1½ cups solidly packed, canned or fresh, cooked pumpkin
3½ cups vanilla ice cream, slightly softened
Glazed pecans (page 212) for garnish

Preheat the oven to 350° F. Combine the crumbs and ¼ cup of the melted butter and mix well. Pat the crumb mixture into a 10-inch pie plate. Mix the pecans with 1 tablespoon of the butter in a baking pan and bake about 12 minutes, stirring occasionally, until they are toasted. Combine ½ cup of the brown sugar with the remaining butter and the toasted pecans and spread over the crumb crust. Bake the crust 8 minutes. Cool completely on a rack.

Combine the remaining ⅓ cup brown sugar, the liqueur, and the spices; blend thoroughly. Beat in the pumpkin until the mixture is smooth. Fold in the softened ice cream and freeze until the mixture holds a mound shape in a spoon. Spread the mixture into the crust. Ring the edge of the pie with glazed pecans and place a glazed pecan half in the center of the pie. Freeze until firm, then cover with plastic wrap and aluminum foil until ready to serve. Before cutting the pie, wipe the bottom of the pie plate with a sponge dipped in very hot water.

MAKES 8 TO 10 SERVINGS.

Variation

9-INCH FROZEN PUMPKIN PIE WITH A PECAN PRALINE CRUST

I love a grand-size pumpkin pie, but it may be too large to fit in some freezers. Here are the proportions for a 9-inch pie.

1 cup and 2 tablespoons butter biscuit crumbs (petit beurre)
½ cup butter (3 tablespoons in the crust, about 1 for the nuts, ¼ cup for the praline)
⅔ cup chopped pecans
⅓ cup plus ¼ cup golden or light brown sugar, packed
3 tablespoons Frangelico or other nut liqueur

½ teaspoon ground cinnamon
¼ teaspoon ground ginger
¼ teaspoon freshly grated nutmeg
About ³⁄₁₆ teaspoon ground cloves
1 cup solidly packed, canned or fresh, cooked pumpkin
3 cups vanilla ice cream, slightly softened
Glazed pecans (page 212) for garnish

Crème de Menthe–Chocolate Chip Pie

It's worth taking a few extra minutes to make the chocolate macaroon crust for this extravagantly delicious pie. But if you want a shortcut, substitute the chocolate cookie crumb crust on page 000.

1½ cups crumbled Chocolate Almond Macaroons (page 211)
¼ cup unsalted butter, melted
1¼ cups chocolate ice cream

1 recipe Quick Crème de Menthe–Chocolate Chip Freeze (page 4) or mint chocolate chip ice cream
Chocolate Leaves (page 213) (optional, for garnish)

Combine the macaroon crumbs and melted butter, blending them thoroughly. Reserve 3 heaping tablespoons of the crumb mixture for garnish. Pat the remaining crumb mixture into an ungreased 9-inch pie pan; freeze until firm. Soften the chocolate ice cream slightly and dot it evenly over the crumb crust. Smooth the ice cream over the crust and around the sides. Freeze several hours, until firm.

Soften the crème de menthe mixture just slightly and pile it into the frozen chocolate pie shell, mounding it in the center. Evenly sprinkle the remaining crumb mixture around the edge of the pie. Pat it into the crème de menthe mixture. Freeze the pie several hours or overnight. Cover with plastic wrap and then foil.

Store up to 4 days. When ready to serve, arrange the chocolate leaves decoratively in the center of the pie.

MAKES 8 TO 10 SERVINGS.

Caramel-Nut-Bottom Ice Cream Pie

3/4 cup golden or light brown
    sugar, packed
1 large egg
3 tablespoons unsalted butter,
    melted
1/4 teaspoon salt
1 teaspoon vanilla extract
1/3 cup all-purpose flour

1/4 teaspoon baking soda
1 1/4 cups medium-coarsely chopped
    walnuts or pecans
3 cups vanilla ice cream or Old-
    fashioned Vanilla Custard Ice
    Cream (page 17)
Bittersweet Chocolate Sauce (page
    199)

Preheat the oven to 350° F. (325° F. for glass pans). Line a 10-inch pie pan smoothly with aluminum foil, folding the edges over the rim. Generously butter the foil with unsalted butter.

Stir together the sugar, egg, butter, salt, and vanilla until well mixed. Sprinkle the flour and baking soda over the sugar mixture and blend them in well. Mix in the nuts. Spread the mixture over the bottom and sides of the pie pan and bake in the center of the oven until the edges are barely firm, about 25 minutes. The center will still be soft. Cool in the pan. Gently loosen the foil from the pan edges and lift the shell from the pan. Peel the foil from the shell and return the shell to the pan.

About an hour before serving, soften the ice cream slightly and spread over the caramel-nut layer. Freeze only until firm. Serve the pie garnished with the chocolate sauce.

MAKES 10 SERVINGS.

Brownie-Meringue-Fudge Cream Pie

A brownie-meringue pie shell smothered in a silky rich chocolate cream and topped with liqueur-flavored whipped cream.

¾ cup plus 3 tablespoons sifted
    powdered sugar
2 tablespoons unsweetened cocoa
    powder
⅓ cup finely crushed chocolate
    wafers
2 large egg whites, at room tem-
    perature
¼ cup sugar
¼ teaspoon vanilla extract
1 ounce unsweetened chocolate
3 ounces semisweet chocolate

⅓ cup (5 tablespoons plus 1 tea-
    spoon) unsalted butter, at room
    temperature
¾ teaspoon vanilla extract
1 tablespoon Cognac or brandy
3 large eggs
1 cup heavy cream, well chilled
3 tablespoons coffee-flavored li-
    queur or Bailey's Irish Cream
Shaved chocolate or Chocolate
    Leaves (page 213) for garnish

Preheat the oven to 325° F. Thoroughly grease the bottom and sides of a 9-inch pie pan.

Combine 3 tablespoons of the powdered sugar with the cocoa; blend well and mix in the wafer crumbs.

In a medium bowl, beat the egg whites until soft peaks form. Very gradually beat in the granulated sugar until stiff, glossy peaks form. Fold in the vanilla and the wafer mixture. Spread evenly on the bottom and up the sides of the prepared pan. Bake in the center of the oven about 45 minutes. Cool to room temperature.

In a small pan within another pan or in the top of a double boiler over simmering water, melt the chocolates. Stir until very smooth, then cool until they are at room temperature but still flowing. With an electric mixer, cream the butter until it is fluffy. Add the vanilla, Cognac, and remaining ¾ cup powdered sugar and beat until smooth. Beat in the melted chocolate well. Add the eggs, one at a time, beating each one in very well. Beat 1 minute longer. Turn the mixture into the meringue shell and freeze until firm. Then cover with plastic wrap and foil until up to 12 hours before you are ready to serve.

At least 4 hours before serving, beat the cream in a chilled bowl until soft peaks will hold their shape, then gently fold in the liqueur only until it is mixed in. Spread the whipped cream onto the frozen pie and freeze 4 hours or more. Garnish with shaved chocolate or Chocolate Leaves.

MAKES 10 SERVINGS.

Strawberry-Margarita Pie

1 cup finely crushed zwieback
   crumbs
¼ teaspoon salt
⅓ cup plus 6 tablespoons sugar
¼ cup unsalted butter, melted
1 (10-ounce) package frozen
   strawberries in syrup, thawed
3 teaspoons unflavored gelatin
4 large egg yolks, at room temperature

6 tablespoons fresh lime juice
3 tablespoons tequila
3½ tablespoons Triple Sec
   liqueur
1½ cups heavy cream, well
   chilled
2 large egg whites, at room temperature
Fresh strawberries (optional, for
   garnish)

Chill beaters and a bowl large enough (4–6-cup volume) to whip the cream. Combine the crumbs, salt, ⅓ cup of the sugar, and the melted butter; reserve 1 tablespoon. Press the crumbs into a 9-inch pie pan and freeze. Drain the syrup from the berries into a very small pan. Sprinkle with the gelatin and allow to soften, about 3 minutes. Cook over low heat, stirring occasionally, until no gelatin granules remain. Stir in the remaining 6 tablespoons sugar until it is dissolved. Beat the 4 egg yolks until they are very thick and ivory-colored. Slowly pour the gelatin syrup over them, beating all the while. Return the mixture to the pan and cook, stirring, about 6 minutes, until the mixture will coat the back of a spoon. Cool to room temperature. Stir in the lime juice, tequila, and Triple Sec. Puree the berries in a blender or food processor and stir them into the cooled custard. In the chilled bowl, whip the cream until soft peaks will hold their shape; fold into the custard mixture and refrigerate until the mixture drops into mounds when dropped from a spoon, about 40 minutes. Do not allow the mixture to set. Beat the egg whites only until curved peaks will hold their shape; fold into the strawberry mixture. Freeze until the mixture is almost firm. Spoon into the pie crust and freeze at least 4 hours. Remove from the freezer 5 minutes before serving and garnish with fresh berries if desired.

MAKES 8 SERVINGS.

Rebeckah's Amaretti–Toffee Crunch Pie

A contribution from my friend Rebeckah Jourgensen, who discovered the recipe from a French chef.

1 cup finely crushed amaretti
    biscuit crumbs
⅓ cup finely chopped almonds
¼ cup unsalted butter, melted
5 cups Old-fashioned Vanilla
    Custard (page 17) or Glo-
    riously Rich French Vanilla Ice
    Cream (page 17)

7 ounces crushed toffee candy
    (homemade recipe on page 213)
2 ounces semisweet chocolate
2 tablespoons heavy cream
1 teaspoon light corn syrup
1 tablespoon Amaretto liqueur

Combine the crushed amaretti, almonds, and butter and mix them together thoroughly. Reserve ¼ cup and pat the remaining mixture into a 9-inch pie pan. Freeze the crust until it is firm.

Soften the ice cream just slightly and stir in the crushed toffee. Spread the ice cream in the crust and freeze until firm.

Combine the chocolate and cream in a small heavy saucepan. Cook over very low heat until the chocolate melts; stir until smooth. Remove from the heat and stir in the corn syrup and Amaretto. Cool the chocolate mixture to room temperature. Drizzle the chocolate mixture decoratively in a swirl pattern over the frozen pie. Sprinkle with the remaining crumbs and freeze until firm. Cover with plastic wrap, then foil.

MAKES 8 SERVINGS.

Karen's Fudge Sundae Pie

My friend Karen Lewis contributes one of her favorite frozen desserts.

½ cup broken pecans
1 cup finely crushed vanilla or
    chocolate wafers
2 tablespoons sugar*
2½ tablespoons unsalted butter,
    melted
2 pints vanilla ice cream

1 cup evaporated milk
1 cup semisweet chocolate morsels
1 cup mini marshmallows
¼ teaspoon salt
¾ cup pecan halves or glazed
    pecans (page 212) for garnish

* Add the sugar only with the chocolate wafers.

Chop the ½ cup pecans to the texture of fine crumbs. If you are using the chocolate wafers, combine the crumbs with the sugar; blend the crumbs with the chopped nuts and the butter and pat into a 9-inch pie plate. Freeze until firm. Slightly soften 1 pint of the ice cream and spoon it evenly over the crust; freeze until firm.

In a medium saucepan, combine the milk, chocolate morsels, marshmallows, and salt. Stir over medium heat until the chocolate and marshmallows melt and the mixture is smooth. Cool to room temperature.

Pour half of the chocolate mixture over the ice cream in the pie shell. Place in the freezer and soften the remaining ice cream just enough to spread it over the pie. Top with the remaining chocolate mixture and freeze until the pie is firm. Top the pie with pecan halves or glazed pecans arranged in concentric circles.

MAKES 8 SERVINGS.

Piña Colada Pie with Coconut-Macadamia Crust

A pie brimming with tropical flavors.

7 ounces sweetened flaked coconut
⅔ cup very finely chopped unsalted macadamia nuts
2 tablespoons powdered sugar
2 tablespoons all-purpose flour
Pinch of salt
½ cup unsalted butter, melted
2 large egg yolks, at room temperature

⅔ cup sugar
2 (8-ounce) containers piña colada yogurt
4 tablespoons dark rum
1 cup plus 2 tablespoons heavy cream, well chilled
Fresh pineapple wedges or chopped macadamia nuts for garnish

Chill beaters and a bowl large enough (4–6-cup volume) to whip the cream. Preheat the oven to 375° F. (350° F. for glass pans). Thoroughly butter the bottom and sides of a 9-inch pie pan.

Stir the coconut and nuts together thoroughly. Blend the powdered sugar, flour, and salt together and blend them into the coconut mixture. Mix in the butter.

Pat the mixture into the bottom and sides of the prepared pan and bake for 8 to 10 minutes, or until the crust is golden brown. Cool on a rack, then chill.

In the top of a double boiler, beat the egg yolks until they are thick and light in color. Place over hot (not boiling) water and gradually beat in ⅓ cup of the sugar until the mixture is pale ivory and the texture of whipped cream. Remove from the heat.

Blend the yogurt, rum, and remaining ⅓ cup sugar together. Gently fold into the egg yolk mixture. In the chilled bowl, beat the cream until soft peaks will hold their shape. Fold one third of the whipped cream into the yogurt, then fold in the remaining whipped cream. Pour into the cooled pie crust and freeze. Garnish with fresh pineapple wedges or a sprinkling of chopped macadamia nuts.

Before cutting the pie, loosen the edges of the crust with a sharp-pointed knife. Set the pie for 5 minutes on a tea towel soaked in very hot water. Remove the pie from the towel and cut into serving pieces with a sharp knife.

MAKES 8 SERVINGS.

Frozen Lime Delight Pie

About 5 large limes★
1⅓ cups butter biscuit (petit beurre) or butter cookie crumbs
¼ cup unsalted butter, melted
4 large eggs
1 (14-ounce can) sweetened condensed milk

1⅓ cups Gloriously Rich French Vanilla Ice Cream (page 17)
½ cup heavy cream, whipped
1½ tablespoons sugar

Cut a thin lime slice from the center of the largest lime, wrap it in plastic wrap, and reserve it for the garnish. Grate the zest from the limes and reserve it. Squeeze ½ cup lime juice.

Combine 2 teaspoons of the grated lime zest with the biscuit crumbs and melted butter; blend well. Pat into a 9-inch pie plate, chill.

In a food processor or with an electric mixer, beat the eggs. Blend in the condensed milk, the ½ cup lime juice, and the remaining 3 teaspoons lime zest and beat until smooth. Pour into the pie crust and freeze until firm.

★ You will need about 5 large limes for the 5 teaspoons lime zest and ½ cup lime juice, plus 1 slice for garnish.

Soften the ice cream and spread it over the frozen pie, smoothing the top. Freeze until firm. To serve the pie, whip the heavy cream with the sugar, spoon into a pastry bag, and pipe a border or rosettes around the edge of the pie. Or garnish similarly with prepared whipped cream. Cut a slit through half of the lime slice from the center through the edge. Twist the slice to form the center garnish (see illustration). Before cutting the pie, set it on a tea towel soaked in hot water for 4 to 5 minutes.

MAKES 8 SERVINGS.

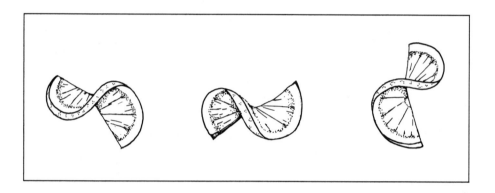

Still-Frozen Desserts: Mousses, Parfaits, and Soufflés

"Parfait!" may have been uttered by French royalty when a chef first presented this sublime frozen dessert: creamy and rich, yet lighter than ice creams, with delicate air bubbles caught in a lacy web of sweetened cream and beaten eggs. The resulting texture glides like satin over the palate. Punctuated with a mellow liqueur or ripe fruit, the flavor clings to the tongue. These days the terms "mousse," "parfait," and "soufflé" seem to be interchangeably used for most still-frozen desserts. Of course, a soufflé is presented in a soufflé dish, with a high collar supporting its shape until serving time. When the collar is removed, the soufflé appears to have risen. But a frozen soufflé or mousse may have the very same composition.

The ancestor of all these desserts was the original French frozen parfait. Chefs had each his own way of arriving at such blissful mixtures. Some cooked a light rich custard, cooled it, and folded in clouds of whipped cream and perhaps beaten egg whites. Others made a sugar syrup, beat the egg whites, then beat the hot syrup into them. This method, known as an Italian meringue, is the base for many still-frozen desserts today.

The dessert's foundation of egg yolks and cream, with their attendant high fat content, prevents large icy crystals from forming during still-freezing. To maintain a velvety texture, it is important not to add too much watery liquid, such as might be found in fresh fruit, in proportion to air, fat, and sugar. Of course, liqueurs don't freeze, so their addition will keep the mixture supple. But if liqueur is overused, the dessert will simply be slushy. As with churned desserts, other ingredients that help maintain creaminess are corn syrup, a little gelatin, fruit preserves, and chocolate (not cocoa).

While testing many of these desserts, I noticed that the smoothest frozen desserts resulted when the eggs had been cooked or heated during the beating stage while uncooked meringue often produced icy crystals. Cooked egg foams are more stable than uncooked ones, and maintain their shape even if air escapes their bubbles, preventing large icy crystals forming in the frozen dessert.

- Just as in chiffon cake batter or cooked soufflés, *eggs must not be overbeaten* or their water-holding capacity will diminish. Beat egg whites without sugar only until curved peaks will stand alone. The peaks should not be stiff, and you should not be able to cut the egg whites into chunks. You may have observed how difficult it is to fold overbeaten egg whites smoothly into other ingredients. If they are folded in too vehemently, the mixture will deflate and encourage large ice crystals in the finished dish.
- Remember to add sugar very gradually to egg whites only after they have been beaten to a soft opaque foam. Beat the egg whites and sugar until there are no sugar granules left. The whites should stand in *curved* peaks.
- Remember to have eggs for beating at room temperature. You can warm them if necessary by placing the eggs in a bowl in hot water.
- Whipped heavy cream is another important ingredient in these desserts. Again, overbeating encourages large ice crystal formation. Whipped cream is actually at its most stable before it is stiffly beaten. Its bubbles should be slightly elastic and not completely filled with air. Beat cream until it mounds upon itself or until very limp peaks will hold up.
- Remember, smooth still-frozen desserts need to freeze as quickly as possible. Opening and shutting the freezer door will slow freezing time.
- Since many of these desserts use more egg yolks than whites, I freeze extra whites in little 3-ounce paper cups. Save them for crunchy meringues, baked Alaska desserts, pie toppings, almond macaroons, and sorbets.

Frozen Chocolate Pâté

What could be more decadent?

*⅓ cup crumbled Almond Maca-
   roons (page 211)*
8 ounces semisweet chocolate
½ ounce unsweetened chocolate
1 tablespoon Cognac
½ cup (1 stick) unsalted butter
1 teaspoon vanilla extract

⅔ cup sugar
*4 large eggs, separated and at
   room temperature*
1/16 teaspoon salt
⅓ cup heavy cream, well chilled
*Chocolate-Dipped Almond Slices
   (recipe below) for garnish*

Line a 8×4-inch (4-cup) loaf pan with foil, extending the foil over the pan edges. Lightly oil the foil with almond or safflower oil. Sprinkle the macaroon crumbs over the bottom of the pan and place it in the freezer. Cut up the chocolates and in the top of a double boiler, over simmering water, melt them, stirring occasionally. Stir in the Cognac and remove the chocolate from the heat to cool.

With an electric mixer, cream the butter until it is smooth and fluffy. Beat in the vanilla and then gradually beat in ½ cup of the sugar until the mixture is very smooth and a creamy ivory color. Beat in the egg yolks, one at a time, beating each one in well. Beat the mixture until it is very creamy. Blend in the melted chocolate.

In a clean bowl with clean beaters, beat the egg whites with the salt until they are just opaque. Gradually add the remaining sugar and beat just until curved peaks will hold their shape. Beat the cream until soft peaks will hold their shape. Fold the beaten whites, one fourth at a time, into the chocolate mixture. Then fold in the cream. Pour the mixture into the frozen foil-lined pan and freeze until firm. Cover with plastic wrap and then foil.

Prepare Chocolate-Dipped Almond Slices.

To serve, let the pâté stand at room temperature about 5 minutes. Slide a knife between the foil and side of the pan. Invert the pâté onto a platter and peel away the foil, carefully shaking the macaroon crumbs onto the top of the pâté. Garnish with Chocolate-Dipped Almond Slices.

Chocolate-Dipped Almond Slices

Melt 1 ounce semisweet chocolate in the top of a double boiler over simmering water. Dip half of each almond slice from ½ cup sliced almonds into the chocolate and place on a piece of waxed paper to harden. Chill the dipped almond slices.

MAKES 10 TO 12 SERVINGS.

Variation

CHOCOLATE PÂTÉ WITH VANILLA SAUCE

Make the pâté as directed. Serve it frozen with Velvety Vanilla Sauce (page 206) at room temperature.

Frozen Calvados Cream with Caramelized Apples

The warm caramelized apples and creamy frozen apple-brandy mousse are a perfect contrast and complement.

1½ cups sugar
8 large egg yolks, at room temper-
  ature
½ teaspoon vanilla extract
⅓ cup Calvados
1 cup heavy cream
3 large cooking apples (Granny
  Smith)

3 tablespoons unsalted butter
1 teaspoon grated lemon zest
2 teaspoons grated orange zest
Caramelized walnuts (page 30)
  or pecan praline (page 27) for
  garnish

Chill a 6-cup soufflé dish or bowl. Chill beaters and a bowl large enough (4–6-cup volume) to whip the cream. In a medium saucepan, combine 1 cup of the sugar and ¾ cup water and cook over low heat. Stir until the sugar is dissolved. Increase the heat and boil for 10 minutes without stirring. Meanwhile, beat the egg yolks until they are thick and light in color. Slowly beat in the sugar syrup in a fine stream while beating constantly. Continue beating until the sides of the mixing bowl are cool. Carefully fold in the vanilla and Calvados.

In the chilled bowl, beat the cream just until soft peaks will hold their shape. Fold half of the cream into the egg yolk mixture, then fold in the remaining cream. Pour into the soufflé dish or bowl. Cover and freeze.

Just before serving or several hours before, peel and core the apples and slice each into 12 lengthwise wedges. Melt the butter in a large heavy skillet and add the remaining ½ cup sugar. Cook and stir about 1½ minutes. Stir in the apple slices and lemon and orange zest. Cook stirring until the sugar melts and becomes golden and coats the apples and the apples are soft but still hold their shape. Remove from the heat and invert onto a plate. If you like, the apples can be reheated just to warm at serving time. Divide the apples among 6 or 8 serving dishes, top with the Calvados cream, and sprinkle with broken caramelized walnuts or any praline.

MAKES 8 SERVINGS.

Melissa's Can't-Fail Liqueur Mousse

Melissa Pugash, a former chef, contributes this velvety-rich mousse, which she says "everyone should have in their recipe file. It is always a hit and you'll usually already have these ingredients on hand."

6 large egg yolks, at room temper-
ature
⅔ cup sugar
½ teaspoon vanilla extract
6 tablespoons Grand Marnier
liqueur

2 cups heavy cream
Fresh orange slices or macaroon
crumbs (page 211) for garnish

Chill beaters and a bowl large enough (6-cup volume) to whip the cream. Beat the egg yolks until they are thick and light-colored. Very gradually add the sugar, beating until a ribbon of egg will remain on the surface 5 seconds when the beaters are lifted. Gently fold in the vanilla and Grand Marnier.

In the chilled bowl, whip the cream until soft peaks will hold their shape. Fold one third of the cream into the egg, then fold in the remaining cream. Spoon into individual goblets or a glass bowl and freeze 4 hours, or until firm.

Garnish with a twisted orange slice or a sprinkling of crumbled macaroons. The mousse is best when consumed within 24 hours.

MAKES 8 SERVINGS.

Flavor Variations

KAHLÚA MOUSSE

Substitute 7 tablespoons Kahlúa or other coffee liqueur for the Grand Marnier. Reduce the sugar to 5 tablespoons. Garnish with Chocolate Leaves (page 213) or shaved chocolate.

AMARETTO MOUSSE

Substitute Amaretto for the Grand Marnier. Add ⅛ teaspoon almond extract along with the vanilla. Garnish with crushed amaretti biscuits and semisweet chocolate shavings.

WHITE CRÈME DE CACAO MOUSSE

Substitute white crème de cacao for the Grand Marnier. Garnish with crumbled Chocolate-Almond Macaroons (page 211) or Almond Macaroons (page 211) and shaved chocolate.

Banana-Rum Parfait with Coconut Praline

2 medium ripe bananas
2½ tablespoons fresh lime or
*   lemon juice*
4 tablespoons dark rum
3½ teaspoons unflavored gelatin
5 large egg yolks, at room temper-
*   ature*

3 tablespoons sugar
½ teaspoon vanilla extract
½ cup light corn syrup
2 cups heavy cream
About 1 cup Coconut Praline
*   (page 28)*

Chill beaters and a bowl large enough (6-cup volume) to whip the cream. In a blender or food processor, puree the bananas with the lime juice until they are completely smooth. Place the rum in a small heatproof cup, sprinkle the gelatin over it, and allow it to soften 3 minutes. Place it in a bowl of hot water and stir until no gelatin granules remain. Blend the rum mixture into the banana puree. In the top of a double boiler, beat the egg yolks until they are pale and fluffy. Place the pan over hot (not boiling) water and gradually beat in the sugar until a ribbon of yolk remains on its surface 15 seconds when the beaters are lifted. Fold the egg yolks into the banana mixture. Fold in the vanilla and corn syrup. In the chilled bowl, whip the cream just until soft peaks will hold their shape, and fold it into the banana mixture. Pour into a large bowl or 6-cup plastic container and freeze 6 hours or until ready to serve.

To serve, allow the mousse to soften in the refrigerator about 15 minutes. Sprinkle about 1½ tablespoons Coconut Praline into each serving goblet or bowl. Scoop in a serving of parfait and sprinkle on additional praline for garnish.

MAKES 8 SERVINGS.

White Chocolate–Raspberry Mousse

1 (12-ounce) bag lightly sweetened, individually frozen raspberries, thawed
½ cup whole milk
5 ounces Tobler white chocolate,
  broken up
⅔ cup sugar
1¼ teaspoons unflavored gelatin

2 tablespoons fresh lemon juice
4 tablespoons Chambord liqueur
2 cups heavy cream
⅓ cup heavy cream (optional)
2 teaspoons powdered sugar (optional)
Fresh raspberries (optional, for
  garnish)

Puree the raspberries in a blender or food processor, then strain to remove the seeds, preserving as much of the puree as possible. Set the puree aside. Chill beaters and a bowl large enough (6-cup volume) to whip the cream.

In a small heavy pan, bring the milk to the simmering point. Stir in the chocolate and cook, stirring, over very low heat until the chocolate melts and the mixture is smooth. Stir in the sugar until it dissolves completely. Do not allow the mixture to boil. Remove from the heat. In a tiny pan or heatproof cup, sprinkle the gelatin over 3 tablespoons water and allow it to soften 3 minutes. Place the cup in a bowl of hot water and stir until no gelatin granules remain. Stir the gelatin, lemon juice, and liqueur into the berry puree. Blend in the chocolate mixture.

In the chilled bowl with the chilled beaters, beat the 2 cups cream until very soft peaks hold their shape. Fold one third of the whipped cream into the berry mixture, then fold in the remaining cream. Pour into a 5- or 6-cup mold and freeze 4 hours, or until firm. Cover with plastic and then foil.

To serve, dip the mold briefly into lukewarm water and invert onto a plate. If desired, whip the ⅓ cup cream and powdered sugar together. Spoon into a pastry bag fitted with a star tip and pipe whipped cream around the edges of the mold and wherever it will enhance the design. Garnish further with the fresh berries.

MAKES 8 SERVINGS.

Maple-Walnut Praline Mousse

½ cup walnuts, chopped about the size of peas	⅓ cup sugar
¾ cup pure maple syrup	½ teaspoon vanilla extract
4 large egg yolks	2 cups heavy cream
2 tablespoons dark brown sugar, packed	Glazed walnuts (page 212)
	Additional whipped cream (optional, for garnish)

Preheat the oven to 375° F. Chill beaters and a bowl large enough (6-cup volume) to whip the cream. Distribute the chopped nuts evenly on a 13 × 9-inch baking pan and bake until the nuts are lightly toasted, about 10 minutes. Turn out onto a plate to cool. Line the baking pan with foil and butter it generously.

In a small saucepan, gradually beat the syrup into the egg yolks. Cook, stirring, over low heat until the mixture is thick enough to coat the back of a spoon and a path drawn across the custard on the spoon remains undisturbed. Pour the custard into a bowl to cool. In a heavy medium pan or skillet, combine the sugars and cook, stirring continuously, until the sugar is liquefied and a caramel color. Stir in the nuts. Immediately pour the praline onto the buttered pan. Cool until the praline is at room temperature and brittle. Place the walnut praline in a plastic bag and break it into fine pieces with a mallet or use a food processor. Add all but ¼ cup of the praline to the custard in the bowl. Stir in the vanilla.

In the chilled bowl, whip the cream until soft peaks will hold their shape. Fold one third of the cream into the maple-nut-custard mixture, then fold the mixture into the remaining whipped cream. Spoon into a 6½-cup mold or bowl. Freeze; when firm, cover with plastic wrap and foil. To serve, dip mold briefly into lukewarm water and invert on a chilled plate. Decorate with the remaining walnut praline and the glazed walnuts. Serve with whipped cream if desired.

MAKES 8 SERVINGS.

Blueberry Mousse

1 teaspoon unflavored gelatin
2 tablespoons plus 2 teaspoons
  fresh lemon juice
1 (12-ounce) package frozen unsweetened blueberries, thawed,
  or 12 ounces fresh blueberries

1 (7-ounce) jar marshmallow
  cream
2 tablespoons light corn syrup
1½ cups heavy cream

Chill beaters and a bowl large enough (4–6-cup volume) to whip the cream. In a small heatproof cup, sprinkle the gelatin over 2 tablespoons water; let soften about 3 minutes. Place in a shallow pan of hot water and stir until no gelatin granules remain.

Blend the lemon juice and berries in a blender or food processor and puree them. Place the marshmallow cream in a large bowl; gradually whisk or beat in the blueberry puree and then the corn syrup until smooth. Blend in the gelatin.

In the chilled bowl, beat the cream only until very soft peaks will hold their shape. Fold half of the cream into the berries. Fold in the remaining cream. Pour into a 6-cup mold or decorative dish. Freeze; when firm, cover with plastic wrap and foil.

Let the mousse soften in the refrigerator about 20 minutes before serving. If molded, invert onto a plate.

MAKES 8 SERVINGS.

Apricot Parfait

Drenched with cream and apricot flavors and garnished with butter-cooked almonds.

5 ounces (about ¾ cup) dried
  apricots
2½ teaspoons fresh lemon juice
½ teaspoon vanilla extract
Pinch of salt
1 teaspoon grated lemon zest

1 teaspoon unflavored gelatin
2 egg yolks, at room temperature
¾ cup sugar
1⅓ cups heavy cream
1½ tablespoons unsalted butter
½ cup sliced almonds

Chill beaters and a bowl large enough (4–6-cup volume) to whip the cream. Cut the apricots into small pieces using a knife or scissors. In a medium saucepan, combine the apricots with barely enough cold water to cover. Bring to a boil, simmer 1 minute, then remove from the heat and allow to stand, covered, until cooled to room temperature. Drain the apricots, reserving the water. In a blender or food processor, puree the apricots with 6 tablespoons of the soaking liquid, the lemon juice, vanilla, salt, and lemon zest until completely smooth; remove to a medium bowl.

Measure ¼ cup of the reserved soaking liquid into a tiny pot or metal cup. Sprinkle the gelatin over it and allow to soften about 3 minutes. Cook, stirring, over low heat until no gelatin granules remain. Stir the gelatin into the apricots.

Beat the egg yolks until thick and light-colored. Very gradually beat in the sugar until the yolks are ivory-colored and a trail of yolk will remain on the surface 5 seconds when the beaters are lifted. In the chilled bowl, beat the cream until soft peaks will hold their shape. Fold one third of the beaten eggs into the apricot mixture. Then fold in one third of the cream. Fold the apricot mixture into the remaining eggs then fold in the remaining cream. Spoon into a 1-quart mold or bowl. Freeze until firm, at least 6 hours. Cover with plastic wrap, then foil.

Melt the butter in a small skillet. Sauté the almond slices until they are golden. Let the almonds cool on paper toweling.

To serve, wipe the mold with a sponge dipped in warm water and invert onto a plate, or spoon out portions. Sprinkle with the almonds.
MAKES 8 SERVINGS.

Chocolate Sabayon

3 ounces semisweet chocolate
½ cup plus 1 tablespoon Madeira wine
2 teaspoons unflavored gelatin
8 egg yolks
6 egg whites at room temperature
1 cup powdered sugar

Pinch of salt
4 tablespoons granulated sugar
2 cups heavy cream
⅓ cup finely chopped candied cherries (optional, for garnish)
Chopped pecans or slivered almonds (optional, for garnish)

Chill beaters and a bowl large enough (6-cup volume) to whip the cream. Chop the chocolate into fine pieces. Combine the wine and gelatin in a heatproof cup and let stand 3 minutes. Place in a bowl of very hot water and stir until no gelatin granules remain. In the top of a double boiler, over simmering water, whisk the 8 egg yolks and powdered sugar together until thick and frothy. Add the wine mixture and cook, beating with an electric mixer, until the mixture is thick and doubled in volume. Remove from the heat and beat in the chopped chocolate until it is completely melted. Cool to room temperature.

Beat the 6 egg whites with the salt until they are completely white. Very gradually add the sugar and beat until they are glossy and stiff. In the chilled bowl, beat the cream until soft peaks will hold their shape. Fold half of the egg whites into the custard. Fold in the remaining whites and then fold in the cream in two batches. Spoon into a decorative bowl or individual goblets or cups and freeze 4 hours or overnight.

Garnish with the cherries or nuts if desired.

MAKES 10 SERVINGS.

Brandied Cherry-Chocolate Mousse Dome

Marinate these cherries several days for great flavor.

1 (16-ounce) can dark, sweet	*1⅓ cups sugar*
cherries	*3 egg yolks*
¼ cup brandy	*1 egg white, at room temperature*
2 ounces unsweetened chocolate	*2¼ cups heavy cream*
3 ounces semisweet chocolate	

Lightly film a 1½-quart bowl with tasteless oil. Line the bowl with plastic wrap, allowing it to extend over the edge of the bowl. Drain the cherries and reserve the juice. Quarter the cherries and pour the brandy over them. Allow to marinate overnight or as long as a week. Chill beaters and a bowl large enough (6–8-cup volume) to whip the cream. Combine the chocolates and 6 tablespoons of the reserved cherry juice in a heavy medium saucepan and melt the chocolates over low heat, stirring occasionally. Add ¾ cup of the sugar and stir until dissolved. Remove from the heat.

Combine the egg yolks and egg white and beat until they are thick and light in color. Gradually beat in the remaining sugar. Beat the chocolate mixture into the eggs. Return to the pan and cook, stirring, until the mixture boils. Remove from the heat and cool completely.

Strain the brandy from the marinated cherries into the chocolate mixture and blend it in. In the chilled bowl, whip the cream until soft peaks will hold their shape. Fold one third of the cream into the chocolate mixture, then fold the chocolate mixture into the cream. Gently fold in the cherries. Pour the mousse into the bowl. Freeze; when firm, cover with plastic wrap, then foil.

To serve, let stand at room temperature 8 to 10 minutes and then wipe the bowl with a sponge dipped in warm water. Wiggle the plastic wrap to loosen the mousse and invert it onto a plate.

MAKES 10 TO 12 SERVINGS.

Creamy Lemon Dessert Squares

A very creamy mixture that can be made into squares, a pie shape, or individual little dessert cups.

¾ cup crushed butter biscuits (petit beurre) or butter cookies
2½ teaspoons grated lemon zest
2 tablespoons unsalted butter, melted
3 large eggs, separated and at room temperature

½ cup plus 5 tablespoons sugar
⅛ teaspoon salt
⅓ cup fresh lemon juice
1 cup heavy cream, well chilled

Chill beaters and a bowl large enough (4-cup volume) to whip the cream. Mash the crumbs and 1 teaspoon of the lemon zest together to release the lemon flavor. Add the melted butter and blend well. Pat the crumb mixture into the bottom of a 10×6-inch glass baking dish or a 9-inch pie plate or 14 to 15 paper-lined muffin cups.

In the top of a double boiler over simmering water, beat the egg yolks until light in color and thick. Gradually beat in the ½ cup sugar, then the salt and the remaining lemon zest. Remove from the heat and immediately fold in the lemon juice. Cool to room temperature.

With clean beaters, beat the egg whites to soft peaks and gradually add the remaining 5 tablespoons sugar, beating the whites to stiff peaks. In the chilled bowl with the chilled beaters, beat the cream until soft peaks will hold their shape.

Fold the egg whites into the lemon–egg yolk mixture, then fold in the cream. Pour into the prepared crust and freeze; when firm, cover with plastic wrap and foil.

MAKES 10 TO 14 SERVINGS.

Optional

Decorate each serving with fresh strawberries or fresh blueberries or a whipped cream rosette.

Frozen Orange-Cointreau Squares

Like the Creamy Lemon Dessert Squares above, this dessert can be made into squares, a pie shape, or individual little dessert cups.

¾ cup crushed butter biscuits (petit beurre) or butter cookies

4 teaspoons grated orange zest

2 tablespoons unsalted butter, melted

3 large eggs, separated and at room temperature

½ cup plus ⅓ cup sugar

⅛ teaspoon salt

⅓ cup frozen orange juice concentrate, thawed

2 tablespoons Cointreau liqueur

1 cup heavy cream, well chilled

Chill beaters and a bowl large enough (4-cup volume) to whip the cream. Mash the crumbs and 2 teaspoons of the orange zest together to release the orange flavor. Add the melted butter and blend well. Pat the crumb mixture into the bottom of a 10 × 6-inch glass baking dish or a 9-inch pie plate or 14 to 15 paper-lined muffin cups.

In the top of a double boiler over simmering water, beat the egg yolks until light in color and thick. Gradually beat in the ½ cup sugar, then the salt and the remaining orange zest. Remove from the heat and immediately fold in the orange juice and Cointreau. Cool to room temperature.

With clean beaters, beat the egg whites to soft peaks and gradually add the remaining ⅓ cup sugar, beating the whites to stiff peaks. In the chilled bowl with the chilled beaters, beat the cream until soft peaks will hold their shape.

Fold the egg whites into the orange–egg yolk mixture, then fold in the cream. Pour into the prepared crust and freeze; when firm, cover with plastic wrap and foil.

MAKES 10 TO 14 SERVINGS.

Optional

Decorate each serving with fresh strawberries or an orange segment or a whipped cream rosette.

FROZEN SOUFFLÉS

Frozen Fresh Lemon Soufflé with Raspberry Sauce

Refreshing and rich at once.

12 large egg yolks, at room tem-
    perature
1⅔ cups sugar
⅔ cup fresh lemon juice
4 teaspoons grated lemon zest
3 tablespoons Cointreau liqueur or
    Triple Sec

6 large egg whites, at room tem-
    perature
Pinch of salt
½ cup heavy cream
Raspberry Sauce (recipe below)

Chill a bowl large enough (4-cup volume) to whip the cream. Cut a strip of aluminum foil long enough to wrap around the top of a 5-cup soufflé dish with some overlap. Fold the foil in half lengthwise. Wrap the foil strip around the dish, letting the foil extend 3 inches above the rim. Tie string around the foil collar to hold it in place. Chill the dish.

In the top pan of a double boiler (not over the heat), beat the egg yolks until they are pale and creamy. Gradually beat in the sugar. Add the lemon juice and zest. Place the top pan over the bottom one and bring the water to the simmering point. Beat the yolks until they are thick and very creamy. Remove from the heat and fold in the Cointreau.

With clean beaters, beat the egg whites with the salt until curved peaks will hold their shape. In the chilled bowl, beat the cream only until soft peaks will hold their shape. Fold both the egg whites and cream into the yolk mixture, half of each at a time. Turn into the chilled soufflé dish and freeze until firm, at least 6 hours. Cover with plastic wrap, then foil.

To serve, remove the collar before bringing the soufflé to the table. Serve with the Raspberry Sauce.

MAKES 8 SERVINGS.

Raspberry Sauce
1 (12-ounce) bag individually frozen raspberries, thawed
¼ cup fresh orange juice
2 tablespoons Cointreau liqueur or Triple Sec
½ cup powdered sugar

Puree the berries in a blender or food processor and strain away the seeds. Blend in the remaining ingredients, stirring until the sugar dissolves. Serve chilled or at room temperature.

Frozen Hazelnut Praline Soufflé

The praline may be made any time in advance of making the soufflé.

⅔ cup hazelnuts
⅔ cup plus ½ cup sugar
2 teaspoons unflavored gelatin
7 tablespoons Frangelico liqueur
6 large egg yolks
Pinch of salt

½ teaspoon vanilla extract
3 large egg whites, at room temperature
1½ teaspoons fresh lemon juice
1¾ cups heavy cream
⅓ cup sifted powdered sugar

Preheat the oven to 400° F. Arrange the hazelnuts in a baking pan and bake about 6 minutes, or until the skins begin to crack. Pour the hot nuts onto the center of a clean towel. Fold the end of the towel over the nuts; rub briskly to remove most of the skins. Chop the nuts coarsely. Line the baking pan bottom with foil and butter the foil. In a small heavy skillet or pan, heat ⅔ cup of the sugar over medium heat, stirring constantly, until it melts and caramelizes. Mix in the nuts, then turn the praline out on the buttered foil. Cool completely, then chop coarsely.

Chill a bowl large enough (6-cup volume) to whip the cream. Cut a strip of aluminum foil long enough to wrap around the top of a 1-quart or 5-cup soufflé dish with some overlap. Fold the foil in half lengthwise. Wrap the foil strip around the dish, letting the foil extend 3 inches above the rim. Tie string around the foil collar to hold it in place. Chill the dish.

Combine the gelatin and ¼ cup of the Frangelico in a heatproof cup or small bowl. Place in a pan of a barely simmering water and stir until no gelatin granules remain. Remove from the heat. In the top of a double boiler, combine the egg yolks, the remaining ½ cup sugar, the salt, and vanilla. Whisk or stir slowly over warm (not boiling) water until the mixture is slightly thick, about 10 minutes. Transfer the egg yolk mixture to the bowl of an electric mixer and beat 10 minutes at high speed, until the mixture looks like whipped cream and will hold soft peaks. Gently blend in the gelatin mixture.

Beat the egg whites until frothy. Add the lemon juice and beat only until curved peaks will hold their shape. Fold one third of the whites into the yolks, then fold the yolks into the remaining whites. In the chilled bowl, whip the cream until soft peaks will hold their shape. Beat in the powdered sugar at the end of the beating time. Fold in the remaining 3 tablespoons Frangelico and 3 rounded tablespoons of the praline. Fold the cream into the egg mixture and pour it into the chilled soufflé dish. Freeze at least 5 hours. When frozen, cover with plastic wrap, then foil.

Before serving, sprinkle the soufflé with the remaining praline. Remove the collar.

MAKES 8 SERVINGS.

Frozen Amaretto Soufflé

Butter
½ cup crushed amaretti biscuits
    (optional)
5 large eggs, at room temperature
4 egg yolks, at room temperature
1 cup plus 2½ tablespoons sugar
Pinch of salt

¾ cup Amaretto liqueur
⅛ teaspoon almond extract
2½ cups heavy cream
2 ounces semisweet chocolate,
    grated, or fresh strawberries for
    garnish

Butter a 6-cup soufflé dish. Chill a bowl large enough (6–8-cup volume) to whip the cream. Cut a strip of aluminum foil long enough to wrap around the top of a soufflé dish with some overlap. Fold the foil in half lengthwise. Butter one side of the foil. Wrap the foil strip around the dish, buttered side in, letting the foil extend 3 inches above the rim. Tie string around the foil collar to hold it in place. Sprinkle the bottom and sides of the soufflé dish lightly with the crumbs.

In the top of a double boiler, whisk together the eggs, yolks, sugar, and salt. Whisk or stir slowly over warm (not boiling) water until the mixture is slightly thick, about 10 minutes. Transfer the egg mixture to the bowl of an electric mixer and beat 10 minutes at high speed, until the mixture looks like whipped cream and will hold soft peaks. Fold in the Amaretto and almond extract.

In the chilled bowl, whip the cream until soft peaks will hold their shape. Fold half of the cream into the egg mixture, then fold in the remaining cream. Turn into the prepared dish and freeze at least 6 hours. When firm, cover with plastic wrap, then foil.

To serve, remove the foil collar. Soften the soufflé at room temperature about 12 minutes. Spoon into dishes and sprinkle with chocolate shavings or berries.

MAKES 8 SERVINGS.

Frozen Irish Cream Soufflé

1 (4-ounce) package Baker's
  German Sweet Chocolate
8 egg yolks
6 egg whites, at room temperature
6 tablespoons sugar
1/8 teaspoon cream of tartar

1/3 cup Irish Cream liqueur
1½ cups heavy cream
Crushed English toffee or Toffee
  Candy (page 213) (optional,
  for garnish)

Chill a bowl large enough (4–6-cup volume) to whip the cream. Cut a strip of aluminum foil long enough to wrap around the top of a 6-cup soufflé dish with some overlap. Fold the foil in half lengthwise. Wrap the foil strip around the dish, letting the foil extend 3 inches above the rim. Tie string around the foil collar to hold it in place. Chill the dish.

Melt the chocolate in the covered top of a double boiler over barely simmering water; stir until smooth. Remove from the heat, leaving the chocolate in a warm place or in a bowl of hot water to prevent it from hardening. In the top of a double boiler, combine the 8 egg yolks and 3 tablespoons of the sugar. Whisk or stir slowly over warm (not boiling) water until the mixture is slightly thick, about 10 minutes. Transfer the egg mixture to the bowl of an electric mixer and beat 10 minutes at high speed, until the mixture looks like whipped cream and will hold soft peaks. In a clean bowl and using clean beaters, beat the egg whites with the cream of tartar until soft peaks hold their shape. Gradually add the remaining 3 tablespoons sugar, until the whites are stiff and glossy. Blend the Irish Cream and chocolate together. Fold the chocolate into the egg yolks, fold in one third of the whites, then the remaining whites, half at a time. In the chilled bowl, beat the cream until soft peaks will hold their shape. Fold in the cream half at a time. Spoon into the chilled soufflé dish and freeze. When firm, cover with plastic wrap, then foil.

To serve, remove the foil collar. Garnish with the chopped English toffee if desired.

MAKES 8 TO 10 SERVINGS.

Lighter, Healthier Delights

We are finally beginning to appreciate that *everything* "good for you" doesn't have to seem unpalatable. Spa food has become fashionable, and restaurants are responding to the increasing demand for more healthful foods. My strategy for remaining slender has been never to diet but to live off nourshing yet delicious snacks—usually light snacks. If I routinely had a rich ice cream sundae for lunch, I might harbor great guilt, but I have absolutely no qualms about savoring luscious homemade frozen yogurts flavored with real fruit or juice. These desserts contain minimal sugar and fat and can be made with a food processor or ice cream machine. For this reason I have prepared the Ice Cream for Breakfast recipes or Frozen Protein Slush; they are a nice, light meal.

The tofulatos, great for people with cholesterol or dairy problems, offered a challenge. I wanted something with a delectable taste and texture, but I didn't want to add butterfat. However, frozen tofu does need something to smoth it out, and a little safflower oil and unflavored gelatin lends a creamy smoothness. The high-protein mixture is enhanced by the addition of concentrated fruit juices.

For Popsicle lovers there is a little collection of pure fruit and juice Popsicles. They rate top scores on sultry summer days.

If you're in the mood to cut back on calories drastically, try some of the light sorbets sweetened with aspartame sweetener. These desserts will satisfy your sweet tooth until you can enjoy a big splurge with a clear conscience.

THE EASIEST FRUIT-FLAVORED FROZEN YOGURTS

Natural frozen fruit juice concentrates give these yogurts wonderful fruit flavor without your having to puree fresh fruit. And since the ingredients are easily kept on hand, you can mix up a quick batch anytime. If you find any one too tart, mix in a little sifted powdered sugar while you are processing the cubes.

To Make Frozen Yogurts in an Ice Cream Machine

All the frozen yogurts may be made in an ice cream machine as well as in the food processor. Follow the recipe, but reduce the amount of gelatin called for from 1¾ teaspoons to 1 teaspoon. Chill the mixture and freeze according to the instructions for your ice cream maker.

Pineapple Frozen Yogurt

1¾ teaspoons unflavored gelatin
⅓ cup sugar
1 cup frozen unsweetened pineapple juice concentrate, thawed
2 cups unflavored yogurt

In a very small saucepan, sprinkle the gelatin over ¼ cup water and allow to stand until it softens, about 3 minutes. Cook over low heat until the gelatin granules dissolve. Add the sugar and stir until it dissolves. Whisk or process the pineapple juice and yogurt together until smooth. Blend in the sugar mixture.

Pour the yogurt mixture into divided ice cube trays and freeze solid.

When ready to serve, place half of the frozen cubes in the food processor work bowl and pulse the machine on and off until cubes are evenly chopped to the texture of coarse snow. Then run the machine continuously until the yogurt is slightly paler and creamy, but not thawed. Process the remaining cubes or save them for another time. Serve immediately or freeze several hours.

MAKES ABOUT 2 PINTS.

Orange Juice Frozen Yogurt

1¾ teaspoons unflavored gelatin
½ cup sugar
¼ cup frozen orange juice concentrate, thawed
2 cups unflavored yogurt

In a very small saucepan, sprinkle the gelatin over ¼ cup water and allow to stand until it softens, about 3 minutes. Cook over low heat until the gelatin granules dissolve. Add the sugar and stir until it dissolves. Whisk or process the orange juice and yogurt together until smooth. Blend in the sugar mixture.

Pour the yogurt mixture into divided ice cube trays and freeze solid.

When ready to serve, place half of the frozen cubes in the food processor work bowl and pulse the machine on and off until the cubes are evenly chopped to the texture of coarse snow. Then run the machine continuously until the yogurt is slightly paler and creamy, but not thawed. Process the remaining cubes or save them for another time. Serve immediately or freeze several hours.

MAKES ABOUT 2 PINTS.

Fruit and Berry Frozen Yogurt

1¾ teaspoons unflavored gelatin
½ cup sugar
1 cup frozen fruit and berry juice concentrate, thawed
2 cups unflavored yogurt

In a very small saucepan, sprinkle the gelatin over ¼ cup water and allow to stand until it softens, about 3 minutes. Cook over low heat until the gelatin granules dissolve. Add the sugar and stir until it dissolves. Whisk or process the juice concentrate and yogurt together until smooth. Blend in the sugar mixture.

Pour the yogurt mixture into divided ice cube trays and freeze solid.

When ready to serve, place half of the frozen cubes in the food processor work bowl and pulse the machine on and off until the cubes are evenly chopped to the texture of coarse snow. Then run the machine continuously until the yogurt is slightly paler and creamy, but not thawed. Process the remaining cubes or save them for another time. Serve immediately or freeze several hours.

MAKES ABOUT 2 PINTS.

Apple-Cinnamon Frozen Yogurt

1¾ teaspoons unflavored gelatin
3½ tablespoons sugar
¼ teaspoon ground cinnamon
¾ cup frozen unsweetened apple juice concentrate, thawed
2 cups unflavored yogurt

In a very small saucepan, sprinkle the gelatin over ¼ cup water and allow to stand until it softens, about 3 minutes. Cook over low heat until the gelatin granules dissolve. Add the sugar and cinnamon and stir until the sugar dissolves. Whisk or process the apple juice and yogurt together until smooth. Blend in the sugar mixture.

Pour the yogurt mixture into divided ice cube trays and freeze solid.

When ready to serve, place half of the frozen cubes in the food processor work bowl and pulse the machine on and off until the cubes are evenly chopped to the texture of coarse snow. Then run the machine continuously until the yogurt is slightly paler and creamy, but not thawed. Process the remaining cubes or save them for another time. Serve immediately or freeze several hours.

MAKES ABOUT 2 PINTS.

Grape Frozen Yogurt

1¾ teaspoons unflavored gelatin
3½ tablespoons sugar
⅔ cup frozen unsweetened grape
  juice concentrate, thawed
2 cups unflavored yogurt

In a very small saucepan, sprinkle the gelatin over ¼ cup water and allow to stand until it softens, about 3 minutes. Cook over low heat until the gelatin granules dissolve. Add the sugar and stir until it dissolves. Whisk or process the grape juice and yogurt together until smooth. Blend in the sugar mixture.

Pour the yogurt mixture into divided ice cube trays and freeze solid.

When ready to serve, place half of the frozen cubes in the food processor work bowl and pulse the machine on and off until the cubes are evenly chopped to the texture of coarse snow. Then run the machine continuously until the yogurt is slightly paler and creamy, but not thawed. Process the remaining cubes or save them for another time. Serve immediately or freeze several hours.

MAKES ABOUT 2 PINTS.

FRESH FRUIT FROZEN YOGURTS

Fresh Lemon Frozen Yogurt

1¾ teaspoons unflavored gelatin
½ cup plus 2 tablespoons sugar
⅓ cup plus 2 teaspoons light corn syrup
¾ cup fresh lemon juice
2 cups unflavored yogurt

In a very small saucepan, sprinkle the gelatin over ¼ cup water and allow to stand until it softens, about 3 minutes. Cook over low heat until the gelatin granules dissolve. Add the sugar and corn syrup and stir until the sugar dissolves. Remove from the heat. Whisk or process the lemon juice and yogurt together until smooth. Blend in the sugar mixture.

Pour the yogurt mixture into divided ice cube trays and freeze solid.

When ready to serve, place half of the frozen cubes in the food processor work bowl and pulse the machine on and off until the cubes are evenly chopped to the texture of coarse snow. Then run the machine continuously until the yogurt is slightly paler and creamy, but not thawed. Process the remaining cubes or save them for another time. Serve immediately or freeze several hours.

MAKES ABOUT 2 PINTS.

Creamy Banana Frozen Yogurt

3 large ripe bananas, peeled
1 cup plus 2 tablespoons unflavored yogurt
2 tablespoons sugar (optional)

Slice the bananas into 1-inch-thick slices. Arrange them on an plate and wrap them in foil or in a plastic freezing bag. Freeze solid, preferably overnight.

When ready to serve, place the frozen banana slices in the food processor work bowl with ½ cup of the yogurt and the sugar. Pulse the machine on and off until the mixture is the texture of coarse snow. Add the remaining yogurt and pulse the machine until the yogurt is evenly incorporated, then process until the mixture is creamy but still frozen. Serve immediately or freeze several hours.

MAKES ABOUT 3½ CUPS.

Fruit and Berry Tofulato

2½ teaspoons unflavored gelatin
⅛ teaspoon salt
½ cup sugar
1¼ cups frozen fruit and berry juice concentrate, thawed

10 ounces soft tofu or silken tofu, drained
¼ cup safflower oil
3 tablespoons fresh lemon juice
½ teaspoon vanilla extract

In a small saucepan, sprinkle the gelatin over ¾ cup water and allow to sit until it softens, about 3 minutes. Cook the mixture over very low heat until no gelatin granules remain. Mix in the salt and sugar and cook over low heat, stirring to dissolve the sugar. Remove from the heat.

In a blender or food processor, combine the juice, tofu, oil, lemon juice, vanilla, and ¾ cup water and process until very smooth. Mix in the gelatin mixture.

Freeze in a 1-quart or larger-capacity ice cream maker according to the manufacturer's directions.

MAKES ABOUT 2 PINTS.

Lemonade Tofulato

2½ teaspoons unflavored gelatin
⅛ teaspoon salt
¼ cup sugar
1 cup plus 1 tablespoon frozen
   lemonade concentrate, thawed

10 ounces soft tofu or silken tofu,
   drained
¼ cup safflower oil

In a small saucepan, sprinkle the gelatin over ¾ cup water and allow to sit until it softens, about 3 minutes. Cook the mixture over very low heat until no gelatin granules remain. Mix in the salt and sugar and cook over low heat, stirring to dissolve the sugar. Remove from the heat.

In a blender or food processor, combine the lemonade concentrate, tofu, oil, and ¾ cup water and process until very smooth. Mix in the gelatin mixture.

Freeze in a 1-quart or larger-capacity ice cream maker according to the manufacturer's directions.

MAKES ABOUT 2 PINTS.

Orange Juice Tofulato

2½ teaspoons unflavored gelatin
⅛ teaspoon salt
¾ cup sugar
1 cup plus 1 tablespoon frozen orange juice concentrate, thawed

10 ounces soft tofu or silken tofu,
   drained
¼ cup safflower oil
4 tablespoons fresh lemon juice

In a small saucepan, sprinkle the gelatin over ¾ cup water and allow to sit until it softens, about 3 minutes. Cook the mixture over very low heat until no gelatin granules remain. Mix in the salt and sugar and cook over low heat, stirring to dissolve the sugar. Remove from the heat.

In a blender or food processor, combine the juice, tofu, oil, lemon juice, and ¾ cup water and process until very smooth. Mix in the gelatin mixture.

Freeze in a 1-quart or larger-capacity ice cream maker according to the manufacturer's directions.

MAKES ABOUT 2 PINTS.

Concord Grape Tofulato

2½ teaspoons unflavored gelatin
⅛ teaspoon salt
½ cup sugar
1¼ cups frozen unsweetened
  grape juice concentrate, thawed

10 ounces soft tofu or silken tofu,
  drained
¼ cup safflower oil
3 tablespoons fresh lemon juice

In a small saucepan, sprinkle the gelatin over ¾ cup water and allow to sit until it softens, about 3 minutes. Cook the mixture over very low heat until no gelatin granules remain. Mix in the salt and sugar and cook over low heat, stirring to dissolve the sugar. Remove from the heat.

In a blender or food processor, combine the juice, tofu, oil, lemon juice, and ¾ cup water and process until very smooth. Mix in the gelatin mixture.

Freeze in a 1-quart or larger-capacity ice cream maker according to the manufacturer's directions.

MAKES ABOUT 2 PINTS.

Boysenberry Tofulato

2¼ teaspoons unflavored gelatin
⅛ teaspoon salt
¾ cup sugar
2½ cups (12 ounces) fresh or frozen unsweetened boysenberries,
  thawed

10 ounces soft tofu or silken tofu,
  drained
¼ cup safflower oil
¾ teaspoon vanilla extract

In a small saucepan, sprinkle the gelatin over ¾ cup water and allow to sit until it softens, about 3 minutes. Cook the mixture over very low heat until no gelatin granules remain. Add the salt and sugar and cook over low heat, stirring until they are dissolved. Remove from the heat.

In a blender or food processor, puree the berries and strain them to remove the seeds. Save the seeds as you strain away the juice. Mix the seeds with ½ cup water and strain again. Combine the strained berries and water, tofu, oil, and vanilla, and process until very smooth. Blend in the gelatin mixture.

Freeze in a 1½-quart or larger-capacity ice cream maker according to the manufacturer's directions. Or if your ice cream freezer is small, split the mixture into 2 batches. Freeze one and chill the other until you are ready to freeze it.

MAKES ABOUT 2½ PINTS.

Honey-Banana Tofulato

2 teaspoons unflavored gelatin
⅛ teaspoon salt
⅔ cup mild honey
3 medium very ripe bananas
10 ounces soft tofu or silken tofu,
    drained

¼ cup safflower oil
3 tablespoons fresh lemon juice
1 teaspoon vanilla extract

In a small saucepan, sprinkle the gelatin over ½ cup water and allow to sit until it softens, about 3 minutes. Cook the mixture over very low heat until no gelatin granules remain. Stir in the salt and honey until the mixture is smooth. Remove from the heat.

In a blender or food processor, puree the bananas. Add the tofu, oil, lemon juice, vanilla, and 1 cup water and process until very smooth. Blend in the gelatin mixture.

Freeze in a 1½-quart or larger-capacity ice cream maker according to the manufacturer's directions. Or if your ice cream freezer is small, split the mixture into 2 batches. Freeze one and chill the other until you are ready to freeze it.

MAKES ABOUT 3 PINTS.

Variations

HONEY-BANANA-NUT TOFULATO

When the tofulato is almost completely frozen, stir in ¾ cup chopped walnuts.

HONEY–BANANA–CHOCOLATE CHIP TOFULATO

When the tofulato is almost completely frozen, stir in ¾ cup chopped semisweet chocolate or semisweet mini chocolate morsels.

Fresh Pineapple Tofulato

2½ teaspoons unflavored gelatin
⅛ teaspoon salt
¾ cup sugar
2⅔ cups finely diced fresh
    pineapple

10 ounces soft tofu or silken tofu,
    drained
¼ cup safflower oil
¾ teaspoon vanilla extract
3½ tablespoons fresh lemon juice

In a small saucepan, sprinkle the gelatin over ½ cup water and allow to sit until it softens, about 3 minutes. Cook the mixture over very low heat until no gelatin granules remain. Add the salt and sugar and cook over low heat, stirring until they are dissolved. Remove from the heat.

In a blender or food processor, puree the pineapple until smooth. Combine the pineapple, tofu, oil, vanilla, lemon juice, and ½ cup water and process until very smooth. Blend in the gelatin mixture.

Freeze in a 1½-quart or larger-capacity ice cream maker according to the manufacturer's directions. Or if your ice cream freezer is small, split the mixture into 2 batches. Freeze one and chill the other until you are ready to freeze it.

MAKES ABOUT 3 PINTS.

Mocha-Almond Tofulato

2¼ teaspoons unflavored gelatin
⅛ teaspoon salt
¾ teaspoon instant coffee granules
¾ cup sugar
2 tablespoons unsweetened cocoa
    powder
10 ounces soft tofu or silken tofu,
    drained

⅔ cup unflavored yogurt
¼ cup safflower oil
¼ teaspoon almond extract
1¼ teaspoons vanilla extract
¾ cup chopped unsalted almonds

In a small saucepan, sprinkle the gelatin over ¾ cup water and allow to sit until it softens, about 3 minutes. Cook the mixture over very low heat until no gelatin granules remain. Stir in the salt and coffee granules and stir to dissolve. Mix the sugar and cocoa together and stir into the gelatin mixture. Cook over low heat, stirring to dissolve the sugar. Remove from the heat.

In a blender or food processor, combine the tofu, yogurt, oil, almond extract, vanilla, and ¾ cup water and process until very smooth. Mix in the gelatin mixture.

Freeze in a 1½-quart or larger-capacity ice cream maker according to the manufacturer's directions. Or if your ice cream freezer is small, split the mixture into 2 batches. Freeze one and chill the other until you are ready to freeze it. Stir in the almonds at the very end of the freezing process.

MAKES ABOUT 3 PINTS.

Maple-Walnut Tofulato

2½ teaspoons unflavored gelatin
⅛ teaspoon salt
10 ounces soft tofu or silken tofu, drained
¼ cup safflower oil
1 cup pure maple syrup
1½ teaspoons vanilla extract
¾ cup chopped walnuts

In a small saucepan, sprinkle the gelatin over ½ cup water and allow to sit until it softens, about 3 minutes. Cook the mixture over very low heat until no gelatin granules remain. Stir in the salt and remove from the heat.

In a blender or food processor, combine the tofu, oil, syrup, vanilla, and 1 cup water and process until very smooth. Mix in the gelatin.

Freeze in a 1-quart or larger-capacity ice cream maker according to the manufacturer's directions. Mix in the walnuts at the very end of the freezing process.

MAKES ABOUT 2 PINTS.

Ice Cream for Breakfast

Yes, you can eat this delicious concoction of milk, eggs, and orange juice for a nourishing breakfast. And it has only 140 calories per serving!

3 large eggs
½ cup honey or 9 tablespoons sugar
½ cup nonfat dry milk
3 tablespoons frozen orange juice concentrate, thawed
⅔ cup evaporated milk
2 teaspoons fresh lemon juice

Separate 2 of the eggs. In a heavy medium saucepan, combine the 2 egg yolks, the remaining whole egg, ½ cup water, and 6 tablespoons honey or 6 tablespoons sugar. If you are using honey, warm it slightly so it will blend smoothly into the eggs. Sprinkle the dry milk into the mixture and blend it in thoroughly. Cook about 5 minutes over very low heat, stirring until the mixture thickens and will coat the back of a spoon. A path will remain on the back of a spoon when drawn across the mixture.

Remove from the heat, place in a mixing bowl, and beat in the orange juice concentrate. Chill the mixture.

Place the evaporated milk in a mixing bowl in the freezer, along with your electric mixer beaters, until ice crystals begin to form around the edge of the milk, about 50 minutes. Beat the milk, gradually adding the lemon juice, until it is the consistency of whipped cream. Clean the beaters and beat the 2 egg whites until curved peaks will hold their shape. Beat while gradually adding the remaining 2 tablespoons honey or 3 tablespoons sugar until the eggs are stiff and glossy. Fold the milk into the chilled custard mixture. Fold in the egg whites, one third at a time. Freeze at least 4 hours,* folding over the mixture 2 or 3 times every hour. Store in a covered bowl.

MAKES 8 SERVINGS.

Vanilla Ice Cream Breakfast

On a summer morning, ice cream, perhaps topped with fresh fruit, is a breakfast everyone looks forward to. So much more interesting than cereal, and only 155 calories a serving.

½ cup nonfat dry milk	*½ cup sugar*
1 tablespoon flour	*1½ teaspoons vanilla extract*
1⅓ cups low-fat milk	*⅔ cup evaporated milk*
3 large eggs	

In a heavy saucepan, combine the dry milk and flour; mix well. Blend in the low-fat milk and 1 whole egg. Separate the remaining eggs and add the yolks and ¼ cup of the sugar to the milk mixture, blending them in well. Cook about 6 minutes over low heat, stirring until the mixture

---

* Or freeze according to the instructions for your ice cream maker. Transfer to freezer containers for storage.

thickens and will coat the back of a spoon. A path will remain on the back of the spoon when drawn across the mixture.

Remove from the heat, place in a mixing bowl, and beat in the vanilla. Chill the mixture.

Place the evaporated milk in a mixing bowl in the freezer, along with your electric mixer beaters, until ice crystals begin to form around the edge of the milk, about 50 minutes. Beat the milk until it is the consistency of whipped cream. Clean the beaters and beat the 2 egg whites until curved peaks will hold their shape. Beat while gradually adding the remaining ¼ cup sugar until the eggs are stiff and glossy. Fold the milk into the chilled custard mixture. Fold in the egg whites, one third at a time. Freeze at least 4 hours,★ folding over the mixture several times every hour. Store in a covered bowl.

MAKES 8 SERVINGS.

Frozen Protein Smoothie

Still-Frozen Method

1 tablespoon unflavored gelatin
¾ cup low-fat or whole milk
¾ cup nonfat dry milk
½ cup sugar or 7 tablespoons honey

2 cups fresh or frozen unsweet-ened strawberries
½ cup heavy cream
2 egg whites

In a small saucepan, sprinkle the gelatin over ⅓ cup milk; allow to soften for about 5 minutes. Warm the gelatin-milk mixture over very low heat, stirring until no granules remain. Remove from the heat. Blend in the remaining milk, dry milk, and sugar or honey. Puree the berries in a blender or food processor. You should have 1 cup puree. Blend in the cream and the gelatin-milk mixture. Freeze in a mixing bowl until almost solid, about 3 hours. Cut into chunks, add the egg whites, and beat until fluffy but not completely thawed. Place in 1-quart or 2-pint containers and freeze at least 4 hours. Allow to soften at room temperature about 8 minutes before serving.

MAKES 6 TO 8 SERVINGS.

★ Or freeze according to the instructions for your ice cream maker. Transfer to freezer containers for storage.

To Make the Smoothie in an Ice Cream Maker

After mixing the gelatin mixture into the berry puree, chill the mixture thoroughly. Beat the egg whites until soft peaks hold their shape. Fold one third of the whites into the berry mixture. Fold the berry mixture into the whites. Freeze according to the directions given for your ice cream maker.

Frozen Berries and Cottage Cheese

Another good breakfast for frozen-dessert lovers.

*¼ cup frozen apple juice concen-
   trate, thawed
4 teaspoons unflavored gelatin
1½ cups fresh or individually
   frozen boysenberries
6 tablespoons sugar*

*⅔ cup cottage cheese
¼ cup heavy cream
½ teaspoon vanilla extract
⅔ cup nonfat dry milk
1 tablespoon fresh lemon juice*

Place the apple juice in a very small saucepan or metal cup and sprinkle the gelatin over it. Allow to soften about 3 minutes. Cook over very low heat until no gelatin granules remain. Puree the berries and strain away the seeds. Combine the sugar, cottage cheese, cream, and vanilla in a blender or food processor and blend until the cottage cheese is smooth. Blend in the berry puree and gelatin mixture. Chill thoroughly.

In a mixer bowl, mix ⅔ cup water and the dry milk together until they are well blended and the milk is dissolved. Freeze about 50 minutes until ice crystals form around the edge of the bowl. Chill the beaters also. Beat the milk, gradually adding the lemon juice, until it is the consistency of whipped cream. Fold one third of the whipped milk into the berry mixture. Fold the berry mixture into the remaining milk. Pour into 2 (1-pint) containers and freeze 4 hours or more.

MAKES 1 QUART, OR 6 TO 8 SERVINGS.

My Own Low-Calorie Ice Cream

This is definitely a compromise. It is not the lowest-fat ice cream but much lower than other good-quality ice cream. I mix sugar with aspartame to get the best flavor with the fewest calories. Of course, you could cut back on the cream and sugar, but then the product would taste like "diet" ice cream.

2 teaspoons unflavored gelatin
4 cups low-fat milk
6 tablespoons nonfat dry milk
¼ cup light corn syrup

¼ cup sugar
⅛ teaspoon salt
2 large eggs, lightly beaten
4½ teaspoons vanilla extract

In a small metal cup or tiny pan, sprinkle the gelatin over ¼ cup water and allow to soften 3 minutes. Heat over very low heat until no gelatin granules remain. Set aside. In a heavy medium pan, combine the milk, dry milk, corn syrup, sugar, and salt. Heat to the simmering point, stirring until the sugar dissolves. Stir about 1 cup of the hot milk into the eggs, then add the egg-milk mixture to the pan. Cook, stirring, until the mixture thickens slightly and will lightly coat the back of a wooden spoon without running. Blend in the gelatin well. Blend in the vanilla. Chill, then freeze according to the directions given for your ice cream maker.

MAKES SLIGHTLY OVER 1 QUART.

Nonfat Ice Cream

For cholesterol watchers.

4 cups evaporated nonfat milk
⅓ cup sugar
⅓ cup light corn syrup
1 tablespoon vanilla extract

In a mixing bowl, chill 2 cups of the milk in the freezer until crystals begin to form around the edge, about 45 minutes. Also chill the mixer beaters. Place the remaining 2 cups milk in a saucepan and bring to the simmering point. Sprinkle in the sugar and cook, stirring, until it is dissolved. Stir in the corn syrup and remove from the heat. Stir in the vanilla and chill thoroughly.

Whip the chilled milk until soft peaks will hold their shape. Blend the whipped milk and sweetened milk together and freeze according to the directions given for your ice cream maker.

MAKES ABOUT 2 PINTS.

Low-Calorie Berry Semifreddo

Italians often like their iced desserts semifrozen. This brings out all the subtle flavors of the dessert that are sometimes lost when iced desserts are frozen solid. The corn syrup is what helps to keep the dessert slightly supple.

2 (12-ounce) bags individually frozen raspberries, thawed
3 teaspoons unflavored gelatin
¼ cup light corn syrup

1½ teaspoons fresh lemon juice
4 tablespoons fresh orange juice
7 (1-gram) packets aspartame sweetener

Puree the raspberries in a blender or food processor. Strain to remove the seeds. Pour the seeds and 1¼ cups water into a dish, mix well, and strain ½ cup of the water into a small pan and the remaining water into the berry puree. Sprinkle the gelatin over the ½ cup water and allow to soften 3 minutes. Heat the water and stir over very low heat until no gelatin granules remain. Stir in the corn syrup until it dissolves. Pour the gelatin mixture into the berry puree. Mix in the lemon and orange juice and aspartame. Freeze following the directions for your ice cream maker.

Eat immediately, or freeze and then soften in the refrigerator about 1 hour before serving.

MAKES ABOUT 2 PINTS.

Low-Calorie Pink Grapefruit Granita

2½ teaspoons unflavored gelatin
2 tablespoons light corn syrup
3 cups freshly squeezed pink grapefruit juice, strained

1 tablespoon very finely grated grapefruit zest
8 (1-gram) packets aspartame sweetener

Measure ¾ cup water and place ⅓ cup of it in a small pan. Sprinkle the gelatin over it and allow to soften about 3 minutes. Cook over very low heat, stirring, until the gelatin granules dissolve. Stir in the corn syrup thoroughly. Remove from the heat. Combine the juice, remaining water, gelatin mixture, grapefruit zest, and aspartame. Freeze according to the directions given for your ice cream maker.

MAKES ABOUT 1 QUART.

Low-Calorie Fresh Lime Sorbet

2½ teaspoons unflavored gelatin
4 tablespoons light corn syrup
¾ cup fresh lime juice
2 tablespoons fresh lemon juice

1 tablespoon finely grated lime zest
14 (1-gram) packets aspartame sweetener, or more to taste
1 egg white

Measure 2¾ cups water and place ⅓ cup of it in a small pan. Sprinkle the gelatin over it and allow to soften about 3 minutes. Cook over very low heat, stirring, until the gelatin granules dissolve. Stir in the corn syrup until it dissolves. Remove from the heat. Combine the lime and lemon juice, remaining water, gelatin mixture, lime zest, aspartame and egg white. Freeze following the directions for your ice cream maker. Allow to soften about 15 minutes in the refrigerator before serving.

MAKES ABOUT 1 QUART.

Pineapple-Yogurt Freeze

2 egg whites, at room temperature
⅓ cup sugar
1 cup unflavored yogurt
1 (20-ounce) can crushed pineapple in juice, drained

Beat the egg whites until soft peaks form. Very gradually add the sugar, continuing to beat until the whites are stiff and glossy. Blend the yogurt and pineapple. Fold the yogurt mixture into the egg whites. Freeze at least 4 hours.

MAKES ABOUT 1 QUART.

FUNSICLES

Real fruit and real fruit juice frozen into delicious bars. Some are creamy, some chunky with fruit, and some pure fruit juice.

Grapejuicesicles

½ teaspoon unflavored gelatin
1 cup frozen sweetened grape juice concentrate, thawed
1 tablespoon fresh lemon juice

Place 1½ cups water in a small saucepan and sprinkle the gelatin over it. Allow to soften about 3 minutes. Cook over very low heat, stirring, until no granules remain. Remove from the heat. Stir in the grape and lemon juices. Pour into 6 (3-ounce) paper cups or Popsicle molds and freeze until slushy. Insert a Popsicle stick or the handle of a plastic spoon into each cup. Freeze solid.

MAKES 6 FROZEN POPS.

Apple-Cranberrysicles

¾ teaspoon unflavored gelatin
½ cup frozen unsweetened apple juice concentrate, thawed
½ cup frozen cranberry juice cocktail concentrate, thawed

Place ¾ cup water in a small saucepan and sprinkle the gelatin over it. Allow to soften about 3 minutes. Cook over very low heat, stirring, until no granules remain. Stir in the juices. Pour into 5 (3-ounce) paper cups or Popsicle molds and freeze until slushy. Insert a Popsicle stick or the handle of a plastic spoon into each cup. Freeze solid.

MAKES 5 FROZEN POPS.

Fresh Orangesicles

1½ teaspoons unflavored gelatin
⅓ cup sugar
2 cups freshly squeezed orange juice
2 tablespoons fresh lemon juice

Place ¼ cup water in a small saucepan and sprinkle the gelatin over it. Allow to soften about 3 minutes. Cook over very low heat, stirring, until no granules remain. Stir in the sugar until it is dissolved. Remove from the heat. Stir in the juices. Pour into 6 (3-ounce) paper cups or Popsicle molds and freeze until slushy. Insert a Popsicle stick or the handle of a plastic spoon into each cup. Freeze solid.

MAKES 6 FROZEN POPS.

Quick Orangesicles

1 (6-ounce) can frozen orange juice concentrate, thawed
3½ tablespoons sugar
1 egg white

Combine juice, 1⅓ cups water, and the sugar and stir until the sugar dissolves. Blend in the egg white. Pour into 6 (3-ounce) paper cups or Popsicle molds and freeze until slushy. Insert a Popsicle stick or the handle of a plastic spoon into each cup. Freeze solid.

MAKES 6 FROZEN POPS.

Strawberry Chunk Pops

Smooth frozen strawberry nectar with little chunks of fresh berries.

¾ teaspoon unflavored gelatin
2 tablespoons sugar
1 (12-ounce) can strawberry
    nectar

2 teaspoons fresh lemon juice
1 cup fresh or frozen unsweetened
    strawberries, chopped the size
    of peanuts

Place 3 tablespoons water in a small saucepan and sprinkle the gelatin over it. Allow to soften about 3 minutes. Cook over very low heat, stirring, until no granules remain. Stir in the sugar until it is dissolved. Remove from the heat. Combine the gelatin with the nectar, lemon juice, and strawberries. Pour into 8 or 9 (3-ounce) paper cups or Popsicle molds and freeze until slushy. Insert a Popsicle stick or the handle of a plastic spoon into each cup. Freeze solid.

MAKES 8 OR 9 FROZEN POPS.

Fruity Cantaloupe Pops

1¼ teaspoons unflavored gelatin
3 tablespoons sugar
⅔ cup frozen fruit and berry juice concentrate, thawed
1 cup finely diced cantaloupe

Place ½ cup water in a small saucepan and sprinkle the gelatin over it. Allow to soften about 3 minutes. Cook over very low heat, stirring, until no granules remain. Stir in the sugar until it is dissolved. Remove from the heat. Stir in the juice. Puree the cantaloupe in a blender or food processor and blend it into the juice mixture. Pour into 6 (3-ounce) paper cups or Popsicle molds and freeze until slushy. Insert a Popsicle stick or the handle of a plastic spoon into each cup. Freeze solid.

MAKES 6 FROZEN POPS.

Lemonade Watermelon Pops

1½ teaspoons unflavored gelatin
5 tablespoons sugar
½ cup frozen lemonade concentrate, thawed
2 cups finely diced watermelon, with all seeds removed

Place 1 cup water in a small saucepan and sprinkle the gelatin over it. Allow to soften about 3 minutes. Cook over very low heat, stirring, until no granules remain. Stir in the sugar until it is dissolved. Remove from the heat. Stir in the lemonade. Puree the watermelon in a blender or food processor and blend it with the juice mixture. Pour into 8 or 9 (3-ounce) paper cups or Popsicle molds and freeze until slushy. Insert a Popsicle stick or the handle of a plastic spoon into each cup. Freeze solid.

MAKES 8 OR 9 FROZEN POPS.

Peachycreamsicles

1 cup heavy cream
1 (16-ounce) can peach slices in juice
5 tablespoons sugar or honey
1 tablespoon fresh lemon juice

Place the cream in a blender or food processor and process until it begins to thicken. Add the remaining ingredients and blend until smooth.

Pour into 9 or 10 (3-ounce) paper cups or Popsicle molds and freeze until slushy. Insert a Popsicle stick or the handle of a plastic spoon into each cup. Freeze solid.

MAKES 9 TO 10 FROZEN POPS.

Apricot Yogurt Pops

1 (16-ounce) can pitted apricots, drained
1½ cups unflavored yogurt
½ cup sugar
Few drops almond extract (optional)

Blend all the ingredients until smooth in a blender or food processor.

Pour into 10 or 12 (3-ounce) paper cups or Popsicle molds and freeze until slushy. Insert a Popsicle stick or the handle of a plastic spoon into each cup. Freeze solid.

MAKES 10 TO 12 FROZEN POPS.

Peanutty Yogurt Pops

⅓ cup honey
¾ cup creamy peanut butter
1 cup unflavored yogurt
1 cup milk
½ teaspoon vanilla extract

In a medium pan over low heat, warm the honey until it liquefies. Blend in the peanut butter until smooth. Remove from the heat and blend in the remaining ingredients.

Pour into 9 (3-ounce) paper cups or muffin tins lined with paper liners. Freeze until the mixture firms up. Insert a Popsicle stick or the handle of a plastic spoon into each cup. Freeze solid.

MAKES 9 FROZEN POPS.

Sauces, Garnishes, Additions

Good Hot Fudge Sauce

An excellent basic sauce. Keeps refrigerated up to 6 weeks. Stir it up before each use.

6 ounces good-quality semisweet chocolate
½ cup unsalted butter
3 cups sugar
⅛ teaspoon salt
1 (12-ounce) can evaporated milk

In the top of a double boiler over simmering water, melt the chocolate and butter together. Stir in the sugar a little at a time, stirring until the sugar dissolves. Blend in the salt and gradually blend in the milk. Remove from the heat.

Reheat in a double boiler. Serve warm.

MAKES ABOUT 1 QUART.

Clingy Hot Fudge Sauce

This sauce becomes like chewy fudge when it coats the ice cream.

4 ounces bittersweet or semisweet
   chocolate, chopped
¼ cup unsalted butter, at room
   temperature

⅓ cup sugar
Pinch of salt
⅓ cup light corn syrup
1 teaspoon vanilla extract

In a heavy small pan over very low heat, melt the chocolate in ⅔ cup water, stirring constantly. Remove from the heat and stir in the butter, sugar, salt, and corn syrup. Return to the heat and cook at the simmering point, without stirring, 10 to 15 minutes, until the sauce thickens. Transfer to a bowl and stir in the vanilla. Cool slightly and serve warm.

MAKES ABOUT 1⅓ CUPS.

Semisweet Chocolate Rum Sauce

8 ounces semisweet chocolate
½ cup unsalted butter
⅔ cup half-and-half
1½ tablespoons dark rum

In a small pan within another pan of water or in the top of a double boiler, melt the chocolate. Stir in the butter, 1 tablespoon at a time, until it is smoothly blended in. Stir in the half-and-half and rum until smoothly blended in. Serve at room temperature. Store refrigerated.

MAKES ABOUT 1½ CUPS.

Bittersweet Chocolate Sauce

¼ cup unsalted butter
2 ounces unsweetened chocolate,
   chopped
⅓ cup sugar

Pinch of salt
⅔ cup heavy cream
¾ teaspoon vanilla extract

In a heavy medium saucepan, combine the butter and chocolate and cook over very low heat, stirring occasionally, until the chocolate is melted and the mixture is smooth. Gradually stir in the sugar, salt, and cream. Cook until the sugar is dissolved. Remove from the heat and stir in the vanilla. The sauce may be served warm or chilled.
MAKES 1½ CUPS.

Chocolate Liqueur Sauce

Change the flavor of this semisweet sauce by adding a liqueur that is compatible with the ice cream you are serving.

3 ounces unsweetened chocolate
1 cup half-and-half
1 cup sugar
1½ tablespoons unsalted butter
2 tablespoons light corn syrup

About 2 tablespoons sweet liqueur
   such as Kahlúa, Chambord,
   Grand Marnier, Amaretto,
   Cassis, or Frangelico

In a heavy small pan over low heat, combine the chocolate and half-and-half. Cook, stirring occasionally, over low heat until the chocolate is melted and the mixture is completely smooth. Stir in the sugar and cook until it dissolves. Stir in the butter. Remove from the heat and stir in the corn syrup and liqueur. Serve at room temperature. Store refrigerated.
MAKES ABOUT 1⅔ CUPS.

Cocoa Fudge Sauce

1 cup heavy cream
6 tablespoons unsalted butter, at
   room temperature
1 cup light brown sugar, packed

⅔ cup sugar
¾ cup Dutch process cocoa powder, sifted
Pinch of salt
1 teaspoon vanilla extract

In a heavy saucepan over medium heat, stir the cream and butter together until the butter is melted and blended into the cream. Blend the sugars, cocoa, and salt together well. Whisk the sugar mixture into the cream and blend it in well. Cook, stirring, over low heat 3 to 4 minutes, until the sauce is glossy. Remove from the heat and pour into a bowl. Stir in the vanilla. Serve warm. Store refrigerated. Reheat over hot water to serve.

MAKES ABOUT 1⅓ CUPS.

Chocolate Marshmallow Sauce

4 ounces unsweetened chocolate, chopped
1½ cups powdered sugar
1 cup marshmallow cream
½ teaspoon vanilla extract

Combine the chocolate, sugar, and ⅔ cup hot water in a heavy saucepan. Cook over low heat, stirring occasionally, until the chocolate is melted and the sauce is smooth. Remove from the heat and fold in the marshmallow cream, one third at a time. Stir in the vanilla. Serve slightly warm.

MAKES 1¾ CUPS.

Praline Ice Cream Sauce

1½ cups golden or light brown
*   sugar, packed*
½ cup granulated sugar
1 cup buttermilk
½ cup unsalted butter

3 tablespoons light corn syrup
1 teaspoon baking soda
1 teaspoon vanilla extract
½ cup coarsely chopped pecans

Combine the sugars, buttermilk, butter, syrup, and baking soda in a heavy saucepan. Bring to the boiling point, then reduce the heat and simmer for 10 minutes, stirring occasionally. Remove from the heat and stir in the vanilla and nuts. Cool completely before serving. The sauce will thicken.

MAKES 1¾ CUPS.

Velvety Mocha Sauce

6 ounces milk chocolate
1 ounce semisweet or bittersweet
chocolate
3 tablespoons unsalted butter
⅓ cup heavy cream

¼ cup milk
3½ teaspoons instant coffee
granules
2 tablespoons sugar

In a small pan within a larger pan of water or in the top of a double boiler over simmering water, melt the chocolates together. Whisk in the butter, 1 tablespoon at a time, until smoothly incorporated. Blend in the cream and remove from the heat. In a tiny pan or metal cup, heat the milk to boiling. Stir in the coffee and sugar until they are dissolved. Blend into the chocolate mixture. Serve the sauce warm. The sauce may be reheated in a double boiler.

MAKES ABOUT 1⅔ CUPS.

Classic Caramel Sauce

1½ cups sugar
⅔ cup boiling water
3 tablespoons unsalted butter
Small pinch of salt
2 tablespoons heavy cream

In a very heavy saucepan, stir the sugar over medium heat until it dissolves into a syrup and is light amber-colored. Remove from the heat. Stirring constantly, and standing well away from the pan, pour in boiling water all at once. Stir over medium heat until the mixture is smooth and is boiling. Boil until you have a light syrup. Stir in the butter, salt, and cream and continue to stir and cook until the sauce is smooth. Plunge the bottom of the pan into a sink or bowl containing cold water until it has cooled. Pour into a bowl. Serve warm or cooled.

MAKES ABOUT 1⅓ CUPS.

Caramel Butter–Rum Sauce

1½ cups light brown sugar, packed
1 tablespoon cornstarch
¼ cup half-and-half
6 tablespoons dark rum
½ cup unsalted butter

In a heavy medium saucepan, combine the sugar and cornstarch. Add the cream, ¼ cup of the rum, and half of the butter. Cook and stir until the mixture boils. Reduce the heat and simmer, stirring occasionally, 8 to 10 minutes, or until the sauce thickens slightly. Pour the sauce into a bowl and whisk in the remaining butter, 1 tablespoon at a time. Stir in the remaining rum. Serve the sauce barely warm or at room temperature.
MAKES ABOUT 1½ CUPS.

Fresh Berry Sauce

Delicious with Lemon Sorbet (page 70) or Lemon Custard Ice Cream (page 50) or peach, vanilla, or chocolate ice cream.

1 (12-ounce) package frozen raspberries, boysenberries, or blackberries, or 3 cups fresh berries
⅔ cup sugar
2 tablespoons cornstarch
¼ cup Chambord liqueur or 3 tablespoons Cointreau or Grand Marnier

Combine the berries, sugar, and cornstarch in a medium saucepan; mix well. Bring to the boiling point, stirring constantly. Cook and continue to stir until juices form and the mixture boils 1 minute. Remove from the heat and stir in the liqueur. Cool completely before serving.
MAKES 2 CUPS.

Brandied Fruit Sauce

½ cup snipped★ julienne dried
   apricots
½ cup snipped★ julienne dried
   pears or peaches
½ cup golden raisins
½ cup diced dried figs or pitted
   dates

½ cup sugar
3 whole cloves
½ cup Cognac or brandy
1 cup diced pared apples
1½ cups diced oranges or tangerines
1½ cups fresh or canned pineapple
   chunks

Place the dried fruit in a bowl and just barely cover with boiling water. Allow to soak 15 minutes. In a saucepan, heat the sugar with ½ cup water and the cloves, stirring occasionally until the sugar dissolves. Continue to cook and boil until the mixture becomes a light syrup, about 5 minutes. Remove the cloves and stir in the Cognac. Cool the syrup to room temperature. Drain the dried fruit and mix it with the fresh fruit. Stir in the cooled syrup. Refrigerate overnight or until ready to use, as long as 1 week. Serve at room temperature.

MAKES ABOUT 7 CUPS, OR 10 TO 12 SERVINGS.

Coffee Sauce

1¼ cups sugar
⅛ teaspoon salt
3 to 4 teaspoons instant coffee
   granules

⅔ cup boiling water
½ cup light corn syrup
2 tablespoons unsalted butter
1 teaspoon vanilla extract

In a saucepan, blend together the sugar, salt, and coffee. Pour in boiling water and stir until the sugar and coffee dissolve. Blend in the corn syrup and swirl the mixture in the pan to be sure there are no sugar crystals clinging to the sides of the pan. Boil the syrup, uncovered, for 10 minutes, until slightly thickened. Remove from the heat and blend in the butter.

★ Scissors are the best tool for this task.

Pour into a bowl and float a piece of plastic wrap directly on the surface of the sauce. When the syrup reaches room temperature, stir in the vanilla. Serve warm or chilled.

MAKES ABOUT 1¾ CUPS.

Very Strawberry Sauce

1 (10-ounce) package frozen strawberries in syrup, thawed
3 teaspoons strawberry jam
2 teaspoons sugar
1 tablespoon cornstarch

Strain the berries, reserving the syrup. Combine the syrup and enough water to make 1 cup liquid. In a medium saucepan, combine the strawberry liquid, jam, sugar, and cornstarch, blending them together well. Cook, stirring, over medium heat until the jam has melted and the sauce is thick and clear. Cool to room temperature, then blend in the berries.

MAKES ABOUT 1⅔ CUPS SAUCE.

Blueberry Ice Cream Topping

1 pint fresh blueberries or frozen unsweetened blueberries
¼ cup sugar
1¼ teaspoons cornstarch
2 tablespoons light corn syrup

Combine the berries, sugar, and cornstarch in a medium saucepan; mix well. Bring to the boiling point, stirring constantly. Cook and continue to stir until juices form and the mixture boils 1 minute. Remove from the heat and stir in the corn syrup. Cool completely before serving.

MAKES 1⅔ CUPS.

Velvety Vanilla Sauce

1½ cups half-and-half   *2 whole eggs*
1 vanilla bean★   *2 teaspoons cornstarch*
1 egg yolk   *6 tablespoons sugar*

Put the half-and-half in a heavy saucepan and add the vanilla bean. Cover the pan and bring to the boiling point. Lower the heat, then place the pot to the side of the heat so that the liquid barely simmers for 10 minutes.

Beat the egg yolk and eggs together. Whisk in the cornstarch. When the vanilla–half-and-half mixture is cooked, stir in the sugar until it is dissolved. Very gradually blend half of the half-and-half into the egg mixture, stirring rapidly. Return the egg mixture to the pan and cook, stirring, over low heat until the sauce thickens and is smooth, about 6 minutes. Strain the sauce into a cool bowl and immediately place a piece of plastic wrap directly on the surface of the sauce. Cool to room temperature. You may refrigerate the sauce to store it, but it is best served at room temperature with icy sorbets or Blackout Chocolate Gelato (page 45). Remove vanilla bean just before serving.

MAKES ABOUT 2 CUPS.

Flavored Whipped Cream Topping

Whip 1 cup well-chilled heavy cream to very soft peaks. Sprinkle in 4 tablespoons powdered sugar and beat in 2 tablespoons Cognac or brandy.

MAKES ABOUT 2 CUPS.

Variation

Whip the cream without the sugar and add 4 tablespoons sweet liqueur, such as Kahlúa, Amaretto, Grand Marnier, Chambord, or Cassis.

★ 1½ teaspoons vanilla extract may be substituted. Simply bring the half-and-half to a boil and add the vanilla when the sauce has cooled.

Cookie Cups for Ice Cream

²⁄₃ cups sifted all-purpose flour
¼ teaspoon baking powder
4 tablespoons butter, at room temperature
¼ cup sugar
1 teaspoon vanilla extract

½ teaspoon almond extract
1 tablespoon milk
1 large egg white, slightly beaten
2 tablespoons very finely chopped almonds or pecans

Cut 8 (7-inch) rounds of baking parchment. Affix 2 rounds on a baking sheet with a few tiny dabs of vegetable shortening. Butter rounds and set aside. Preheat the oven to 375° F.

Stir the flour and baking powder together. Beat the butter and sugar together until smooth. Beat in the extracts. Mix in the flour mixture, milk, and egg white just until smooth. Blend in the nuts.

Spread a thin layer of batter on each parchment circle, leaving a ¼-inch border of parchment. Bake about 8 minutes, or until the edges are slightly browned. Invert each cookie onto an upside-down custard cup; quickly peel away the paper and press the cookie around the cup to shape the shells. Let cups cool 4 to 5 minutes, then remove the cups to a rack. Repeat with the remaining batter.

MAKES 8 CUPS.

Praline Cookie Cups for Ice Cream

¼ cup unsalted butter, melted
⅓ cup golden or light brown sugar, packed
⅛ teaspoon salt

2 tablespoons plus 2 teaspoons light corn syrup
½ cup sifted all-purpose flour
⅓ cup very finely chopped pecans

Preheat the oven to 375° F. Lightly grease 1 or 2 large baking sheets. With your finger, draw a line through the grease horizontally across the center of the baking sheet. In a bowl, combine the butter, sugar, salt, syrup, flour, and pecans. Mix only until blended. Spoon 1 rounded tablespoon batter 3 inches from the top left-hand corner of the baking sheet. Repeat with a second tablespoon of batter in the lower right portion of the sheet. Bake the cookies 6 to 8 minutes, or until golden brown and lacy. Cool on the baking sheet about 1 minute, or until the cookie is firm enough to lift with a spatula but still pliable. Invert the cookies over upside-down custard cups and press lightly into cup shapes. Cool on the cup, then remove to a rack. Wipe each baking sheet clean before baking another batch.

MAKES 6 CUPS.

Easy Chocolate Cups for Ice Cream

Line 12 large muffin cups with paper liners. Melt 8 ounces semisweet or bittersweet chocolate in a double boiler over simmering water. Stir until smooth. Remove the top pan from the bottom. Keep the water in the lower pan hot. Spoon about 1 rounded tablespoon of the melted chocolate into a muffin cup. With the back of a spoon, smooth the chocolate over the bottom and up the sides of the paper cup. Repeat with the remaining cups. If the chocolate becomes too stiff to work with, set it over the hot water and stir for a few moments. Chill the cups until they harden, then peel away the paper.

MAKES 12 CUPS.

Glamorous Chocolate Cups

These are larger and more delicate than the easy chocolate cups above.

Melt about 1 pound semisweet or bittersweet chocolate to make 6 to 8 cups. You won't be able to use all the chocolate because you need enough depth to dip in the mold. The chocolate may be used again, however.

Chill 10 large oranges or small grapefruit. In a double boiler, melt the chocolate over hot but not boiling water; stir until it is smooth. Remove the top pan from the lower pan, keeping the water in the lower pan hot. Let the chocolate cool until it thickens but still flows.

Prepare 10 pieces of plastic wrap large enough to cover each orange. Cover two plates with waxed paper. Place each orange in the center of a piece of plastic wrap and wrap it by drawing the plastic around it and twisting the wrap at the top. The wrap need not be smooth around the fruit. Once wrapped, return all but 2 oranges to the refrigerator. Holding the fruit by the twisted portion of the wrap, dip each orange halfway into the chocolate. Hold the fruit there about 40 seconds, or until a substantial layer of chocolate has coated the fruit. Place on the wax-paper-covered plate in the refrigerator. Repeat with 7 more oranges (extras are chilled for trial and error). Reheat the chocolate slightly as needed.

After the chocolate hardens on the oranges, carefully remove the orange from the plastic, then remove the plastic from the chocolate cup.

With practice, you will get 8 cups.

Meringue Shells for Ice Cream or Sorbets

You can get very creative with these. Combine sorbet and ice cream in one cup if you like, and serve topped with a sauce. Try Irish Coffee Sorbet (page 77) and Extra-Rich Processor Vanilla Ice Cream (page 8) and top it with a chocolate sauce. Or try Ultra Boysenberry Sorbet (page 78) topped with Velvety Vanilla Sauce (page 206).

4 large egg whites, at room temperature
¼ teaspoon cream of tartar
Pinch of salt
1 cup superfine granulated sugar

1½ tablespoons vanilla extract
2 teaspoons cornstarch, strained
¼ cup very finely chopped almonds (optional)

Preheat the oven to 225° F. Line 2 baking sheets with baking parchment, affixing it to the sheet with dabs of vegetable shortening. Draw 4 (3½-inch) circles on each paper.

Beat the egg whites until white and foamy. Add the cream of tartar and salt and beat just until very soft peaks form. Very gradually add the sugar, 1 tablespoon at a time, and beat until stiff peaks will hold their shape and the sugar is dissolved. Gently fold in the vanilla, cornstarch, and nuts, if you are using them. Using about two thirds of the meringue, drop equal mounds of meringue onto the circles drawn on the parchment. Spread the meringue about ⅓ inch thick inside each circle to form a thin base. Then, with the back of a spoon or a pastry tube and a #5 tip, add some of the meringue to form a decorative edge about 2 inches high, to create a shell. Bake about 1 hour, or until the meringue is crisp and dry. Turn oven off and let the shells cool in the oven.

MAKES 8 SHELLS.

Variation

CHOCOLATE CHIP MERINGUE SHELLS

Make Meringue Shells, substituting ½ cup mini semisweet chocolate morsels for the almonds.

Chocolate Meringue Shells

5 tablespoons unsweetened Dutch process cocoa powder
⅔ cup powdered sugar
½ cup plus 1 tablespoon granulated sugar

4 large egg whites, at room temperature
¼ teaspoon cream of tartar
⅛ teaspoon salt
¾ teaspoon vanilla extract

Preheat the oven to 225° F. Line 2 baking sheets with baking parchment, affixing it to the sheet with dabs of vegetable shortening. Draw 4 (3½-inch) circles on each paper.

Sift together the cocoa, powdered sugar, and 3 tablespoons of the granulated sugar. Beat the egg whites until white and foamy. Add the cream of tartar and salt and beat just until very soft peaks form. Very gradually add the remaining granulated sugar, 1 tablespoon at a time, and beat until the meringue will hold stiff peaks and the sugar is dissolved. Gently fold in the vanilla, and the cocoa mixture, half at a time. Using about two thirds of the meringue, drop equal mounds of meringue onto the circles drawn on the parchment. Spread the meringue about ⅓ inch thick inside each circle to form a thin base. Then, with the back of a spoon or a pastry tube and a #5 tip, add some of the remaining meringue to form a decorative edge about 2 inches high, to create a shell. Bake about 1 hour, or until the meringue is crisp and dry. Turn oven off and let the shells cool in the oven.

MAKES 8 SHELLS.

Almond Macaroons

These macaroons are made in large pieces to save time, since they are designed to be crumbled up for piecrusts.

Vegetable shortening
1 cup slivered almonds
1 cup sugar
2 large egg whites
¼ teaspoon almond extract

Preheat the oven to 350° F. Line a baking pan with parchment paper, affixing it to the pan with dabs of shortening. Grease the paper lightly.

Finely grind the almonds in a blender or food processor with ⅓ cup of the sugar. In the bowl of an electric mixer, combine the almonds, egg whites, remaining sugar, and extract. Beat on low until mixed; increase speed and beat for 3 minutes.

Fold a 3-foot-long piece of wax paper in half horizontally. Gather the cookie dough into a ball. Pat it out between the wax paper halves to a 3/16-inch-thick rectangle. Try to make it as even as possible. Cut into 3-inch squares and place about 1 inch apart on the parchment. Bake about 12 minutes, or until edges are crisp. Cool the cookies several minutes, then loosen from paper and cool on a rack. If the cookies are not crisp when they cool, dry them out an hour or so in a barely warm oven. (If you have a pilot, there's no need to warm the oven.) Use crumbled for piecrusts.

Chocolate-Almond Macaroons

Like the cookies in the preceding recipe, these are designed to be used in ice cream piecrusts or as a garnish.

3 ounces semisweet chocolate
1 cup slivered almonds
1 cup sugar
2 large egg whites
¼ teaspoon almond extract

Preheat the oven to 350° F. Line a baking pan with parchment paper, affixing it to the pan with dabs of shortening. Grease the paper lightly. In the top of a double boiler over simmering water, melt the chocolate.

Finely grind the almonds in a blender or food processor with ⅓ cup of the sugar. In the bowl of an electric mixer, combine the almonds, egg whites, remaining sugar, and extract. Beat on low until mixed; increase to medium speed and beat for 3 minutes. Beat in the chocolate for 1 minute more.

Fold a 3-foot-long piece of wax paper in half horizontally. Gather the cookie dough into a ball. Pat it out between the wax paper halves to a 3/16-inch-thick rectangle. Try to make it as even as possible. Cut into 3-inch squares and place about 1 inch apart on the parchment. Bake about 12 minutes, or until the edges are crisp. Cool the cookies several minutes, then loosen from the paper and cool on a rack. If the cookies are not crisp when they cool, dry them out an hour or so in a barely warm oven. (If you have a pilot, there's no need to warm the oven.) Use crumbled for piecrusts.

Glazed Nuts

An opulent sundae topping or pie or cake decoration.

2 tablespoons light corn syrup
2 tablespoons unsalted butter
1/16 teaspoon salt
1/2 teaspoon vanilla extract
2 cups pecan or walnut halves

Preheat the oven to 250° F. Line a rimmed baking sheet with foil. In a heavy saucepan, combine the syrup, butter, salt, and 2 tablespoons water. Bring the mixture to a boil, mixing everything together well. Remove from the heat and immediately stir in the vanilla and nuts. Coat the nuts evenly with the syrup mixture. Turn out onto the baking sheet, spreading them out evenly. Bake for about 50 minutes to 1 hour, stirring occasionally, until the nuts are dry. Cool on the baking sheet.

Toffee Candy

Wonderful crushed up in many flavors of ice cream or sprinkled over the top as a last-minute garnish.

⅔ cup unsalted butter	1 teaspoon vanilla extract
1 cup sugar	⅔ cup ground or finely chopped
½ teaspoon salt	almonds or pecans

Butter a 9 × 13-inch baking pan. Have a cup of cold water at the stove. In a heavy saucepan, combine the butter, sugar, 3 tablespoons water, and the salt. Cook over medium heat, stirring, until the mixture boils and the sugar is dissolved. Continue to boil, shaking the pan occasionally until the mixture is golden brown and will form a brittle thread when a small amount is dropped in the cup of cold water. (A candy thermometer will register 305° F.) Pour into the baking pan and let cool until hardened. To break up the candy, place pieces of it in a plastic bag and crush with a mallet.

MAKES ABOUT 1 POUND.

Chocolate Leaves

10 large or 15 small fresh green leaves (camellia and rose leaves work well)
4 ounces semisweet chocolate

Rinse the leaves in cool water; pat both sides with a towel until completely dry. Line a tray or baking sheet with wax paper.

In a small pan in a larger pan over simmering water or in a double boiler, melt the chocolate. Turn off the heat, and leave pan in hot water.

Hold the stem of a leaf with one hand. Using a pastry brush or small spatula, spread a thin, even layer of melted chocolate on the underside of the leaf; do not let chocolate extend over the edges to the front of the leaf. Place coated leaves on the baking sheet chocolate side up; refrigerate about 5 minutes, until set. Keep the chocolate warm over hot water. When the chocolate on the leaves has hardened, spread another thin layer of chocolate over the first; chill until hard. Repeat the procedure until the chocolate has built up to a thickness of about ⅛ inch. Chill at least 1 hour, until very firm.

Twist several ice cubes in a towel. Cool your hands by grasping the towel-wrapped cubes. With chilled hands, peel away leaves from chocolate from stem end. Refrigerate the chocolate leaves until ready to use.

MAKES 10 LARGE OR 15 SMALL LEAVES.

Index